Philippians,
First and Second Thessalonians,
and Philemon

Westminster Bible Companion

Series Editors

Patrick D. Miller
David L. Bartlett

Philippians,
First and Second Thessalonians,
and Philemon

FREDERICK W. WEIDMANN

WESTMINSTER
JOHN KNOX PRESS
LOUISVILLE • KENTUCKY

First edition
Published by Westminster John Knox Press
Louisville, Kentucky

13 14 15 16 17 18 19 20 21 22—10 9 8 7 6 5 4 3 2 1

Book design by Publishers' WorkGroup
Cover design by Drew Stevens

Library of Congress Cataloging-in-Publication Data

Weidmann, Frederick W.
  Philippians, First and Second Thessalonians, and Philemon / Frederick W. Weidmann.
        p. cm. — (Westminster Bible companion)
    Includes bibliographical references (p.   ).
    ISBN 978-0-664-23852-0 (alk. paper)
  1. Bible. N.T. Philippians—Commentaries.   2. Bible. N.T. Thessalonians—Commentaries.   3. Bible. N.T. Philemon—Commentaries.   I. Title.
    BS2705.53.W45   2012
    227'.077—dc23

                                              2011039954

Most Westminster John Knox Press books are available at special quantity discounts when purchased in bulk by corporations, organizations, and special-interest groups. For more information, please e-mail SpecialSales@wjkbooks.com.

Philippians,
First and Second Thessalonians,
and Philemon

FREDERICK W. WEIDMANN

WESTMINSTER
JOHN KNOX PRESS
LOUISVILLE · KENTUCKY

© 2013 Frederick W. Weidmann

First edition
Published by Westminster John Knox Press
Louisville, Kentucky

13 14 15 16 17 18 19 20 21 22—10 9 8 7 6 5 4 3 2 1

Scripture quotations from the New Revised Standard Version of the Bible are copyright © 1989 by the Division of Christian Education of the National Council of the Churches of Christ in the U.S.A. and are used by permission.

Book design by Publishers' WorkGroup
Cover design by Drew Stevens

Library of Congress Cataloging-in-Publication Data

Weidmann, Frederick W.
  Philippians, First and Second Thessalonians, and Philemon / Frederick W. Weidmann.
    p. cm. — (Westminster Bible companion)
  Includes bibliographical references (p.   ).
  ISBN 978-0-664-23852-0 (alk. paper)
  1. Bible. N.T. Philippians—Commentaries. 2. Bible. N.T. Thessalonians—Commentaries. 3. Bible. N.T. Philemon—Commentaries. I. Title.
  BS2705.53.W45 2012
  227'.077—dc23

                                                            2011039954

Most Westminster John Knox Press books are available at special quantity discounts when purchased in bulk by corporations, organizations, and special-interest groups. For more information, please e-mail SpecialSales@wjkbooks.com.

Contents

Series Foreword

This series of study guides to the Bible is offered to the church and more specifically to the laity. In daily devotions, in church school classes, and in listening to the preached word, individual Christians turn to the Bible for a sustaining word, a challenging word, and a sense of direction. The word that Scripture brings may be highly personal as one deals with the demands and surprises, the joys and sorrows, of daily life. It also may have broader dimensions as people wrestle with moral and theological issues that involve us all. In every congregation and denomination, controversies arise that send ministry and laity alike back to the Word of God to find direction for dealing with difficult matters that confront us.

A significant number of lay women and men in the church also find themselves called to the service of teaching. Most of the time they will be teaching the Bible. In many churches, the primary sustained attention to the Bible and the discovery of its riches for our lives have come from the ongoing teaching of the Bible by persons who have not engaged in formal theological education. They have been willing, and often eager, to study the Bible in order to help others drink from its living water.

This volume is part of a series of books, the Westminster Bible Companion, intended to help the laity of the church read the Bible more clearly and intelligently. Whether such reading is for personal direction or for the teaching of others, the reader cannot avoid the difficulties of trying to understand these words from long ago. The Scriptures are clear and clearly available to everyone as they call us to faith in the God who is revealed in Jesus Christ and as they offer to every human being the word of salvation. No companion volumes are necessary in order to hear such words truly. Yet every reader of Scripture who pauses to ponder and think further about any text has questions that are not immediately answerable simply by reading the text of Scripture. Such questions may be about historical and geographical details or about words that are obscure or so loaded with meaning that one cannot tell at a glance what is at stake. They may be about the fundamental meaning of a passage or about what connection a particular text might have to our contemporary world. Or a teacher preparing for a church school class may simply want to know: what should I say about this biblical passage when I have to teach it next Sunday? It is our hope that these volumes, written by teachers and pastors with long experience studying and teaching Bible in the church, will help members of the church who want and need to study the Bible with their questions.

The New Revised Standard Version of the Bible is the basis for the interpretive comments that each author provides. The NRSV text is presented at the beginning of the discussion so that the reader may have at hand in a single volume both the Scripture passage and the exposition of its meaning. In some instances, where inclusion of the entire passage is not necessary for understanding either the text or the interpreter's discussion, the presentation of the NRSV text may be abbreviated. Usually, the whole of the biblical text is given. We hope this series will serve the community of faith, opening the Word of God to all the people, so that they may be sustained and guided by it.

From almost the beginning of our work on the Westminster Bible Companion, Stephanie Egnotovich of Westminster John Knox Press was our editor, encourager, and friend. Her death was a great loss to us and to this project, and with gratitude we dedicate these volumes to her memory.

Introduction

"It's not about you." That's a mantra for some educators who lead workshops and otherwise work with pastors or seminarians who are studying to be pastors. And it's good advice, because it is not about the given church leader and the gifts and particulars that that person brings to a given position. It's about God, mission, the gospel, and the church. The advice, "it's not about you," at its best, serves to protect and support both the individual leader and the local and broader church.

But—there's always a "but"—it *is* about the church leader at some level, isn't it? All that she or he brings to a given place and a given position will vary from what any other individual brings and is informed by upbringing, education, vocations, and avocations before the call to ministry, current commitments both within and outside of the church, and a plethora of social markers. And further, it is commonplace within many churches that teachers or preachers will comment from time to time—if not often—on their own tastes, foibles, and life experiences in order to illustrate or prove a point. Many will recognize themselves, or a beloved colleague or church leader, in that last sentence.

All of which leaves us at an important place in approaching this extraordinary collection of letters from a person at once so familiar and yet so distant, mysterious, challenging, and even confusing. To return to our mantra above, how does Paul negotiate the distinction between the "it" of his calling, mission, and gospel, and the "you" of his own self and identity? And, to the degree he fuses, or confuses, himself with the broader mission, why does he do so? How are we, the reader/hearer/recipient, *now*, to react? How did members of the churches at Philippi, Thessalonica, and Philemon's house, who were among Paul's first hearers, *then*, react to Paul and his message? Such questions are particularly appropriate to studying the letters of Paul, and will, along with many others, guide our reading.

PHILIPPIANS, 1 AND 2 THESSALONIANS, AND PHILEMON AMONG THE EPISTLES OF PAUL

Of course, answers are to be found primarily through reading the letters of Paul. The letters contained in this study are only part of the whole collection of Paul's letters within the New Testament. Further, we know from Paul himself (2 Cor. 2:3–4) and from other ancient sources that Paul wrote letters beyond those that are preserved for us in the New Testament. To complicate matters further, Colossians, Ephesians, 1 and 2 Timothy, and Titus are considered by many modern scholars not to have been composed by Paul but by members of later communities wishing to speak with the authority of Paul. So, simply defining or describing the collection of Paul's letters is not as easy a task as it may at first seem.

What we know, at least by scholarly consensus, is that Romans, 1 and 2 Corinthians, Galatians, 1 Thessalonians, Philippians, and Philemon represent the "undisputed" letters of Paul. This volume considers Philippians, 1 Thessalonians, Philemon along with 2 Thessalonians, whose authorship is itself disputed by some scholars but which many other scholars, including myself, consider on balance of historical and literary considerations to have been composed by Paul.

This is a commentary on Paul's earliest (those to the Thessalonians), friendliest (Philippians), and most personal (Philemon) letters, as well as what may be the earliest Christian literary composition (the so-called Christ Hymn, Phil. 2:6–11). These letters span the better part of the years of Paul's ministry through which all the letters that we have were written (late 40s through mid-late 50s) and so, to the degree that such might have occurred, provide an opportunity to observe and gauge changes and developments in Paul's own thought and practice.

Each of these letters was written to a Christian community (including, it's fair to say—given the direct address to others within the local community and to the community itself—the letter to Philemon), which Paul had been active in founding. That said, "Christian" is a designation not found in these letters and that Paul, so far as we know, did not use. First and Second Thessalonians were written "from the field" after Paul had left and moved onto another site in his ongoing missionary work and church development; Philippians and Philemon were likewise written following some period of time at other mission sites and are particularly notable for having been written from prison.

IDENTITY

Above, I raised a question about Paul's "own self and identity." Paul speaks to that question repeatedly and very directly in these letters. Several things mark who Paul was *and continued to be*. Many speak of Paul's "conversion," and on the face of it the designation makes sense. Within Paul's letters, particularly in the autobiographical sections of Philippians (Phil. 3:3–8) and Galatians (Gal. 1:13–2:21; cf. 2 Cor. 11:21–12:13), it is evident that Paul separates his life into two distinct sections: the section before his encounter with Christ and the section after. Once God had "called" him to a new life and mission, he dropped everything and "went away" (Gal. 1:15–17) from his former life, both literally and figuratively. Further, he even writes that he counts "all gains" from his pre-encounter life to be "loss" or "rubbish" (Phil. 3:6–8). Many who have had "conversion" experiences themselves, or know individuals who have, will recognize such behavior and descriptions. That said, we who read and associate ourselves with Paul and his message need to be careful both about the language we use and what it means.

Does conversion mean leaving your religion? Well, Paul didn't do that. At least, not according to descriptions in the book of Acts (roughly half of which is devoted to descriptions of Paul and his ministry) or in Paul's letters broadly, and certainly not in the letters herein. Paul remains committed to, and associates with, Jews and Judaism throughout, as we see in Romans 9–11 and in the strong language in his letter to the Galatians (for further discussion, see Weidmann, *Galatians*, passim, in this commentary series).

Paul's is a movement and a mission within Judaism. That is a position that has been in the ascendancy for decades now and has gained consensus status among scholars to the point where it now makes "common sense." Both Christian and Jewish scholars, whose work both independently and with continuing benefit and insight, together, agree. It is true historically and socially (and, again, a simple glance at the book of Acts will indicate Paul's continued interaction with synagogue communities). So too is it true theologically (as is confirmed within the letters themselves). Paul could not conceive of himself or his ministry outside of Judaism and Jewish Scripture and patterns of thought and behavior.

But what, then, about Paul's "conversion"? It remains a good and descriptive word for Paul and Paul's ministry provided we have some clarity about what it does and doesn't mean. The work of Alan Segal has been particularly influential is this area of Pauline studies (*Paul the Convert* and "Response: Some Aspects of Conversion and Identity Formation"). According to Segal, "Paul is a convert in the basic sociological sense of that term—a person who changes religious communities. That does not necessarily have to apply to changing from one religion to another. . . . Paul continues to be a Jew and he continues to believe that his new faith is part of Judaism" ("Response," 185). In this book, I refer both to Paul's "conversion" and, using a word closer to his own description, to his "call" (Gal. 1:15).

Beyond his own identity, within these letters (as within his letters in general) Paul is much more concerned with the corporate identity of individuals and communities who are formed "in Christ." Perhaps nowhere is this evidenced more than in Paul's use of and introduction to the so-called Christ Hymn (which, as indicated above, may be the earliest Christian literary composition we have). The Christ Hymn is indeed a "hymn" or selection of composed verse. Presuming, as many scholars do, that Paul borrowed it more or less in tact from the liturgical practice of an early Christian community, perhaps that of Antioch, it may very well have been composed and in regular use years before Paul composed Philippians (in the mid-50s). In it we find an expression or model—certainly Paul presents it as such—of the sorts of behaviors and orientations toward others that can and should mark the actions of the members of the community and of the community as a whole. By way of introducing the hymn, Paul writes,

> If then there is any encouragement *in Christ*, any consolation from love, any sharing in the Spirit, any compassion and sympathy, make my joy complete: be of the same mind, having the same love, being in full accord and of one mind. Do nothing from selfish ambition or conceit, but in humility regard others as better than yourselves. Let each of you look not to your own interests, but to the interests of others. Let the same mind be in you that was *in Christ Jesus*. (Phil. 2:1–5, emphases mine)

Clearly, community identity is "in Christ."

MISSION

In Philippians, Paul has been stopped "dead," we might say, in his tracks: he is in prison, "in chains" (Phil. 1:7; the NRSV translation arguably understates the case by not including mention of "chains"). No matter. Paul writes, "I want you to know, beloved, that what has happened to me has actually helped to spread the gospel. . . ." (Phil. 1:12). Is Paul indicating that when life hands you a lemon, you ought to make lemonade? Perhaps. But it is more than that. Some "proclaim Christ out of love," while "others proclaim Christ out of selfish ambition, not sincerely but intending to increase my suffering in my imprisonment." What does it matter? Just this, that Christ is proclaimed "in every way" (Phil. 1:16–18).

Paul's first letter to the Thessalonians, which portrays a free and mobile Paul, provides something of a contrast to the period of imprisonment in Philippians. Or does it? Paul is describing a period in which he is on the move, having left Philippi for Thessalonica, and then Thessalonica for points south, including Athens. But along the way, as he writes to the Thessalonians, "we wanted to come [back, north] to you—certainly I, Paul, wanted to again and again—but Satan blocked our way" (1 Thess. 2:18). However, "when we could bear it no longer, we decided to be left alone in Athens; and we sent Timothy, our brother and coworker for God in proclaiming the gospel of Christ" (1 Thess. 3:1–2). Whether the way be clear or not, and whether Paul be the bearer or not, the mission goes on.

Paul would, I think, agree wholeheartedly with the previous sentence. He worked hard and proactively to achieve that mission, and he celebrated it. Part of inspiring mission is doing just that: inspiring the hearers in your mission to take on the mission. Paul was certainly aware of that.

In the earliest letter we have, Paul writes to the community he has just developed:

> And you became imitators of us and of the Lord, for in spite of persecution you received the word with joy inspired by the Holy Spirit, *so that you became an example to all the believers* in Macedonia and in Achaia. *For the word of the Lord has sounded forth from you* not only in Macedonia and Achaia, but in every place your faith in God has become known. . . . (1 Thess. 1:6–8; emphases mine)

So, not only did Paul preach his gospel, he variously nurtured, inspired, and called for those who heard to imitate him and his team in spreading the mission.

The letter to Philemon arguably involves something of a twist on this idea of imitation and mission spread. Here again, Paul is imprisoned—he cannot physically spread the gospel. Nor does he ask Philemon, outright, to imitate him. Rather he appeals to Philemon as a "partner" and, by way of inserting himself into the scenario, suggests that Philemon "welcome" the one on whose behalf Paul writes "as you would welcome me" (Phlm. 17). Again, Paul is sedentary, but the community and the mission continue to develop. And again, whether via imitation or partnership, Paul calls his hearers to act.

END TIMES

"These times demand the *Times*," so says a popular ad campaign for the well-known *New York Times* newspaper. What did "these times" in which Paul lived demand from him and his contemporaries? For many who, like Paul, were Jewish and committed to Pharisaism, an awareness of traditions about the end times was necessary to understand oneself and one's community, the political and social world, and God.

To the casual reader, at least, the earliest letters in our collection (1 and 2 Thess.) are the most overtly interested in the end times. In a rare quotation of—or, at least, allusion to—a familiar saying of Jesus, Paul writes, "Now concerning the times and the seasons . . . you yourselves know very well that the day of the Lord will come like a thief in the night" (1 Thess. 5:1–2). Similarly, in 2 Thessalonians 2:1, Paul introduces a sustained discussion of episodes and activities associated with the end times.

But what more broadly, and programmatically for Paul, marks these end times? Our earliest letter, 1 Thessalonians, provides the answer(s) toward the beginning: "we know, brothers and sisters beloved by God, that [God] has chosen you, because our message of the gospel came to you. . . . [who] turned to God from idols, to serve a living and true God, and to wait for his Son from heaven, whom he raised from the dead—Jesus, who rescues us from wrath that is coming" (1 Thess. 1:4, 9–10). Paul is using a collection of words and images familiar in traditions regarding the end times. First, among the actors there is God's "Son from heaven"; that is, the messiah. The coming of the messiah, as also the coming of the wrath, marks the end times. Also among the actors are "you" who have "turned to God from idols, to serve" God. These are, of course, non-Jews, or pagans, who have forsaken their former idol worship in favor of worshiping God.

According to scriptural tradition, "In the days to come the mountain of the LORD's house shall be established . . . [and] all the nations shall stream to it. Many peoples shall come and say, 'Come, let us go up to the mountain of the LORD, to the house of the God of Jacob'" (Isa. 2:2–3; also Mic. 4:1–2). Using imagery closer to Paul's, the noncanonical text 1 Enoch 91:14 describes how the nations will "bury their idols" and turn to the ways of God.

Paul is living and working and informed by the end times.

THE TIME IS NOW

I am aware, as I write these words, that "the end times" has a very particular connotation in our popular entertainment and news media. One thinks of particular and peculiar images informed by particular and peculiar readings of the book of Revelation, including individuals being suddenly raptured into heaven. Further, one thinks of a callous disregard toward the world that some who, in our world, are (mis)informed by the end times assume. This is neither Paul's nor his tradition's notion of the end times. As we will discuss further in this volume, when Paul writes in Philippians 3:20 that "our citizenship is in heaven, and it is from there that we are expecting a Savior, the Lord Jesus Christ," he is not leaving or urging others to leave their relationships with and for each other and for the world. Quite the opposite, he is urging the very direct and ongoing engagement of individuals within the community and of the community with the world.

I am also aware of the very influential "existentialist" impulse in biblical scholarship and in American religion, which is often (and, for the most part, correctly) associated with the New Testament scholar Rudolf Bultmann, that focuses on the individual/individual's engagement with Scripture and the urgent call and pull that engagement can have on the individual. There is much to commend in that impulse and much that is positive in biblical scholarship and in American religious expression that has come from it. It can also lead to a kind of theological blindness.

When I title this short section "The Time Is Now," I mean neither to suggest that the end of the world is coming in a "the sky is falling" sort of way nor do I mean to suggest—at least not solely—that a deep and certain moment of truth awaits the individual who would encounter, or be encountered by, God; though I should hasten to add that given the choice of those two alternatives, I would tend toward the latter, and do so with enthusiasm. What I do mean to suggest is that for Paul the time has come and is now for the (reconstituted?) people of God to respond to the gospel.

And so Paul challenges his congregations, other congregations, his tradition, his opponents, potential converts, and all who would listen that the time has come, and it is now the time to respond to the gospel message *as the people of God*. And so he writes to communities about life in community in and for the world. Indeed, even when he writes to an individual, Philemon, he addresses not an individual but a collective of several individuals as well as, corporately, the whole community in and of that place: "To Philemon our dear friend and co-worker, to Apphia our sister, to Archippus our fellow soldier, and to the church in your house" (Phlm. 1–2). He does so on behalf of a particular individual within that community and on behalf of the "partner[ship]," which is the gospel.

The time is now for God's people to constitute themselves as God's people and respond, and live, and preach, and teach, and act accordingly. No easy task. For Paul it was worthy of never ending prayerful care and effort—even when he was in chains, in jail. I hope and pray that for us that that task is worthy of the same dedication. May our own engagement of these letters of Paul be a continuing part of that effort.

Philippians

Introduction

The Letter to the Philippians is arguably Paul's greatest testimony to the challenges and joys of life together in Christ. It includes what is possibly the earliest Christian composition in the Bible (the "Christ Hymn" of chapter 2), perhaps the earliest Christian confession in the Bible (the phrase "Jesus Christ is Lord," as found within the Christ Hymn), and the most detailed autobiographical sketch of Paul's early life (3:4–7). Through masterful use of these and many other statements, arguments, and sketches, Paul establishes an energizing and abiding foundation for life in Christ, in community, and in the world.

The broad and specific themes of the letter gain added poignancy and punch given Paul's predicament as a prisoner within the imperial system, as indicated by his statement on his own imprisonment as a factor in the "spread of the gospel" (1:12–14), his musings on "living" and "dying" (1:21), and by his pointed use of the rhetoric of empire (2:11; 3:20). Related to his imprisonment, or to the immediate circumstance of the writing of the letter, is the mutual concern that Paul and the Philippians have for each other. Imprisonment and mutual concern come together right near the beginning of the letter in 1:7: ". . . all of you share . . . in my imprisonment and in the defense and confirmation of the gospel." Words for "share" and the use of a particular prefix indicating "with" or "co-" are fairly evident throughout the letter in the English of the NRSV translation, and even more so as we unpack Paul's Greek.

In some sense, Philippians stands in stark contrast to Galatians, in which Paul indicates grave concern for the direction the Galatians seem to be headed; that is, toward "a different gospel" than that which Paul had preached and established among them (Gal. 1:6). As is evident in the quote from Philippians 1:7 above, the Philippians are clearly partners with Paul on behalf of "the gospel." And it is no mistake that that theme of "gospel" mission, whether with regard to Paul's circumstance (1:12) or theirs (1:27), keeps coming up in Philippians. Indeed, the very notion of separating Paul's circumstance from theirs (however much that might make sense on the surface of things) is itself questionable in light of the common mission (1:30).

But that is not to say that all is rosy. As in Galatians, here, too, Paul has concerns about the community that he addresses in the letter. Not least of these is the concern of "opponents" looming (1:28), who may or may not be akin to the rivals in Galatians. And as in Galatians though far more pronounced here, the language and themes of friendship are evident.

Indeed, Paul's particular sense of fondness for the churches of Macedonia (which include the Philippians along with the Thessalonians) is evident not only in this letter and 1 Thessalonians (see esp. 1 Thess. 1:7–10; 2:7, 11–12, 17), but also in a letter to another church in another region entirely: "We want you to know, brothers and sisters, about the grace of God that has been granted to the churches of Macedonia; . . . their abundant joy . . . for the privilege of sharing in this ministry. . . ." (2 Cor. 8:1–4). We have already seen how Paul states that the Philippians "share" in his ministry (Phil. 1:7). Even earlier than that, both "sharing" and "joy" are found in the same sentence (vv. 4–5), as they are in this quote from 2 Corinthians. Clearly, Paul feels a deep, significant, and joyful bond with this church and its response to his mission.

So, where's the rub? There are three immediate answers to the question which, fittingly, involve Paul, the Philippians, and the very embodiment of their ongoing relationship with each other. These form the precipitating events for the letter.

First, there is the matter of Paul's imprisonment. This is no small matter. Apparently some have suggested that this unfortunate fact points to a downturn in the Pauline mission (1:12). Indeed, such rivalry (1:15) that would spawn such remarks is present. More so, the rigors of prison and of pending legal judgment, and perhaps even of life in this mortal frame more broadly, weigh heavily on Paul (1:19–24). The pathos and intensity of these verses, and others in Philippians, are not to be missed.

Second, there is some threat to the mission and the integrity of community that the Philippians are experiencing and to which Paul feels compelled to respond. Already in the comments above, "rivalry" (1:15) and "opponents" (1:28) have been named (see also 3:2–3, 18–19). There may be real or potential negative influences and threats from without, or perhaps even from within, the community. What is clear is that inside the community at least two named current and past leaders (both women, showing that women had leadership roles in these early churches) are at odds (4:2). This threatens their own work on behalf of the mission and threatens the community.

Third, and perhaps most immediately, is the plight of a particular "co-worker" and "fellow soldier," Epaphroditus. Because of Epaphroditus's recent health struggles, Paul is sending him back to the Philippians so that they might "[w]elcome him . . . with all joy, and honor such people, because he came close to death for the work of Christ. . . ." (Phil. 2:29–30). The last part of the sentence, which follows the explanatory "because," is important. Is Epaphroditus returning, bearing this letter, for the sake of his health? Not so much, as it seems he has recovered already. The return of Epaphroditus allows concrete testimony to service "for the work of Christ" as evidenced in his own person. The letter that he bears, written by Paul, provides its own testimony "for the work of Christ." These provide the dual occasion for the letter to the Philippians.

When the letter was written, and from where, are two closely related questions. The arguments among scholars are endless. But it is Paul's language and imagery that trump the discussion of the letter, regardless of where it was written. The direct clues are at the beginning and end of the letter.

In 1:13 Paul indicates that his imprisonment is at or within "the whole imperial guard" (or, as in the NRSV alternative translation, "the whole praetorium"), while in 4:22 he brings greetings, notably, from within "the emperor's household." These descriptions, on the face of it, suggest a Roman provenance. If so, then the obvious answer for a time of composition would be during the Roman imprisonment at or toward the end of Paul's career, most likely the early 60s CE. However, a case can also be made for Paul's writing from Ephesus. Two passing remarks in the Corinthian correspondences ("I fought with the animals at Ephesus" [1 Cor. 15:32] and ". . . the affliction we experienced in Asia . . . [in which] we despaired of life itself" [2 Cor. 1:8]) may well indicate a time of imprisonment in the capital city of the province of Asia, or Ephesus (2 Cor. 11:23 directly mentions multiple "imprisonments," but with no indication of location). Further, the description that Paul "despaired of life itself" during such an Ephesian imprisonment would appear consistent with Philippians 1:19–24.

Perhaps more so than Rome, Ephesus, which lies to the southeast across the Aegean Sea from Philippi, allows for the travel back and forth that is presumed in the letter. There were members of the praetorian guard stationed in and around Ephesus, and members of the "household of Caesar" were throughout the empire. (This is evidenced, for example, by such familiar names as the historian Flavius Josephus or by the names of King Herod's children, which include Herod Marcus Julius Agrippa). If an Ephesian imprisonment is indicated herein, then the letter was written in the mid 50s, after Galatians and, arguably, at about the same time as Philemon. That is my presumption, though nothing in the commentary that follows stands or falls on the time and place of Paul's imprisonment. It should be noted that some, particularly older, commentaries speculate that Paul wrote the letter from an imprisonment in Caesarea, such as is indicated in Acts 23:33–35. Let alone other reasons, the great unlikelihood of such travel between Philippi and Caesarea that that would entail renders a Caesarean provenance very unlikely.

If Paul is writing from Rome, the imperial city itself, some of the rhetoric of the letter perhaps takes on even deeper meaning. But that said, the very goal of the empire was in spreading its influence and in defining and enforcing its reality. So, whether written from the mother city itself or from an important provincial capital such as Ephesus, Paul's rhetoric has bite.

The city of Philippi, with its particular and unique history, provides quite a context for the letter. Philippi was a Roman colony with a great and august history. Its particularly Roman history stems from an important event following the assassination of Julius Caesar. The forces of Brutus and Cassius were cornered by those of Mark Antony and Octavian (who would become Caesar Augustus) at Philippi. Brutus and Cassius were killed—or, more accurately, granted the option of killing themselves—by the victorious Antony and Octavian, after which time the city was, at the direction of victors, settled by Roman soldiers as a formal colony of Rome. It was renamed Colonia Julia Philippensis—that is, the Julian colony of Philippi. Following Octavian's eventual defeat of Antony, the colony was expanded, as was its name, to Colonia Augusta Julia Philippensis.

Philippi is the one city in that whole portion of the empire that stretches from Greece through the easternmost boundaries that was governed using the Latin (not Greek) language and in which Latin (not Greek) inscriptions predominate. That being the case, even more so than in other cities of the eastern part of the empire, the direct ties to the imperial city of Rome were strong and obvious to resident and visitor alike. Whether Philippians was written from Rome or Ephesus, the context of a Roman colonial city settled at, or near, the birth of the empire by Roman soldiers provides a very rich backdrop for Paul's rhetoric.

Finally, a word about the story of the initial formation of the Christian community at Philippi as recorded in the book of Acts. Notable in Acts 16:11–15 are (1) the lack of an established Jewish synagogue within the city

(at least, one of which Paul was aware) and (2) the very significant role of women in general and of a female leader/patron for the worshiping community, Lydia, who is also apparently a Gentile. Each of these elements is consistent with what we find in Paul's letter to the Philippians: a predominantly, if not solely, Gentile Christian community in which women play an important role as leaders. That Lydia invites Paul and his mission to "stay at my home" (Acts 16:15) may be an indication of the foundation of the house church model at Philippi, which may have expanded by the time of the writing of this letter, to include several house churches also led or supported by prominent women (see discussion of 4:2).

Commentary

SALUTATION AND ADDRESS
Philippians 1:1–2

1:1 **Paul and Timothy, servants of Christ Jesus,**
   To all the saints in Christ Jesus who are in Philippi, with the bishops and deacons:
   [2] **Grace to you and peace from God our Father and the Lord Jesus Christ.**

The beginning of Philippians shows both similarities and variations relative to the patterns Paul establishes within his letters. Paul usually refers to himself as "apostle" at the top of the letter (see Rom., 1 and 2 Cor., Gal.). But not here. Usually Paul names one or more coauthors, as he does here. In the Romans salutation Paul refers to himself as a "servant" (or better, "slave," see discussion below), but in that instance he is referring only to himself. Here, the plural "servants" refers to both him and Timothy.

The alternative NRSV reading, "slaves," is to be favored over "servants," because Paul was writing within a slave society—one whose economic and social structure presumed and depended on slavery. The word he uses simply and straightforwardly means "slave." This same term is also a term used in Scripture (e.g., in the Septuagint, the Greek version of the Hebrew Bible). An interesting parallel within the New Testament, particularly given the presence of the Christ Hymn in Philippians 2:6–11 (see especially "slave," v. 7), is Jesus' teaching as recorded in Mark 10:44–45 (see also Matt. 20:27–28): ". . . whoever wishes to be first among you must be slave of all. For the Son of Man came not be served but to serve, and to give his life a ransom for many." Paul's great statement of 2 Corinthians 4:5 may itself suggest the Christ Hymn looming not far beneath the surface: "For we do not proclaim ourselves; we proclaim Jesus Christ as Lord and ourselves as your slaves for Jesus' sake."

Within the context of Hebrew Scripture, such a designation places Paul and Timothy in the tradition of the great figures of the Bible. In Exodus 32:13, for example, Moses refers to "your slaves" Abraham, Isaac, and Israel, while at the beginning of the book of Joshua, God refers to Moses as "my slave." In the context of Galatians 1:10, the designation "slave of Christ" reinforces Paul's conviction that his is a divine, not a human, calling. The designation "slave" calls to mind also the Prophets (Jer. 7:25 and Amos 3:7).

Timothy appears as coauthor with Paul in each of the Macedonian correspondences (Phil. and 1 and 2 Thess.) as well as in Philemon. Along with Silvanus (who is named in 1 and 2 Thess.; see "Silas" as one who accompanies Paul and Timothy in Philippi and Thessalonica in Acts 16:11–17:15), Timothy accompanied Paul and is named as a recipient of two Pauline epistles. Timothy's projected role here (2:19) is akin to that reported in 1 Thessalonians 3:2. Clearly Paul is wont to send him back to communities that he has—or perhaps better, they have—founded, in order to bring back news to Paul from the community and enforce or strengthen the community in and for mission. The closeness of Timothy and Paul is affirmed within the body of the letter, as is the nature of their relationship (with Paul as the senior figure, 2:22). This is consistent with the portrait presented in Acts (see especially 16:1; 17:14–15; 18:5).

Unique among the letters of Paul is the absence of the designation "church" or "churches" within Paul's address (1 and 2 Cor., Gal., 1 and 2 Thess., and even Phlm. [see Phlm. 1:2]). Also notable is the bare designation "saints" or "holy ones," familiar in one form or another in several addresses (see Rom., 1 and 2 Cor.), but not in this simple way. 1 Corinthians, which uses both the noun form and a verb form of "saint" or "holy one" within the address, probably gets at Paul's general understanding and sense of the word with regard to the churches he addresses and mentions: ". . . to those who are sanctified in Christ Jesus, called to be saints" (1 Cor. 1:2). Use of the term also conjures up biblical language, such as "a holy nation" (e.g., Exod. 19:6) or "holy ones" (Ps. 16:3, 34:9). Perhaps more to the point for Philippians, the designation is used in the book of Daniel, in the context of apocalyptic, to refer to the community of God's people (Dan. 7:18, 21, 22). Such an apocalyptic context (i.e., one in which God's people are aware of, and participate in, God's direct intervention on earth) is particularly apropos given Paul's message to the Philippians.

As for the added phrase that Paul includes here, "with the bishops and deacons," the slightly confusing alternative reading provided in the NRSV is important: "overseers and helpers." Whenever and wherever Philippians was written,—Ephesus in the early to mid 50s or Rome in the early

60s—it was composed at a time prior to the formalization of offices within Christian communities. That there were formal and recognized bishops and deacons at this time within the community at Philippi is unlikely.

For example, limiting ourselves to Paul's letters, a simple comparison with the list of offices or positions within the community named by Paul in 1 Corinthians 12:28 indicates the designations "apostles . . . prophets . . . teachers" (repeated in 12:29), along with those with other "gifts." Among the "gifts" are "forms of leadership" (1 Cor. 12:28) but no designation for "bishops" or "deacons." The NRSV alternative reading captures well the nontechnical usage of these terms here in Philippians. Paul is referring broadly to leaders within the community. By adding this phrase about leadership, he is also setting up his concern regarding leadership within the community, particularly in 4:2.

The actual greeting at verse 2 is quite standard for Paul (Rom. 1:7; 1 Cor. 1:3; 2 Cor. 1:2; Gal. 1:3; 1 Thess. 1:1; 2 Thess. 1:2; Phlm. 3). Its repeated use by Paul in his letters' addresses reflects a simple but creative modification of the standard word for "greeting" regularly found at the front of a standard Greek letter. Paul's use, of course, is pointed to his addressees and to his and their relationship to God and God's action (see, e.g., Jer. 31:2). Indeed, the use of "grace" in verse 7 not only suggests the bond that Paul shares with the Philippians (and, by extension, all in community in Christ) but also helps to set up one of the pervasive themes in the letter: partnership in and for "the gospel." Further, while the first word gives a nod to the convention of greetings in Greek letters, the second, "peace," favors a broadly Semitic or distinctly Jewish idiom, recalling the *shalom* greeting (see, e.g., Dan. 4:1) standard in epistolary and other addresses. That Paul found meaningful this balance of "grace" and "peace" is illustrated by the way he employs a modification of the greeting by balancing phrases, within just a few verses of each other, that use one element or the other (Phil. 4:9, 23; see also Gal. 6:16, 18; 1 Thess. 5:23, 28; 2 Thess. 3:16, 18).

THE PRAYERFUL AND FOCUSED THANKSGIVING
Philippians 1:3–11

> 1:3 I thank my God every time I remember you, [4] constantly praying with joy in every one of my prayers for all of you, [5] because of your sharing in the gospel from the first day until now. [6] I am confident of this, that the one who began a good work among you will bring it to completion by the day of Jesus Christ. [7] It is right for me to think this way about all of you, because

you hold me in your heart, for all of you share in God's grace with me, both in my imprisonment and in the defense and confirmation of the gospel. [8] For God is my witness, how I long for all of you with the compassion of Christ Jesus. [9] And this is my prayer, that your love may overflow more and more with knowledge and full insight [10] to help you to determine what is best, so that in the day of Christ you may be pure and blameless, [11] having produced the harvest of righteousness that comes through Jesus Christ for the glory and praise of God.

As is standard in Paul's letters, Philippians moves from greeting to thanksgiving. (The famous and glaring exception to this is Galatians. Another exception is 2 Cor. 1:3–7, which includes a word of hope and consolation instead of a thanksgiving.) As is relatively standard practice for Paul, prayer is a significant component within the thanksgiving (Rom. 1:9, 1 Thess. 1:2, Phlm. 4). Several items are notable within Paul's thanksgiving herein, which drive to the heart of Paul's concerns.

In verse 4 Paul notes that his prayer is marked by "joy." It may or may not be coincidence that Paul uses a word here that in the Greek differs from "grace" just slightly. Both are two syllables and have the same first syllable. "Grace," as noted in the comments on verse 2 above, will return in verse 6, while "joy" is to mark both the Philippians' experience of "faith" (1:25) and their reception of those whose own efforts are indicative of "the work of Christ" (2:29; see also 2:2, and the use of the related verb "rejoice" in 1:18; 2:17, 18, 28; 3:1; 4:1, 10). On a closely related note, not only are the Philippians to recognize in others "the work of Christ," but Paul establishes at the beginning of the letter that God has already begun "a good work" among the Philippians themselves (verse 6; see also, comments on vv. 13 and 14 below).

From verse 3 on, Paul directs his letter to "you," the Philippians. The "you" is unambiguously plural in the Greek, and that is significant. Paul throughout is addressing the plurality of the Philippian church and its common work, even across individual differences (see especially 4:2). This is confirmed and affirmed right at the top, in v. 4, with Paul's stressing of "all of you."

That hallmark of the relationship that Paul establishes here, and continues to be concerned with, is "your"—all of you together—"sharing in the gospel" (1:5). Both of the terms, "sharing" and "gospel," are vital to Paul's message. We will turn to each in a moment.

The "in" within the phrase, "sharing in the gospel," provides a far more ambiguous translation than need be. Paul's statement here is strong and clear, through the use of a standard preposition and a standard construction

of Greek syntax: the "sharing" is *for the purpose of* "the gospel." From the top of the letter Paul is clear that this common work (of the Philippians and him) has its purpose in the gospel. That has been the case "from the first day" of Paul's own mission preaching in Philippi and the concurrent founding of the Philippian community (v. 5). To "remember" them (v. 3) is to remember their common work on behalf of the gospel.

Interestingly, and perhaps counterintuitively for many who know and read the New Testament today, "gospel" is a Paul word. Many tend to split the New Testament into the Gospels and the Letters, among other categories, or even more narrowly "the Gospels and Paul." But Paul uses the term early and often (Rom. 1:1, 3, 16; 10:16; 11:28; 15:16, 19; 1 Cor. 4:15; 9:12, 18, 23; 2 Cor. 2:12; 4:4; 8:18; 9:13; 10:14; 11:4; Gal. 1:6–9; 2:2, 5; Phil. 1:5, 27; 2:22; 4:3, 15; 1 Thess. 1:5; 2:4; 3:2; 2 Thess. 1:8; Phlm. 13). That is, through shear amount and regularity of usage he makes it his word. His usage predates any of the written Gospels as we know them. Further, the context and regularity of his usage, as in Philippians, suggests strongly that the word was part of his missionary teaching and preaching. Both in his in-person presentations and in his letters, Paul's addressees would have heard and become familiar with Paul's "gospel."

What does the word mean? Or, more particularly, how does Paul use it? Paul uses the term consistently throughout the Letters to indicate his mission and message regarding "Christ" (See, e.g., Rom. 1:16; 1 Cor. 4:15; 9:23; 2 Cor. 8:18; Phil. 1:5, 1:27; 2:22; 4:3; 1 Thess. 2:4). In Galatians 1:6–9, and indeed throughout Galatians, he is at pains to distinguish his "gospel" message from that which others preach. Whether or not there is anything akin to that concern behind his usage in Philippians is unclear (see especially comments on Phil. 1:15). One thing that marks Paul's "gospel" consistently from its appearance/presentation in his first extant letter (see 1 Thess. 1:5, esp. in light of 1:9) to his last (Rom. 1:16; 11:25–28) is its inclusion of and outreach toward Gentiles (in Gal., esp. 2:2).

As many readers of this volume will know, the basic meaning of the Greek term generally translated "gospel" is "good news." Also familiar to many, its usage in the New Testament (besides Paul, perhaps most famously in Mark 1:1; cf. Matt. 3:3–4, Luke 3:3–6) owes some debt to the book of Isaiah. Just beyond the passage from Isaiah 40:3 as quoted at or near the top of Matthew, Mark, and Luke, appear these words (in Isa. 40:9):

> O Zion, herald of good tidings;
> lift up your voice with strength
> O Jerusalem, herald of good tidings,
> lift it up, do not fear.

Two things are immediately relevant in Paul's usage of "gospel" herein, and a third may be looming. First, the term translated "good tidings" in the NRSV of Isaiah 40:9 is, in the Septuagint (the Greek version of Hebrew Scripture familiar in Paul's day) the same word, "gospel," that Paul uses here. Paul, as a Greek-speaking and Greek-writing Jew, is certainly familiar with that word in Isaiah. Second, this very portion of Isaiah, beginning with 40:1, serves as a kind of entrée into that broad section of Isaiah that variously suggests or describes the opening up of the "gospel" to the "nations" or the "Gentiles." (Both English words translate the same Greek word; see esp. Isa. 42:6; 43:9; 45:22–25.) That this broad section of Isaiah is influential for Paul may be indicated directly in his use of the Christ Hymn, the end of which is itself influenced by Isaiah 45:22–25.

The NRSV translates well Paul's use of closely related terms for "sharing" or "partnership." Virtually impossible to translate into proper English would be Paul's intensifying of the word "share" in verse 7. "Co-sharers in God's grace with me" is a translation that approximates Paul's Greek. What is more, that intensifier "co-" and the word for "with" are precisely the same in Greek. Arguably Paul doubly overstates his case. Wouldn't the simple repetition of "share" in verse 7 have sufficed? In Philippians, Paul uses the base word for "share" many times (as a noun, 1:5; 2:1; 3:10; a noun with the intensifier, "co-," 1:7; as a verb, 4:15; as a verb with the intensifier, "co-," 4:14). Further, he uses the intensifier, "co-," repeatedly with other words (1:27; 2:2, 25 [twice], 3:10, 17; 4:2 [in reference to what may be a proper name], 4:3 [twice]). Partnership, sharing, and mutuality are at the heart of this letter from beginning (1:5) to end (4:15). Of course, it is a focused partnership for the purpose of "the gospel" (1:5).

Verse 6 reinforces one feature and introduces another into the letter. The mutuality that Paul so intensively and deliberately writes about has to do with "work" or "spread" or "progress" (1:12, 25). Paul is concerned with the growth and activity of his mission. On some level he is an actor, and the Philippian community is an actor. On another level their separable actions and predicaments are in fact fused and mutual and inseparable (v. 7). And on the most basic and profound level it is neither he nor they, individually or mutually, but rather "God" (v. 3) who is the actor who "began," nurtures, and will "bring . . . to completion" all that he and they do on behalf of the gospel.

Further, there is a recognizable (if not measurable) sense and location of the gospel's "completion" in "the day of Jesus Christ" (see also "the day of Christ," v. 10). Doubtless influenced by the Prophets' use of the phrase, "day of the LORD" (see esp. Isa. 13:9, 11; 27:13; 28:5; Joel 1:15; 2:1, 11, 31;

3:14, 18; Zech. 2:11; 9:16; Mal. 3:17), "day of Jesus Christ" is a concept and a phrase that (with slight variations) Paul uses throughout his extant letters, from the earliest to the latest, and doubtless in his preaching and teaching more broadly (1 Thess. 5:2; 2 Thess. 2:3; 1 Cor. 1:8; 5:5; 2 Cor. 1:14; cf. the broader descriptions surrounding "that day," 2 Thess. 1:10, and "the day," Rom. 2:16). Clearly the introduction of "the day of Jesus Christ" early in the letter sets up an eschatological tension and focus, to which Paul will return directly (3:20) and indirectly (2:10–11; see comments on v. 5, above). The question of the relationship between the state of an individual who dies prior to "the day of Jesus Christ" and the occurrences that will accompany that day is addressed directly in Paul's earliest extant letter, 1 Thessalonians (see esp. 4:13–17) and is arguably raised anew by Paul's statement regarding death in Philippians 1:23 ("to depart and be with Christ") but is left unconsidered in this verse.

Verses 7 and 8 contain important statements of deep feeling and compassion consistent with the mutuality that Paul has already established or affirmed in these initial verses of the letter. The NRSV's alternative reading is a wonderful case in point; how fitting that as presented in the NRSV, it may mean, "because you [Philippians] hold me [Paul] in your heart" *or*, "because I [Paul] hold you [Philippians] in my heart" (NRSV alt.) The particular grammatical structure used in the sentence renders the subject and the object ambiguous. Frankly, given the word order, a strong argument could be made for swapping the primary and alternate readings as presented in the NRSV. Regardless, both are perfectly reflective of the phrase as it appears here in the letter. Has Paul purposely planned it this way? Why not? Each of the mirrored statements, taken singly or together, is perfectly consistent with the thrust of verse 7 and indeed of the letter as a whole.

Arguably, the whole of verse 8 confirms, directs, and intensifies what has been presented in verse 7. The simple statement about "how I long for all of you" reflects usage that Paul does not turn to often, but does employ throughout the extant letters that we have, from the earliest (1 Thess. 3:6), to mid-career (2 Cor. 5:2), to the latest (Rom. 1:11). Only in Philippians does Paul repeat the statement (see also 2:26). Further, he uses an adjective, built from the same word, "long for" (it is one word in Greek), in 4:1.

By way of intensifying, the action of longing is modified by the phrase "with the compassion of Christ Jesus." Paul has already used the term "heart" in verse 7 in the same idiomatic sense that English speakers do, as the seat of compassion. Here he turns to another available term in the Greek which carries the same connotations regarding compassion, though it literally refers to intestines or entrails; the closest idiom available in English would be something along the lines of, "I feel it in my guts." Often, including within the NRSV, this particular word is simply and somewhat misleadingly translated with the English "heart" (see 2 Cor. 7:15, Phlm. 12, 20; Paul also uses it at 2 Cor. 6:12 and within this letter, Phil. 2:1 ["compassion"]). The full phrase, "compassion of Christ Jesus" is only used here among Paul's extant letters. What does it mean? Perhaps there is no better answer than that given by the Christ Hymn of Philippians 2:5–11, which, as noted above, is introduced, in part, via this same word (2:1).

Beyond the words and phrases indicating compassion, there is another very important term and concept introduced in verse 7 that is captured by the word "think." Paul uses the word repeatedly in Philippians (1:7; 2:2 [twice], 5; 3:15, 19; 4:2, 10 [twice]), usually in the same or a similar phrase. The consistency of Paul's use of this word, variously translated as *think* or *mind*, is impossible to gauge using the English of the NRSV.

One of the definitions in the standard Bauer *Greek-English Lexicon of the New Testament* captures well Paul's usage in Philippians: "to develop an attitude based on careful thought, be minded/disposed." Perhaps 2:5, more than any verse in Philippians, captures that sense. But all of Paul's usages are consistent, even when used within a negative example (3:19).

Paul is setting up for the community an ethos, or an ethical framework, with(in) which to act. He begins by putting himself in the role of the thinker/disposed one, and the Philippians themselves in the role of the model (the ones being observed). In verse 7, as the object of Paul's mindedness, the Philippians become the first of a series of models for how to act (esp. Christ, 2:5–11; Timothy, 2:19–20; Epaphroditus, 2:25–30; Paul 3:3–14) and how not to act (3:2, 18–19). (See also 1:15–18, which provides a back and forth of negative and positive inclinations and examples).

The terms "knowledge" and "full insight" work together. The first has to do particularly with recognition; it is a modification or intensification of the word from which the English terms "gnosis" and "gnostic" are derived. The second, "insight," suggests experience or having a sense of something. Perhaps the most direct parallel in Paul's letters is Philemon 6 which, in some ways, serves a kind of distillation of much of this whole section: "I pray that the sharing of your faith may become effective when you perceive all the good that we may do for Christ." In Philippians in particular, Paul is calling for and providing the content and models with which his addressees might recognize and perceive "what is best" (v. 10).

The sense of "determine" that Paul is after in verse 10 is given a particular bent as it is introduced with the very same sense of purpose with which

Paul first introduces "gospel" in verse 5. And this is no abstract determining, but has to do with real action and discernment in real time. A helpful parallel is 2 Corinthians 8:8, in which Paul confesses to his addressees that "I am testing the genuineness of your love against the earnestness of others." In other words, it's not just about talk, but action—a sentiment which is affirmed by the production and harvest language of verse 11. In a sense, verse 11 is a restatement of verse 6; where verse 6 focused on God as actor, verse 11 approaches the matter from the point of view of the Philippian community as actor. What the community is called to and equipped for (by no less than God, v. 6) is "work" (v. 6), and production and "harvest" (v. 11) on behalf of the "gospel" (vv. 5, 7). This community activity occurs within the timeframe, but perhaps even more profoundly within the ethical framework, provided by the anticipated, eschatological day of Jesus Christ (vv. 6, 10; see 3:20).

THE GOSPEL-INFUSED NARRATIVE OF PAUL'S CURRENT CIRCUMSTANCE
Philippians 1:12–26

1:12 **I want you to know, beloved, that what has happened to me has actually helped to spread the gospel, [13] so that it has become known throughout the whole imperial guard and to everyone else that my imprisonment is for Christ; [14] and most of the brothers and sisters, having been made confident in the Lord by my imprisonment, dare to speak the word with greater boldness and without fear.**

[15] **Some proclaim Christ from envy and rivalry, but others from goodwill. [16] These proclaim Christ out of love, knowing that I have been put here for the defense of the gospel; [17] the others proclaim Christ out of selfish ambition, not sincerely but intending to increase my suffering in my imprisonment. [18] What does it matter? Just this, that Christ is proclaimed in every way, whether out of false motives or true; and in that I rejoice.**

Yes, and I will continue to rejoice, [19] for I know that through your prayers and the help of the Spirit of Jesus Christ this will turn out for my deliverance. [20] It is my eager expectation and hope that I will not be put to shame in any way, but that by my speaking with all boldness, Christ will be exalted now as always in my body, whether by life or by death. [21] For to me, living is Christ and dying is gain. [22] If I am to live in the flesh, that means fruitful labor for me; and I do not know which I prefer. [23] I am hard pressed between the two: my desire is to depart and be with Christ, for that is far better; [24] but to remain in the flesh is more necessary for you. [25] Since I am convinced of this,

I know that I will remain and continue with all of you for your progress and joy in faith, [26] **so that I may share abundantly in your boasting in Christ Jesus when I come to you again.**

An interesting comparison can be made between this section and its equivalent in 1 Corinthians 1:11–17. In both cases, Paul provides a narrative of events that set up, speak to, or provide examples of concerns that Paul will address in the letter. In 1 Corinthians, he writes about events at Corinth. Here, ostensibly, the subject of the narrative is Paul. He is in prison, and as if that alone is not enough cause for alarm, there seem to be rivals who want to augment their own importance and diminish that of Paul and his mission. But in another sense, it is not Paul but the gospel that stands front and center (vv. 12, 16). Following the mutuality established in the Thanksgiving section (1:3–11), the section fittingly draws to a close with a most personal set of musings over life and death that moves seamlessly from individual (1:20–24) to community (1:24–25) focus and mutuality (1:26).

The section picks up where the previous one left off: the already established (v. 5) and eagerly anticipated (v. 11) work and accomplishment on behalf of the gospel. This crucial idea of the "progress" (v. 25 NRSV), or spread (v. 12), of the gospel is forwarded by Paul through this one word (it is the same word in Greek) that he uses only in Philippians among his extant letters (see also 1 Tim. 4:15). What is its relevance? Perhaps Sirach 51:17 is looming behind this verse:

> I made progress in her;
> to him who gives wisdom I will give glory.

In both there is the spread/progress word. Important too are the "in" and "glory." In verse 11 Paul speaks of that "harvest of righteousness" associated with "the glory . . . of God." So too in Sirach 51:17, "glory" is due to God. But Paul's use of the simple "in" in verse 13 is not evident in the NRSV translation. What Paul writes in Greek is, "it has become known . . . that my imprisonment is *in* Christ" (translation and emphasis mine; see "in the Lord," v. 14, which reflects this same usage of "in").

The progress, or spread, that has occurred via Paul's imprisonment is *in* Christ, just as the progress described in Sirach is *in* wisdom (the "her" in Sirach 51:17 refers to "wisdom"). Like that of Sirach, this progress is God blessed, God given, and *in* the sphere or realm of the divine. Further, this same progress word, tied here directly to "the gospel," can be tied in verse

25 to humans, just as it is in Sirach. And its dual use in Paul, verse 12 (gospel) and verse 25 (the community), is indication of Paul's profound fusing of the two—the progress of the gospel and the progress of the community whose identity is "in faith" (v. 25), "in Christ" (v. 13, my translation).

Paul's "imprisonment" is given prominence in several ways in verses 13 and 14. In verse 13, in a manner not reflected in the NRSV translation, "imprisonment" stands at the front of the sentence, immediately following "so that," and so is stressed simply via word order. It is repeated in verse 14 and therein serves as the agency whereby those believers who are present are "made confident" and "dare to speak the word with greater boldness and without fear." All of this happens "in the Lord," which parallels directly the phrase "in Christ" (my translation) in verse 13.

Notice the development: in verse 13 the imprisonment is centered "in Christ"; in verse 14, the imprisonment is itself the agency or vehicle whereby the believers are ramped up "in the Lord" to induce the progress of the gospel. That transition corresponds to the use of "confident" in verses 6 and 14. The former references the "good work" begun in you, the latter provides an example whereby the work of community is enabled to flower even amidst adversity for Paul and—one may rightly read between the lines—a sense of threat among the believers present.

Through the direct address at the beginning of verse 12 and the descriptor or label used for believers in verse 14, Paul accomplishes much in terms of an understanding of community formation and identity. Indeed, as suggested by the alternative reading of the NRSV at verse 12, the word translated "beloved" (v. 12) and "brothers and sisters" (v. 14) is the same word. This would have been obvious to the Philippians. (To further add to the confusion promoted by the NRSV translation, Paul does, indeed, use the Greek word for "beloved" at 2:12 and 4:1.) By referring to "brothers and sisters" in both verse 12 and 14, Paul lays the foundation for the familial language and the sense of familial relationship with God and within the community that he will be promoting broadly and repeatedly within the letter. Here he implicitly makes the point that the believers in Philippi and the believers at his prison site (and, by extension, believers anywhere) are members of, and siblings within, the same family "in Christ," or "in the Lord."

The term used in verses 13 and 14 for "imprisonment" is, as has already been discussed, given prominence in several ways in these verses. It is also given prominence simply in its repetition throughout the first sections of the letter (1:7, 13, 14, 17). What is more, Paul doesn't use an abstract term, as the NRSV translation "imprisonment" suggests, but rather the very colorful and concrete "chains." And, given contemporary practice, it is very likely the case that Paul literally was "in chains," under guard, perhaps even chained to a guard. Besides the obvious effects of lack of mobility and general discomfort, the type of chain and method of chaining could, and often did, result in acute pain and wounding. In *Moralia*, 165E, Plutarch writes of "the inflammation surrounding wounds, the savage gnawing of ulcers in the flesh, and the tormenting pains" of the "chains of prisoners." There is little doubt that when Paul refers to the "increase" of "suffering in my imprisonment," he is starting from a baseline of considerable suffering. At the very least, that is what his addressees would have presumed, given the practices of chained imprisonment.

Fittingly for Paul, the location or context for the imprisonment is given in passing, in reference to the spread of the gospel. To what does "the . . . imperial guard" or, as per the alternative reading, the "praetorium," refer? The latter is simply the English version of the term that Paul actually uses, which is a Greek version of the Latin word *praetorium*. This means, simply, "governor's palace." If used in reference to a place outside of Rome, that simple meaning makes sense. However, the term had come to also be used to refer to something else entirely, which is reflected directly in the NRSV primary reading: the "imperial" or "praetorian" guard dedicated to the empire and stationed in Rome. Which does it mean here? Given the ambiguity of the term, the answer can only be had as part of the broader consideration of the origin of the letter. As discussed in the introduction to Philippians above, if the letter is written from Rome, then Paul here refers to "the imperial guard" and, more broadly, its headquarters. If written from Ephesus (or, for that matter, another place outside of Rome), then it refers to the governor's palace and the troops and prison facilities associated with it.

We have already noted the direct connection between the spread/progress of the gospel in verse 12 and that of "you" Philippians in verse 25. In verse 14, through a cluster of words, Paul begins to put some particular shape on the response or (re)action that this spread/progress entails. Being "confident" (v. 14) is manifest in that the siblings or believers around Paul "dare to speak the word with greater boldness and without fear." The term "boldness" does not actually occur here (confusingly, the NRSV used it to translate an adverb employed by Paul to indicate how "exceedingly" the siblings now "dare to speak" and "without fear"). That said, this verse sets up Paul's actual use of the term "boldness" regarding himself in verse 20. These are, in a real sense, "fightin' words." First, Paul's use of "dare" in Romans 5:7 shows a willingness to carry on even to the point of death.

Second, "boldness" in Philippians 1:20 indicates both a lack of fear and a willingness or orientation to speak frankly in the face of power. This is captured well in Acts 26:26, in which Paul claims to "speak freely" before King Agrippa using a verb form of the same word translated "boldness" in Philippians 1:20.

The portrait of Paul in Acts and Paul's use of "boldness" here draw on a philosophical motif that dates back at least to Socrates. It is used to great affect by the moral philosopher Epictetus, a contemporary of Paul, who speaks of "kings and tyrants of this world" who use "bodyguards and their arms" to derive their ability to speak and act as they wish *and* squelch the ability of others to do the same. He contrasts them to the one who as "friend and servant to the gods" has no such power over others via force or governmental means but simply seizes the right, "if it so pleases the gods" (itself a quote from Plato's *Crito*, 43D), "to speak freely" (*Discourses* 3.22.94–96). Such is the model for Paul and the believers around him as they recognize that Paul's imprisonment, and their confidence in the work of spreading the gospel, is "in Christ," or "in the Lord."

In verses 15–18, Paul steps back as if to reflect on the spread of the gospel broadly and on the place of his imprisonment in particular. He knows and wants the Philippians to know that his current predicament has had a positive effect on the spread of the gospel. That said, the very way this section is introduced in verse 12, captured well by the NRSV translation, has some sense of defensiveness and urgency. Surely there are those who believe and want others to believe that what happened to Paul is not good for him, for those who would associate themselves with him, or for the spread of the gospel. These ones carry out their own proclamation of the gospel through "envy and rivalry."

Because of the vagueness of the language ("some," v. 15, "the others," v. 17) and lack of any detail or direct information about their teachings or positions, it is unclear who these rivals of Paul's are. Perhaps Paul is here referring to those he counters in Galatians (see Weidmann, *Galatians* [Westminster Bible Companion series; Louisville, KY: Westminster John Knox Press, 2012] or ones akin to them. Both of the words used here occur in the list of "the works of the flesh" in Galatians 5:19–21 ("envy," Gal. 5:21; the word for "rivalry," translated as "strife," Gal. 5:20). If the rivals in Philippians are the same rivals as those in Galatians, then the rhetorical question of verse 18 along with the statement of inclusivity across lines of rivalry that follows it are all the more interesting. Paul labels that which he opposes in Galatians as "a different gospel" (Gal. 1:6) whose promotion is in contrast with "the truth" (Gal. 4:16). Indeed, precisely what is at stake in Galatians is "the truth of the gospel" (Gal. 2:5, 14; cf. 5:7) that Paul preaches—*not* the others, not even Peter (2:14). Here Paul is able to "rejoice" regardless of whether the proclamation moves from "false motives or true." Has Paul's position changed with regard to that "different gospel"?

What appears clear is that whomever Paul has in mind in verses 15 and 17, they are not present in Philippi and are of no direct threat to the Philippians (see 1:28, "your opponents"; see also 3:2, 18). On the other hand, they likely are present or otherwise influential in and around Paul's place of imprisonment (or they may be present and influential in other places that Paul has a stake in), since through their activity Paul believes they are "intending" to increase his "suffering."

In the comments on verse 7, above, Paul's pattern of establishing models for behavior (both positive and negative) throughout the letter is noted. Verses 15–18 provide a compact example of that. Here, without naming names, Paul moves from considering a negative model for proclaiming Christ (v. 15a), to positive examples (v. 15b, 16), and then again a negative example (v. 17). But these are not abstract examples. In a real sense it's personal; in both verse 16 and verse 17 Paul is present ("I," "my").

In a sense, Paul's addressees are also present in these verses. In verse 16, there are direct echoes as "these" who are modeling positive proclamation, like the Philippians in 1:7, have Paul's "defense of the gospel" in their sights. As regards verse 17, the description in verse 1:7 of the Philippians' willingness to "share" "in [Paul's] imprisonment" stands in sure contrast to "the others" who model negative behavior vis-à-vis Paul and his predicament, looking to increase his "sufferings." Later, in a parallel lost in the NRSV translation, Paul states that "you [Philippians] share my distress" (4:14). "Suffering" (1:17) and "distress" (4:14) translate the same Greek word.

In verse 18 Paul transitions into a remarkably nuanced and forceful statement, the crux of which is easily lost on many readers today. The verb "rejoice," which is directly related to the word for "joy," is used twice herein. It bridges the transition out of the dense discussion of positive and negative models (vv. 15–18a) and into the consideration of death and deliverance (vv. 18b–26). Even when not named or referenced in any way, the addressees (and *their* "joy," 1:25) are quite present through these verses as well, particularly in the resolution of verses 24–25 and continuing into the next section (1:27–29).

In both verse 4 and 18a, "joy" and "rejoice" are tied directly to gospel and proclamation. At least indirectly that is also the case in verse 25 (see discussion of spread/progress in v. 12, above). Here Paul uses "rejoice" in the context of his own ("my") "deliverance." The word is a strong and nuanced one and may mean "deliverance" from prison or, more broadly, "salvation" (as it is translated in Phil. 1:28 and 2:12). Both are relevant here, and both may be in play. But, given Paul's language, particular arguments and concerns, and the way he structures these verses, the broader sense of "salvation" would seem better to capture the resonances herein.

First, in verse 19 Paul is quoting word for word from Job 13:16. That is easily missed as there is no quotation formula present, or introductory remarks of any kind. But comparison with the Septuagint (ancient Greek) version of the Hebrew Bible indicates that the phrase, "this will turn out for my deliverance" is a direct quote from Job. Of course, Paul's context and Job's are quite different. Nonetheless, a simple comparison with Job's predicament broadly and within the section around the quoted verse (wherein he turns away from others' understandings of his suffering to take his case directly to God, who will "vindicate" him [Job 13:18]) would suggest that it is "salvation" that is at stake.

Paul does not spell out what "this" (which, again, is part of the direct quote taken from Job) might refer to in his case. The simplest grammatical answer is that it would refer to the nearest antecedent, which would be the phrase "that Christ is proclaimed in every way, whether out of false motives or true" (v. 18a). The emphasis, presumably, would be on the first part of the statement. That is, put another way—and consistent with what he has been at pains to show through these beginning verses of the letter—his focus is on this: that his mission and the spread of the gospel continue.

If indeed it is Paul's mission and the spread of the gospel more broadly that "this" refers to, then what follows begins to fall into place. First, "this" connects the surrounding uses of joy/rejoice (vv. 4, 18a, 25) with "rejoice" in verse 18b: Paul's deliverance/salvation is in some manner dependent on the continuing of his mission and the spread of the gospel more broadly. Second, and consistent with the first, Paul is gravely concerned with his predicament. As he presents the situation, his life and death literally hang in balance. Regardless, the record will show that "by my speaking with all boldness, Christ will be exalted now as always in my body, whether by life or by death."

So, it is not Paul's death or life that will determine whether the mission and spread of the gospel continue; which is not to say that Paul's actions in prison are indeterminate. Quite the opposite! Paul is clear that he will put his "body" on the line as an instrument for, or location of, the exaltation of Christ. As we have already seen (above), Paul introduces a series of words and concepts into the letter, "speaking with all boldness" being significant among them. This forwards the notion of seizing authority, in concert with God, regardless of what station one finds oneself in. The next verses are a study in that theme.

In the discussion of verse 14, the moral philosopher, Epictetus, a contemporary of Paul, is cited. In another passage, Epictetus waxes philosophic about what to do in a predicament analogous to that in which Paul finds himself. Such was a recurring topic of discussion among moral philosophers and their students, not least because "speaking with all boldness" could and did get philosophers, teachers, and others (including religious figures) in trouble. Imprisonment, exile, torture, and the sentence of death were realities to be reckoned with. They served as reference points for consideration of the moral life. Epictetus writes:

"Will you not, as Plato says, study not merely to die, but even to be tortured on the rack, and to go into exile, and to be severely flogged, and, in a word, to give up everything that is not your own? If not, you will be a slave among slaves . . ." (*Discourses* 4.1.172–73). Epictetus goes on to contrast the life of a philosopher (i.e., the moral life that he is promoting) with that of "a rich old man" (counter to the moral life that he is promoting). Later in the same passage, he uses a form of the word "shame" in a way similar to that of Paul here in verse 20. This indicates that such intention and such action as he prescribes, though counter to prevailing notions of success, safety and security, will not be perceived as shameful.

Epictetus's references both to Plato and (disparagingly) to slaves are shorthand. The great model for how to live *and* die is Socrates, Plato's great teacher and the subject and source of many of Plato's writings. From the teachings of Socrates to the burlesque of Roman writers, slaves are used as examples of shameful activity. Though Paul interestingly and forcefully uses "slave" language for very different reasons and in very different ways (see discussion 1:1, above), he is consistent with Epictetus and others in striving for the avoidance of shame.

Though moving from a very different place both literally (prison) and figuratively (promoting mission and community "in Christ"), Paul proceeds in a manner strikingly akin to that of Epictetus. In verse 21 Paul manages to lay the foundation for the next few verses and, more broadly, establish a kind of worldview and moral framework for all of Christian life and death. He also takes a swipe at worldly wisdom and wealth in a way that might have even dazzled Epictetus. The last phrase of verse 21, "to die is gain," is both simply a truism (at least for Paul and his gospel) and a backhanded poke at worldly gain (see 3:7). The first part of the verse is a reassertion of his mission and purpose in life: "[the gospel of]

Christ." Though it is a very personal, bold, and existential statement of a prisoner enduring life in chains and facing possible execution, it is also a paradigmatic statement for all who would identify themselves with life in Christian community.

The beginning of verse 22 extends and focuses the first part of verse 21, connecting it to the harvest imagery of verse 11 (lost in the NRSV translation is that in both verses precisely the same word, meaning simply "fruit," is used).

It is with the second part of verse 22 that Paul extends and focuses the second part of verse 21—the consideration of death. Lost in the translation of the NRSV is Paul's direct consideration of, and assertion of control regarding, death. This is uncomfortable for Christians and others in our society to recognize. Speaking as a Christian and a member of our society, I would concur. But as a student of Paul, I do not want to miss the depth of his writing. Simply put, Paul does not write, "I do not know which I prefer." No. The verb Paul uses is in the future tense and it means plainly and simply, "choose." What Paul writes in verse 22b is, "and I do not know which I will choose." Those strong words and that bold assertion of control brilliantly set up the next verses.

In recent Roman history, Cato had famously chosen to take his own life while holding "Plato's book" in his hand. The book was Plato's *Phaedo*, regarding the trial and death of Socrates (and, in particular, the intimate and difficult dialogue about his taking of the poisonous hemlock). Weighing the "desire . . . to depart" had been (for centuries prior to Paul) and was (during Paul's time) a familiar theme of philosophical discourse. So Epictetus's reference to Plato as cited above, so Paul's words here in Philippians.

In another passage, Epictetus counters those who, in his opinion, have veered too far in their desire to depart. First he lays out their position: "Are we not in a manner akin to God and have we not come from him? Allow us to go back from whence we came . . . to be freed from these chains that are fastened to us and weigh us down. Here there are thieves and robbers, and courts of law, and those who are called tyrants. They think that they have some power over us because of this paltry body and its possessions. Allow us to show them they have no power over us" (*Discourses* 1.9.13–16, with slight revisions of the Loeb translation).

The broad strokes of this stance regarding death (or more particularly what we would call suicide) and Paul's framing of the matter is striking. Some of the parallel points: Death is attractive. It (re)connects with God; in Paul's case, "Christ." The "chains" referenced above translate precisely the same word for "imprisonment" that Paul uses repeatedly in 1:7, 13, and 14. The last line regarding power is consistent with Paul's assertion of such in these verses.

Having set out these positions, Epictetus responds in his own voice: ". . . wait upon God. When [God] shall give the signal to depart and set you free from this service, then you shall depart to him; but for the present, endure to abide in the place where he has stationed you (*Discourses* 1.9.16, with slight revision of Loeb translation).

So, asserts Epictetus, suicide is not the answer, at least not so in some aimless fashion. Such desire to "show them" who have legal and military power is best tempered via relationship with, and direction from, God. Here Epictetus shows himself, consistent with the passage cited above, a good student of Plato indeed. As he presents it in the *Phaedo* 62B–C, Plato makes it clear that the great teacher Socrates did not choose the hemlock until it had become perfectly clear to him that God had ordained it as "necessary."

Consideration of relationship with, and direction from, God are precisely the sorts of things one would expect from Paul as well. Further, especially given the thrust of the teachings regarding mutuality and sharing thus far in the letter, one would expect not only consideration of relationship with God but with the community of "siblings" as well. On these matters, Paul does not come up short.

Verse 24 begins with a very telling "but," as Paul begins to explain his choice (v. 22). (Again, the NRSV's "prefer" does not accurately convey Paul's word choice.) On the face of it, the sentence is strong and makes sense: "to remain in the flesh is more necessary for you." More so, Paul is using code language familiar to students of Plato and, interestingly, familiar to any of us who would claim even a surface familiarity with the broad sweep of the Gospel story regarding Jesus' life and death. (See Mark 8:31 and parallels on how "the Son of Man *must* undergo great suffering . . . and be killed"; emphasis mine.) As noted above, Plato's story of Socrates establishes the matter of divine necessity; according to *Phaedo* 62c, in the voice of Socrates: "An individual must not kill himself until God brings some necessity upon him, such as has now come upon me." For Paul, it has become clear that it is "more necessary" to remain. Case closed.

What is more, as Paul writes, it is more necessary "for you." For what it is worth, Epictetus would likely have approved heartily. His great teacher, Musonius Rufus, had written: "One who by living is of use to many has not the right to choose to die . . ." (fragment 29, in Lutz). And the great orator Cicero, who a few generations earlier has been stationed for a time in Paul's city of Tarsus as governor, writes as follows regarding his decision not to carry through with the possibility of (what we would call) suicide: "the one argument which called me back from death was everybody's saying that no small portion of your life was vested in mine" (Letters to His Brother Quintus [Quint. fratr.] 1.3.2). We have already seen how deeply the mutuality of the Philippians and Paul has been indicated in the letter (1:4, 7, 8, 12 [and 25, as discussed above regarding v. 12]). So the Ciceronian or Musonian resolution, consistent with the great Socrates: it is not necessary for me to die, rather it is in fact even "more necessary" to remain "for you."

Did Paul *really* consider taking his own life? Who can know, short of God, Paul, or perhaps Paul's closest associates? What is important to recognize is that as he presents himself here in these verses, Paul takes on the role of the teacher-philosopher, facing possible execution and considering suicide. Just as Paul paints the picture of Paul the runner in Philippians 3, or portrays himself and his addressees as soldiers in 1 Thessalonians 5, or portrays himself as a boxer in 1 Corinthians 9, so here Paul paints the picture of Paul the prisoner contemplating suicide in order to make a point. His Philippian addressees would have recognized as much; indeed, to the degree that they were familiar with the trope, they might have expected as much from their teacher and founder. That the portrait corresponds in significant detail to his actual predicament certainly adds depth, texture, and pathos to these extraordinary verses.

Paul chooses to remain and, more pointedly, to remain in ongoing relationship with the community. As we have already seen, that ongoing relationship is all about Paul's mission and the spread of the gospel more broadly. In verse 25, something that is unfortunately lost in the NRSV translation, Paul uses precisely the same word he has used in verse 14 and verse 6: "confident." Yes, he is "convinced," as the NRSV says, but more pointedly he is confident. "I know that I will remain and continue with all of you for your progress and joy." As already noted several times (see esp. discussion of v. 12, above) this use of "progress" here reprises the "spread" of verse 12. Each translates the same, somewhat unique word in Greek. In short, "your progress" (v. 25) and the "progress of the gospel" (v. 12) are connected, and Paul is *the*, or at the very least *a*, link. Also linked is "your . . . joy" and Paul's (1:4, 18; see esp. discussion of v. 4, above), and, of course, their joy is linked to the spread of the gospel.

As stated regarding verse 19, Paul's deliverance and salvation is in some manner dependent on the continuing of his mission and the spread of the gospel more broadly. That matter is resolved in verses 25–26 and particularly through the pointed use of "boasting" in verse 26. We have already seen in Philippians that Paul's theology is apocalyptic in orientation, with repeated focus on "the day of Christ" (or some variation thereof, 1:6, 10; see discussion above). In 2:16 these two foci, *boasting* and *day of Christ*, will converge: "It is by your holding fast to the word of life that I can boast on the day of Christ that I did not . . . labor in vain." As is so evident in the manner that Paul works out his (re)commitment to his mission and the spread of the gospel in verses 18b–24b, so in 2:16 he will not entertain—whether in life or death—extracting himself from that mission and that spread. The Philippians are an integral part of that whole. Their success is his success and evidence that he has faithfully served.

In a different letter in different circumstances, Paul in 2 Corinthians similarly raises the matter of boasting. 2 Corinthians 1:14, with its densely stated mutuality and focus on the day of the Lord, could be extracted and dropped into Philippians seamlessly: ". . . on the day of the Lord Jesus we are your boast even as you are our boast." 2 Corinthians 5:6–9 in similar terms considers matters crucial to Philippians 1, including confidence and life and death. Sandwiched between that set of verses and a consideration of "boasting" (5:12) and of mission "for God" and "for you" (5:13), appears this sentence in 5:10: "For all of us must appear before the judgment seat of Christ, so that each may receive recompense for what has been done in the body. . . ." Paul has cast his lot with his mission and the spread of the gospel; so the remainder of 2 Corinthians 5 (see vv. 16–21) and so here. As for this section of Philippians, just as it is necessary (the "must" of 2 Cor. 5:10, whether by coincidence or not, recalls the Socratic necessity discussed above) to appear before the judgment seat of Christ, so is it all the more necessary for Paul to remain and carry on his mission, however hampered his physical predicament may be, in concert with the Philippians (Phil. 1:24). His eyes are on the twin prizes of the mission and spread of the gospel (so the "this" of 1:19; see discussion above), and on more fruitful labor (1:22; see also 1:11), which will accrue to their, and his, record (1:26).

For good and centuries-old theological reasons, many readers will be somewhat uncomfortable with the notions of boasting and accruing records. Indeed, part of the broader issue at play is touched on in the introduction to this volume: "It's not about you, it's about Jesus Christ." That is all true, and all for the good. As Paul proceeds through the letter, we will see how he orients the community to the model of Christ and others. A quick return to 2 Corinthians 5, in this case verse 20, makes part of the point well: "So we are ambassadors for Christ, since God is making his appeal through us. . . ." It is not, finally, about Paul, or about you, or about us. It is about the gospel of Christ, instituted by God, for which we are ambassadors and through whom God makes his appeal (see esp. 1:28b–1:30, below).

CITIZENSHIP WORTHY OF THE GOSPEL OF CHRIST
Philippians 1:27–30

> 1:27 **Only, live your life in a manner worthy of the gospel of Christ, so that, whether I come and see you or am absent and hear about you, I will know that you are standing firm in one spirit, striving side by side with one mind for the faith of the gospel,** [28] **and are in no way intimidated by your opponents. For them this is evidence of their destruction, but of your salvation. And this is God's doing.** [29] **For he has graciously granted you the privilege not only of believing in Christ, but of suffering for him as well—** [30] **since you are having the same struggle you saw I had and now hear that I still have.**

It is a tribute to the depth and breadth of Paul's interest in mutuality and mission in this letter, that the thanksgiving (1:3–11) and narrative (1:12–26) sections resonate so deeply with each other and with other sections and verses throughout the letter. Here in these few verses, between the narrative section and the lead in (2:1–5) to the Christ Hymn (2:6–11) and beyond, Paul provides something of a summary or focus of his major arguments and appeals throughout the letter.

The break with the previous sections is clear—or, as clear as can be in Philippians, given the understandings and descriptions of mutuality—as Paul moves from primarily considering his predicament to a focus on and the delivery of a command to his Philippian addressees. The break with the following sections is less clear. Indeed, a pattern is available whereby one can observe major terms and themes introduced in verse 1:27 regarding citizenship and "standing firm" (see discussions below), which are then reprised at the close of chapter 3 (v. 20) and the very beginning of chapter 4 (v. 1), respectively. That pattern suggests something of bookending of one long unit of advice and modeling, from 1:27 through 4:1, followed by a distinct section of advice beginning with 4:2 ("I urge . . ."). Below, we will consider this broader framework, 1:27 through 4:1, while also recognizing smaller sections.

This section begins strongly and assertively with a command. That much is relatively clear in the English translation of the NRSV: "live your life. . . ." It is not evident in the NRSV translation that Paul here uses a verb form of the same word that in 3:20 is translated "citizenship." This is crucial to an understanding of Paul's teaching and the structuring of the letter. He writes: "Be citizens . . ." or "live as citizens." In terms of the social context for which the letter was written and within which it was first read and heard, that constellation of terms around citizenship would have resounded in particular ways. As noted earlier, Philippi enjoyed the status of being a Roman colony. It was governed, locally, not through the use of the Greek language but in Latin (the mother tongue of the imperial city of Rome) and boasted an array of civic inscriptions in Latin. This was unusual in this part of the Roman empire (where governing was done, and the vast majority of public inscriptions were written, in the Greek language) and marked Philippi as particularly, even uniquely, Roman in this part of the empire. What could it mean, then, for Paul to command his addressees to "be citizens"?

Paul begins to spell it out immediately; indeed, in the word order of the sentence, this phrase comes first: ". . . in a manner worthy of the gospel of Christ." The very phrase and concept "gospel of Christ" hooks the command into much that we have already seen in 1:6–1:25, including the mutuality of Paul and the Philippians, the notion of spread/progress (1:12 and 25) and, of course, the sense of mission, rootedness in Christ, *and* potential for rivalry (v. 15) and "suffering" (v. 17) that "gospel" suggests. The letter thus far has already yielded models for behavior befitting "the gospel," in Paul (vv. 12–14), the Philippians themselves (vv. 5, 7, see esp. discussion of the latter), and the unnamed "others" of verse 15–16.

Knowledge and mind are very important as Paul builds his ethic of community action on behalf of the gospel (see below, esp. 2:2). Though the NRSV translation would suggest otherwise, neither of these important notions is included here in verse 27 in the Greek. Paul writes simply that he would want to "hear" (not "know") about them, and it is "soul," not mind, that follows "spirit" in verse 27. Operative in this part of the verse, and introduced for the first time in the letter, is the term and idea of "standing firm." As noted in the introduction to this section, above, "standing firm," like the directive to "be citizens" serves to delineate the first broad section of exhortation in Philippians through 4:1 (the verse in which the verb "stand firm" is again used). Here, as there, it is followed by a prepositional phrase beginning with "in."

Simply stated, the "in" phrase indicates location. Unlike the next prepositional phrase in the verse (in the NRSV, "with one mind," or better, "soul") it does not indicate the manner in which some action is taken, but rather the place in which that action occurs. Just as "in the Lord" in

4:1 points to God, so "in one spirit" does here. According to the conventions of the NRSV, it is better translated as "in one Spirit," with a capital "S" (for the same phrase, see 1 Cor. 12:13; one might conjecture that the phrase is itself shorthand for Paul's teaching about baptism as reflected in 1 Cor. 12).

In verse 19, Spirit is very closely associated with Jesus Christ and with "the help" that is afforded one member of the community "through" the action of others. The same elements are advanced in this verse. The Spirit is present, as has just been discussed. The verb form, "striving side by side," suggests the mutuality of effort, each for the other and for the whole, that is characteristic of the community. By using the same intensifier for "with" or "co-" as discussed regarding verse 7, above, Paul creates a graphic word for co-striving (the "striving" part is from the Greek word that forms the basis of the English word, "athlete") to which he will return in 4:3. Thus he links the second exhortation section of the letter, 4:2–20, with this. He also sets up the broadly athletic imagery of 3:12–14.

As has already been noted, "mind" is an important term and concept within Philippians. However, here Paul further describes the Philippians' co-striving with the phrase "with one soul," not as indicated in the NRSV, "with one mind." That sort of language, "one mind," is introduced toward the end of 2:2. For all the talk of mutuality and sharing, it is perhaps curious that Paul only uses "one soul" here within the letter. It is familiar in early Christian literature (see Acts 4:32) and very familiar as a concept in Greek moral philosophy from Aristotle's *Nicomachean Ethics* (1163b6–7) and beyond; Aristotle notes that it is a time honored expression in his day.

In verse 28, Paul ties the Philippians' circumstance to his in a much more pointed way than before. Up until this point, one might infer that the Philippians are themselves under no immediate threat regarding their organization around, identity in, and work on behalf of mission for "the gospel." Clearly Paul is under a threat, and those believers in and around the place of his imprisonment feel at least some sense of that threat as well (see discussion of vv. 13–14 and 15, 17 above). Here Paul ties the knot: the Philippians too are in a position, potentially at least, to be frightened or intimidated by some opponents.

Who these are and what sort of threat they pose is unstated—the Philippians knew already, but we probably never will. In terms of the letter, what relationship, if any, these "opponents" in 1:28 have either to those of 1:15, 17 or those of 3:2 or 3:18–19 is a complicated question. The question is rendered even more complicated by the question of what possible relationships any of those other opponents have with each other. What we know about the opponents is that those described in 1:15, 17 are Christian opponents: that is, they "proclaim Christ" in one way or another and for one purpose or another. Similarly, the description of those in 3:2, especially in light of 3:3, indicates that they are part of a Christian mission. (More so, they promote a similar understanding of circumcision of Gentile Christians as Paul's rivals in Galatians; see Galatians passim, esp. 5:12.) There appears in the letter nothing linking those in 1:15, 17 with those of 3:2. If the opponents in 3:18–19 are linked in some way to those in 3:2 (their descriptions bookend Paul's self-described Christian walk) then they are Christian. If not, they may or may not be Christian. The immediate descriptions in 3:18–19, and the broader context within the surrounding verses, render the matter unclear. An interesting observation from this little exercise, which may or may not gain us ground in understanding the Philippians' opponents in 1:28, is that of all these opponents introduced into the letter, those in 1:28 and those in 3:18–19 are the only ones who are not necessarily part of a Christian mission. Do those in 1:28 and those in 3:18–19 have something to do with each other? Are those in 1:28 freestanding? Are they Christian or non-Christian?

"Destruction," and in particular destruction of the opponent under discussion, links 1:28 and 3:19. At this point in the development of Christianity, those in Christian community are very much still under the umbrella of Judaism. Most who would identify with community in Christ were practicing Jews. In Romans 9:22–24, Paul seems to reserve "destruction" for those of Jewish or Gentile communities whom God "has called." In 2 Thessalonians 2:3, Paul reserves the term for that which will happen to "the lawless one." In 1 Corinthians 1:18, a form of this same word, regularly translated "destruction" in the NRSV, is used in contrast to those "who are being saved": "For the message about the cross is foolishness to those who are perishing, but to us who are being saved it is the power of God." Indeed, both the word for perish/destruction and the word for "save" are related to the two terms in this part of Philippians 1:28: destruction and salvation. Given the consistency of 1:28 with 1 Corinthians 1:18 and the lack of anything tying them to Judaism, Christianity, or "the gospel," it is likely that those in 1:28 (and perhaps also 3:18–19) refer to non-Jewish, non-Christian individuals or communities who have some capability of exercising influence or power over the Philippians: perhaps formal governmental officials or perhaps those representing broader social or economic institutions, formal or informal.

"Salvation" in verse 28, like the citing of opponents, is another direct link of the Philippians' plight with Paul's. As discussed at some length above, the word translated in the NRSV as "deliverance" in verse 19 and that translated "salvation" here are the same. Now, if there remains any doubt regarding the intimate connection between Paul's circumstance and the addressees', verse 30 drives the matter home in no uncertain terms.

The whole of verses 29–30 is one sentence. Its dense rhetoric is not, perhaps, as gracious as the NRSV translation suggests—for example, there is no "privilege" in Paul's sentence—but it is affective. Of course, consistent with the whole of Philippians, the plural "you" refers to the whole community. "Christ" stands much more front and center than is conveyed in the NRSV translation; indeed, "you" and "Christ" stand in a neat tension: "For to you has been granted this thing on behalf of Christ. . . ." The next two phrases, then, begin to spell "this" out: "believing in him" and "suffering for him"—"Christ" is stated up front, and both of these parallel phrases include the simple pronoun referring back to Christ. So, between the use of the term and the double use of the pronoun, "Christ" is referenced three times in verse 29, further underlining the difference—in identity, in community, in practice, in mission—between the addressees and their opponents. Certainly verse 29 puts further content on the command to be citizens or live as citizens "worthy of the gospel of Christ . . ." (1:27).

The particular phraseology regarding believing *in* Christ is pointed and is employed on occasion by Paul. It might more forcefully be rendered "believing into Christ" (for fuller discussion, see Weidmann, *Galatians*, 55–56). Though Paul has been keen to link the Philippians' plight with his plight throughout this section, and though the broad concept of "suffering" certainly accomplishes as much (see 1:17), Paul introduces two separate words for "suffering" in 1:29–30. The first is used only here in Philippians. Interestingly, this same word for "suffer" is used in 1 Thessalonians 2:14 in the context of discussing local Christian communities (one Gentile, the Thessalonians themselves; one Jewish, in Judea) and the suffering they receive from those in broader culture, whether Gentile (in the case of the Thessalonians) or Jewish (in the case of the Jewish Christian communities referenced in Judea). Is Paul using the same word here with the same nuance? That would confirm that the opponents of 1:28 are non-Christian and have something to do with the struggle of the Philippian Christian community living in its broader, Gentile, social and economic context. The term used for "struggle" in 1:30 also appears only this one time in Philippians. It is a term Paul uses regarding himself in 1 Thessalonians 2:2. That is, perhaps, fitting enough given the mutuality and linking of circumstance and struggle for the gospel here in verse 30 and throughout the letter. But what is more, 1 Thessalonians 2:2 refers to Paul's "struggle" in Philippi. Does use of this word link Paul's experience and his addressees' in their native city and, more particularly, do the opponents named in 1:28 have something to do with Paul's earlier struggles in Philippi as well as with the Philippian community's current struggles?

The verb form that Paul uses to introduce the whole of verses 29–30 is, as indicated by the NRSV translation, related to the noun form, "grace." As Dietrich Bonhoeffer famously says in *The Cost of Discipleship*, God's grace is no cheap matter. But it is as free as it is costly. Paul's presentation in Philippians would seem to affirm as much. It is the noun "grace" that ties together the descriptions in both verses 29–30 and verse 7. Whether "imprisonment" (v. 7) or "struggles" (vv. 29–30) of various kinds, "grace" calls the Philippians to God and to action and binds them together with God, with Paul, and with each other.

THE COSMIC AND LOCAL CHRIST
Philippians 2:1–11

2:1 If then there is any encouragement in Christ, any consolation from love, any sharing in the Spirit, any compassion and sympathy, [2]make my joy complete: be of the same mind, having the same love, being in full accord and of one mind. [3]Do nothing from selfish ambition or conceit, but in humility regard others as better than yourselves. [4]Let each of you look not to your own interests, but to the interests of others. [5]Let the same mind be in you that was in Christ Jesus
[6] who, though he was in the form of God,
did not regard equality with God
as something to be exploited,
[7] but emptied himself,
taking the form of a slave,
being born in human likeness.
And being found in human form,
[8] he humbled himself
and became obedient to the point of death—
even death on a cross.
[9] Therefore God also highly exalted him
and gave him the name
that is above every name,
[10] so that at the name of Jesus
every knee should bend,
in heaven and on earth and under the earth,

¹¹ **and every tongue should confess**
   that Jesus Christ is Lord,
   to the glory of God the Father.

In a sense, the whole of the letter thus far has been leading to this point and, in turn, the first part of this section (2:1–5) is a lead-up to the Christ Hymn (2:6–11). Throughout chapter 1 Paul has referred to "Christ," either alone or in some combination with Jesus (and in v. 2 with Lord as well). Particular phrases have been used—including "compassion of Christ" (v. 8), "imprisonment . . . for Christ" (v. 13), and "gospel of Christ" (1:27)—which are indicative of the role that Christ plays for Paul's sense both of engagement and mission *and* for modeling or defining behavior. The last sentence of the previous section, particularly in verse 29, has put a kind of exclamation point on that. There, Christ is referred to no less than three times—once with the term, "Christ," and twice via pronoun (the English of the NRSV, as discussed above, only captures two of these references, not three). Here Paul turns directly to the cosmic Christ as model for community.

Paul marks this turning point in the letter directly toward the Christ Hymn with a rhetorical flourish or, better, a set of rhetorical flourishes. In the Greek, the whole of verses 1–4 is one sentence, which verse 5 then punctuates by focusing that which has preceded into one command and provides direct entrée into the hymn as found in verses 6–11.

As it appears in the Greek, the "If" which begins the sentence is repeated prior to each following phrase, rendering a total of four uses of the word in verse 1. This is a rhetorical flourish lost in the NRSV translation. The NRSV's repeated "any" captures well another of set of repetitions Paul uses. To the four-times repeated rhetorical statement, "if there is any," clearly the answer Paul is looking for from his addressees is "yes, of course there is."

Not surprisingly (given the whole of ch. 1 and esp. the last sentence, vv. 29–30), it does not take long for Paul to mention Christ, who binds him to them and provides their common sense of identity and mission. Also not surprisingly, given much of what we have seen in chapter 1, mutual encouragement is affirmed and forwarded through this sentence and beyond (verses 1–4). The particular use of "then" at the beginning of the sentence directly links it to the previous sentence and by extension links the sweep of 2:1–5 through 2:6–11 back to what precedes.

Each of the phrases is very simple and, in Greek, does not even include the "there is" or any such equivalent; simply "if any" plus a proposition.

Of the four phrases, the middle two jump out for their direct association with what has been stated in chapter 1. "Love" is part of the final sentence which brings the thanksgiving and prayer section to a close and puts the stamp on Paul's prayer (v. 9). Further, "Love" sounds the keynote for what will be their "harvest" (vv. 9–11), which Paul then, as we have seen, echoes in verse 22 regarding his own "fruitful labor."

As important as that "harvest" or "fruitful labor"—indeed part and parcel of it—is mutual support and shared engagement of and for the gospel. And so Paul here stresses the "consolation," which is a rough equivalent of the previous term "encouragement." Paul uses these two terms (or very closely related forms of them) together on two other occasions in his extant letters. Both 1 Thessalonians 2:12 and 1 Corinthians 14:3 are consistent with Paul's usage in Philippians. The latter parallels more closely what Paul is expressing here, since the activity he is forwarding in 1 Corinthians 14:3 is about "upbuilding" those within the community.

The third phrase reprises two different terms and concepts that are encountered in chapter 1, "sharing" and "Spirit," and links them directly. As discussed above (see esp. comments on 1:5), Paul uses "sharing" and related forms repeatedly throughout the letter. It is a key term in setting out Paul's overall goal within the letter, which is to reinforce and build "sharing *for the purpose of* the gospel" (see comments on 1:5 above). "Spirit" appears twice in chapter 1 (vv. 19 and 27) and again here within the letter. It does not appear throughout the letter as do the variations on "share." Nevertheless, it is important and reinforces Paul's message of "sharing" and mutuality. As discussed in comments on 1:27 above, the NRSV's choice of the lowercase "spirit" in 1:27 is misleading in light of the NRSV convention of indicating the divine, or Holy, Spirit by way of capitalization. As indicated externally by the parallel with 1 Corinthians 12:13, and internally via phrase structure (see 4:1, "in the Lord") and content (the close tie of "Spirit" with both "Jesus Christ," 1:19, and with the community, 1:19 and esp. 1:27), the presence of the "Spirit" is part and parcel of the relationship and mutuality between Paul and the Philippian community. By extension, the mutuality extends to all who identify with, and work on behalf of, "the gospel." Further, unlike 1:27, here the phrase in Greek reads simply "sharing of the Spirit"; there is no "in." Given that structure, an indicated behavior ("help," 1:19; "sharing," 2:1) followed by "Spirit" in the genitive case, the phrase much more so picks up directly on 1:19, and the "help" or support suggested there. Interestingly, then, insofar as the link with 1:19 is made, Paul is urging the inclusion of the Philippians, via their "sharing," in the helping activity associated with the Spirit.

The rest of the sentence, verses 2–4, resolves the four "if . . . any" phrases of verse 1. The rhetoric, especially in verse 2, is dense and nimble. Paul uses different grammatical structures in virtually every phrase, sometimes for purposes that are lost in English translation and subtly underline the pattern of sharing and mutuality that he has already so well established. The first clause of verse 2 is, in a sense, *the* statement, with the rest modifying it. It is a command—"make my joy complete"—which picks up on the theme of "joy" already established in the letter (see discussions of 1:4 and 1:18 above), and which, in turn, is associated with "sharing in the gospel" (1:4–5) and proclaiming Christ (1:18). It also directly draws on verse 11, importantly, in a manner lost in the NRSV translation; "complete" in 2:2 and "produced" in 1:11 are precisely the same word: making Paul's joy complete (2:2) and producing "for the glory and praise of God" (1:11) are congruent.

The next phrase is, it turns out, crucial for the development and focusing of Paul's message through this section and throughout the whole of the letter. As discussed above in 1:7, Paul uses in a very distinct and pointed way one particular verb that the NRSV translates using two separate words: a verb ("think") and a noun ("mind"). This renders it all but impossible to observe and gauge Paul's usage (1:7, 2:2 [twice], 2:5; 3:15, 19; 4:2, 10 [twice]). In the comments on verse 1:7, above, the sense of be minded/disposed was forwarded, and that indeed captures well Paul's usage here and throughout. Nowhere more urgently than here, in the lead-up to the Christ Hymn, is Paul striving to construct an ethos, or an ethical framework, with(in) which the community is to act. In the comments on 1:7, the various role models found within Philippians, including the Philippian community itself, are noted. None of those is more central, of course, than Christ, as verse 5 and the Christ Hymn itself will make clear.

Here in verse 2 it is the Paul-Philippians relationship, established so firmly and repeatedly in chapter 1 that is stressed and (re)affirmed. In its own (somewhat subtle) way, the NRSV captures well the structuring of verse 2. The balance of the verse, following "make my joy complete," is a result clause. This is introduced in English by a phrase such as "in order that," or "with the result that." The NRSV simply has a colon. But the symbol is, or at least can be, potent: "make my joy complete" *in these following ways*. That's what the structure of verse 2 is facilitating. And, as we've seen, the two phrases including "mind" or, better, be minded/disposed, are key. So too is the use of "love," which draws on and reminds the reader of the very pointed usage of "love" in 1:9–11 and 2:1. Before moving onto verses 3–4 it should be noted that the NRSV's "being in full accord" actually renders one of the many and creative compound words using "co-" or "with" that Paul employs in Philippians. (See comments on 1:5 and 1:7 above; besides the usages in 1:7 and here, Paul uses the intensifier "co-" to form compound words in 1:27, 2:25 [twice], 3:10, 3:17, 4:2 [in reference to what may be a proper name], 4:3 [twice], and 4:14.) The final two phrases of the NRSV translation of verse 2, "being in full accord and of one mind," would be better rendered as one phrase: "co-souls being minded/disposed to the same thing."

In verses 3–4 Paul moves out of the Paul-Philippians system established in verse 2 to a consideration of behavior toward "others." Key to these verses is the use of "humility" in verse 3. Arguably, the bulk of verses 3–4 is a comment on what that concept means or entails. Moreover, it introduces into the letter and into the overall ethic that Paul is constructing a disposition or virtue that is evidenced in Christ (2:8) and in the community (3:21). But, what sort of virtue is this?

Clearly "humility" is not something to be strived for, or put on display in one's actions, within the broader Greco-Roman world. Paul's contemporary, the moral philosopher Epictetus, will have nothing of it. Using both the same word and a closely related one built on the same root, he writes: ". . . do not go humbly. . . . Where is there yet a place . . . for humility?" (*Discourses* 3.24.54–56). Put simply, what Paul says makes no sense, yet he says it. There is some scriptural warrant, of course, to bolster such a case as Paul is making, of which he is more than likely fully aware: "wisdom is with the humble"; "humility goes before honor" (Prov. 11:2; 15:33). More central is Job 5:11, which captures and supports the narrative twist of the Christ Hymn (2:8–9) and the ethic Paul derives from it (see esp. Phil. 3:21, and the attendant comments below): "[God] sets on high those who are lowly." As found in the Septuagint (ancient Greek) version of Hebrew Scripture, the word for "lowly" shares the same root Paul uses here and might be rendered "humble." But Paul is not interested, at least overtly, in such scriptural warrant as he drives his addressees to the Christ Hymn of 2:6–11 and, as we will see therein, the use of "humbled" in verse 8.

Verse 5 serves as the transitional sentence from the introduction of 2:1–4 into the Christ Hymn itself. There are several simple yet profound points that cannot and should not be missed with regard to this sentence, especially for readers familiar with popular American religiosity. First, the form of minded/disposed used here, as in both cases within verse 2, is verbal. It is not a noun as suggested by "mind" in the NRSV. Here in verse 5, the form is a simple imperative—"Be so minded." Second, as is crystal clear in the Greek, the imperative is directed to a collective. "You [Philippians, as a collective] be so minded." The directive is to the whole church, the community, not to an individual or even to a group of independent individuals. Third, Paul's guiding ethical question is not, "What would Jesus do?" Rather it is, "What has Christ Jesus done?" Fourth, Paul does not shy away from consideration of Christ Jesus's divine identity or from the divine context within which Christ's emptying (2:7) begins. Quite the opposite, these are key for locating and understanding the mindedness or disposition toward which Paul points his addressees in verse 5. And, as will become clear, such mindedness with regard to Christ is not reckoned by Paul as comfortably distant or readily detachable from individual consideration or consumption. As indicated by the eschatological context of the second half of the Christ Hymn (2:9–11), the exhortation immediately following the Christ Hymn (2:12–13), and the revisiting of the Christ story in 3:20–21, "we" the addressees—are very much part and parcel of that story and of God's action with regard to it.

Verses 6–11 form a narrative and lyrical whole. The NRSV, in its presentation and formatting of these verses, captures well their hymnic nature. This passage is not epistolary narrative, thanksgiving, greeting, or exhortation, but something markedly different. Regarding both form and content, there is a notable degree of symmetry and structure within the hymn in the following ways:

- Of the six total verses, the first set of three are regarding Christ's actions while the second set of three are regarding God's, and others', actions on behalf of, or with regard to, Christ;
- There are three distinct or separable statements per verse (though see discussion of verses 7 and 8, below);
- There are other notable sets of three, including "heaven . . . earth . . . under the earth" in verse 10;
- The hymn begins where it ends—in heaven, that supramundane and eternal realm above earthly reality and perception.

Regarding content, the second part of the hymn is dominated by, and draws on, the eschatological vision of Isaiah 45, especially verse 23. The first part arguably also draws on Isaiah (the so-called Servant Songs of Isaiah, chapters 42–53, though a different word for "slave" or "servant" is used in the Septuagint [ancient Greek] version of those songs than is used in v. 7 here) as well as on any number of biblical and extrabiblical understandings of one or more divine attendants in consort with, or within, the godhead. (E.g., there is the presentation of personified Wisdom in Prov. 8 or in Sir., as referenced in the discussion regarding 1:11, above. Within the New Testament, see Jesus' comment regarding Satan in Luke 10:18, which takes the reader back to the same eternal, heavenly realm found in this hymn.)

Did Paul write the Christ Hymn? Characteristic of the hymn are its several unusual or unique terms, including "form" (vv. 6 and 7), "something to be exploited" (v. 6), "highly exalted" (v. 9), and "under the earth" (v. 10). Further, matters that one might expect to see addressed in such a piece composed by Paul—such as the resurrection (which is glossed over or left unstated) or justification (not considered)—are notably absent. Of course, such considerations can wear thin. One would be hard pressed to compare 1 or 2 Thessalonians or even Philippians theme for theme or term for term with Galatians or Romans. Further, there is much within the hymn that resonates loudly and clearly with passages and themes elsewhere in Paul's letters. Two ready examples of this are the use of Isaiah 45 (referenced above and discussed further regarding vv. 10–11 below) in Romans 14:11 and the description of "our Lord Jesus Christ" in 2 Corinthians 8:9 (". . . though he was rich, yet for our sakes he became poor . . ."). At the very least, these examples are quite consistent with the treatment and description of Christ Jesus herein.

Whether from Paul's hand originally (which is perfectly possible) or not (the more likely, in my opinion), the composition of this hymn would seem to predate that of the letter. If indeed the last line of verse 8 is an insertion into an otherwise strictly structured, balanced hymnic whole, then that very addition might indicate the mark of Paul inserted within the hymn. Regardless of whether the hymn was composed or borrowed (or both) by Paul for use within Philippians, and regardless of whether Paul has altered the structure of the hymn with a later insertion, what is clear is this: Paul sets up this hymn as a crucial element within the overall letter. This element influences and informs both that which precedes (as we have seen through the lead-in to these verses) and that which follows it (as we will see, e.g., in verse 3:20–21).

As discussed above, the hymn begins in heaven. Not surprisingly in so structured and dense a composition, many of the words are charged. A recent United States president, in a context and a setting far more mundane than those under discussion here, famously said: "It depends upon what the meaning of the word *is* is." Here in verse 6, it is the meaning of "was" that is charged and worthy of deeper consideration. Though the NRSV translation rightly captures one level of its meaning, the particular Greek verb used here has at its root to do with "beginning" or "foundational" things or existences. The hymn begins by establishing that Christ

Jesus "was existing" or even, "was existing originally." Further, since it is a compound that includes a preposition, the very form of the verb propels the reader forward. What is already suggested in the verb is spelled out more fully in the prepositional phrase, "in the form of God." And strikingly, that very word, "form," is repeated in verse 7 connecting the heavenly and the earthly existences of Christ in direct and startling ways. By comparison, the archetypal fairy tale *The Prince and the Pauper* would seem to be about two socioeconomic equals relative to what is being described here.

The point is made in several ways throughout verses 6–7. The single word that is translated "something to be exploited" is only found in this verse within the New Testament, and the NRSV captures well its range of meaning, from a prize or prized possession to (stolen) booty.

Interestingly, the word "form" is unique within the letters of Paul and exceedingly rare within the whole of the New Testament. Its one other usage is in a passage that many text critics believe was later added to the Gospel of Mark, Mark 16:12. There it has the sense of appearance or shape that, perhaps, captures something of its meaning in verse 7 where its usage is largely metaphorical; after all, Christ, or Jesus, was not, literally a slave (so far as we know or so far as is reported in the New Testament or broader early Christian literature). Was Christ literally "in the form of God"? It depends, to a significant degree, on what the meaning of "form" is. Does it mean "shape" or "appearance"? Perhaps either or both of those approach(es) its meaning. In Galatians 4:19, Paul uses the verbal form of this same word, "to form," in the passive voice: "Christ is formed in you." Therein a closer, integral, all-pervasive sense of formation is suggested, beyond or separate from (mere) shape or appearance.

"Equality" is also uniquely used only here among Paul's letters, though it is used several times elsewhere within the New Testament. It is used generally with the sense of equivalency or consistency (e.g., Mark 14:56, 59; Acts 11:17). Particularly relevant for understanding this passage may be John 5:18 regarding reaction to Jesus' statements. The narrator comments that Jesus "was also calling God his own father, thereby making himself equal to God." The whole phrase, "equality with God," might have suggested to the Philippians—living, as they were, in a Roman colony founded by Julius Caesar—a particular imperial honorific, with its attendant affirmations and understandings of leadership and power. A contemporary of Julius Caesar, Nicolaus of Damascus, writes in his biography of Caesar that Caesar "was honored even as the equal of God" (translation mine; for further discussion, see Heen, "Phil. 2:6–11 and Resistance to Local Timocratic Rule. . . ."). It may indeed be that this whole hymn, having to do with the opposite of attending to or progressing toward honor in the Roman imperial way, is something of a parody of that system (see esp. comments on 2:11 and 3:20–21).

The first physical (if that's the right word) positive action by Christ is described as such: Christ Jesus "emptied himself." Unlike several other terms discussed above, this one *is* used several other times by Paul (and only by Paul, within the New Testament: Rom. 4:14, 1 Cor. 1:17; 9:15, 2 Cor. 9:3), though in contexts quite different from this. The simple sense of "emptied" well suggests the root meaning of the word. Among the documents within the so-called *Apostolic Fathers* (Christian writings from in and around the second century) a passage in the *The Shepherd of Hermas* would seem to capture the meaning of the term, interestingly in the context of a spirit leaving, or emptying, a human, earthly body (Mandate 11:14).

The use of "himself" here is arguably troublesome: who or what precisely does it refer to? Presumably not to the subject of the hymn, Christ Jesus, in an essential way, since he would appear to maintain a fixed identity/integrity throughout the whole of the hymn even as he undergoes changes; indeed, the hymn would lose much of its power and meaning were that not the case. Presumably "himself" is a reference more particularly to the heavenly or eternal state or form in which we, the reader/listener/reciter/singer of the hymn, first meet Christ Jesus.

In the above discussion of the structure of the hymn I noted that each of the six verses of the hymn (as presented in the text of the New Testament) contains three separable lines or units; that structure is captured well in the NRSV. The exception to this rule would appear to be verse 7 which contains four units: (1) ". . . emptied . . ."; (2) "taking the form . . ."; (3) "being born . . ."; and (4) ". . . being found. . . ." Simply stated, if you shift that fourth element over into verse 8 (leaving a neat list of three in v. 7), then you end up with another neat list of three: (1) ". . . being found . . ."; (2) ". . . humbled . . ."; and (3) ". . . became obedient . . ." This is followed by a final extra statement in verse 8, which appears as though it might be a nonmetrical add-on or insertion into an otherwise neatly structured whole: "even death on a cross." As suggested in the discussion on structure above, that insertion, if it is an insertion, may be the hand of Paul at work in making the hymn his own (by analogy to the way a great vocalist like Ray Charles, Billie Holliday, or Frank Sinatra will make a song his or her own through characteristic expressions or turns of phrase). Certainly the use of "cross" and the closely related verb, "crucify" is characteristic of Paul (e.g., Phil. 3:18; 1 Cor. 1:18; 2:8; 2 Cor. 13:4; Gal. 5:11, 24; 6:12, 14).

Beyond this arguably very Pauline focus on the cross, the hymn provides other foci for Christ's earthly or human existence, following the emptying. On analogy with 2 Corinthians 8:9 cited above, the reference to "slave" may indicate the vast and unfathomable change in Christ's status, from (equality with) God to human. It may also suggest a reference to the Servant Songs of Isaiah 42–53, though, as noted above in the discussion of the hymn's structure, the word for "slave" or "servant" in the Septuagint version of Isaiah is different than the word used here.

There are a couple of elements in the fourth or final Servant Song (Isa. 52:13–53:12) that seem to be quite alive within the Christ Hymn. In the Septuagint version of both Isaiah 53:8 and 53:12 it is stated that the servant was "led" or "given over" unto "death" (the same word for "death" as found [twice] in Phil. 2:8). Further, extant only in the Septuagint version of Isaiah 53:8 is the use of the noun form of the verb found in Philippians 2:8, "humbled." It is "in humbleness" or "by way of humbleness" that the servant is "led to death" (Isa. 53:8 LXX; "LXX" is shorthand for "Septuagint"). Beyond the possible allusion to Isaiah 53:8 LXX and to the servant, what is the role of "humbled" in Philippians 2:8? Paul picks up on this same word/concept in Philippians 3:21 where it is a virtue, not a shame (something that is easily missed; see further discussion regarding 3:21, below). Similarly, Paul picks up directly on "became obedient," which follows "humbled," raising it immediately following the close of the hymn (2:12; see further discussion below).

In 1 Peter 5:5–6, which is a telling parallel both to Philippians 3:21 and to Philippians 2:8–9, it is God who will exalt the "humble." The same is true here. Notably, these two markers "humbled" and "exalted," are located at the turning point of the hymn. As noted in the discussion of structure above, half of the Christ Hymn reports on the activities of Christ while the other half reports on God's, and others', response to those activities. It is verses 8–9 that provide that transition, as the first half closes with "death" (and particularly, in the possible Pauline addition to the hymn discussed above, the "cross"), and the second half begins with "God also highly exalted him." It is the word "therefore" (v. 9) that sits at the turning point, rightly pointing back to what has been as that which results, in what is about to be narrated. Though the particular term for "highly exalted" used here is not found elsewhere in the New Testament, it is a compound word formed from the same word for "exalt" used in 1 Peter 5:5–6, and is immediately recognizable as such (just as "highly exalted" and "exalted" are immediately recognizable as sharing the same word). More to the point, this very same word, "highly exalted," is employed in the Septuagint version of Psalm 37:35: "[God] saw the impious one very highly exalting himself." Of course, God "passed by" that one and did not acknowledge him (due to a different numeration system for the Psalms as found in the Septuagint, the parallel is Psalm 36:35–36 LXX; translations mine). Here God responds positively and decisively to Christ and "highly exalted him."

The cosmology depicted in these final verses of the hymn is perfectly consistent with that which is indicated at the top of the hymn. The realms of "heaven" and "earth" are evident in verses 6–7; the realm of "under the earth" is not referenced or alluded to until verse 10. We have already noted an interesting parallel to 1 Peter. Within the New Testament, the famous passages regarding the so-called (according to traditional Western church language) harrowing of hell are also from 1 Peter 3:19–20 and 4:6. Therein Christ "went and made a proclamation to the spirits in prison" (3:19); that is, "the gospel was proclaimed even to the dead" (4:6). The reference to those "under the earth" would seem to be to these same ones.

Not to be missed is that after Christ's exaltation, God "gave him the name that is above every name." Does that suggest a divine realm or godhead within which there are more identifiable divine consorts than simply this one, Christ? It may, and parallels for such are readily found in the cosmologies within any number of gnostic documents. But one need look no further than that passage from Luke 10:18 cited in the introductory discussion to the Christ Hymn, above. What exactly is "the name that is above every name"? Presumably, "Lord." The Greek word order of verse 11 puts stress on "Lord" in a way difficult to capture in English: "Lord is Jesus Christ" is a close approximation. Finally, on the basis of Isaiah 45:23–25 and more broadly on the basis of use of "Lord" throughout the Servant Songs section of Isaiah, it is clear that "Lord" is, indeed, the ultimate name: ". . . I am he. Before me no god was formed, nor shall there be any after me" (Isa. 43:10). Of course, such giving or gracing of Christ Jesus with such a unique, honored, and worshiped name for God from biblical literature is striking. Interestingly, and consistent with Paul's letters broadly, the place of God "the Father" as that one who enacts Christ's resurrection (e.g., Rom. 10:9; 1 Cor. 6:14; 15:15; Gal. 1:1) and to whom glory is directed (Phil. 4:20; see similarly Rom. 6:6; 16:27; 2 Cor. 1:20; 4:6) remains firm and unquestioned.

Further, there is political bite to this statement about the granting of the "name," especially as it informs the confession in verse 11, "Jesus Christ is Lord." But Caesar is Lord, no? Well, yes. For example, extant references to Nero (emperor 54–68 CE) as "Lord" include "Nero the Lord" (Oxyrhynchus papyri no. 246) and "Nero, Lord of the whole world" (No. 814 in W. Dittenberger, *Sylloge inscriptionum graecarum* [Leipzig: Hirzel, 1915–1924]; translations mine). We have already noted that Julius Caesar was reckoned as being "equal to God" (see discussion of v. 6, above). There can be little doubt that for Paul's addressees in Philippi, as indicated in discussion of verse 6 above, these would have resonated as honorifics for Caesar.

What were they to make of it? As we have already seen, the pointed language of 1:27 (see discussion, above), which is lost in the translation of the NRSV, suggests a critique and a creative response. Further, as we will see below, the very notion/concept that "Jesus Christ is Lord" may have threatened some level of fear or questioning within the community (esp. 3:1), while Philippians 3:20–21 would seem to provide a more definitive Christian framework on which to found a notion of Christian citizenship.

OBEDIENCE AND MUTUALITY (AND BOASTING)
Philippians 2:12–18

2:12 **Therefore, my beloved, just as you have always obeyed me, not only in my presence, but much more now in my absence, work out your own salvation with fear and trembling; [13] for it is God who is at work in you, enabling you both to will and to work for his good pleasure.**

[14] Do all things without murmuring and arguing, [15] so that you may be blameless and innocent, children of God without blemish in the midst of a crooked and perverse generation, in which you shine like stars in the world. [16] It is by your holding fast to the word of life that I can boast on the day of Christ that I did not run in vain or labor in vain. [17] But even if I am poured out as a libation over the sacrifice and the offering of your faith, I am glad and rejoice with all of you— [18] and in the same way you also must be glad and rejoice with me.

We have repeatedly seen the mutuality and sharing that connects Paul with the Philippian community (see esp. discussions above regarding 1:7 and 1:26). This hortatory section begins by picking up on the notion of obedience as found in the Christ Hymn (2:8) in a particularly hierarchical way (2:12). It then moves through pointed directives (2:12, 14) toward a reestablishing of the mutuality (and attendant boasting) that Paul feels, and promotes, toward his addressees.

Paul proceeds, following the hymn, in a very active, deliberate manner. The "therefore" at the top of the sentence ties the exhortation, which is to come, directly into the hymn (or, by extension, into all of 2:1–11 or even all of 1:27–2:11). The address, "my beloved," or better (to reflect the plural of the word that Paul uses), "my beloved ones," reaffirms the close relationship he has with the Philippians (see comment on 1:12, above). Does Paul's use of "beloved" introduce a different metaphor than, or build on the same one that, he has established via the family terminology of 1:12, 14? That "beloved ones" can and did refer to family members in biblical tradition is indicated immediately in the telling of the Abraham-Isaac story of Genesis 22 within the Septuagint, in which Isaac is repeatedly referred to as "your son, your beloved" (Gen. 22:2, 12, 16 LXX; translated differently in the NRSV given the Hebrew text tradition). Elsewhere Paul uses the term consistently with that tradition (so regarding Timothy in 1 Cor. 4:17) and consistently with the "brother and sister" or "sibling" language he has established herein (so regarding Onesimus in Phlm. 16; see discussion of that verse in commentary on Philemon, below).

Given the established mutuality that has predominated within the letter, there is arguably something of a change in tone here as Paul recounts in a rather teacherly way the "obedience" that his addressees have shown him "not only in my presence, but much more now in my absence." Paul's first sentence here suggests that, vis-à-vis the matter of obedience, he is in the role of God while the Philippian community presumes the role of Christ. Those are pretty high stakes and quite a set of models! On the matter of rhetoric and language, Paul elsewhere merges intimate language of friendship with the notion of obedience; Philemon includes precisely the same term, "beloved" (Phlm. 1, 21 [the word translated "friend" in the NRSV is the same as that translated "beloved" here]), as does 2 Corinthians 7:1, 15 [the latter of which is discussed further below]).

The first directive picks up on the plurality of the term, "beloved." Unclear in the English is that both the command, "work out," and the possessive, "your," are in the plural; tellingly, "salvation" is not. Paul is addressing the community: "you all work out [together] your own [common] salvation." Particularly in the United States, where common notions of religion posit salvation and relationship to God as personal matters, it is important to recognize the repeated and consistent thrust of Paul's words and concepts; they are directed to, and defined by, the community of faith. Anyone who has done the "work" called for by life in community will appreciate the particular verb form here, which suggests ongoing "work": "continue to work out," "be working out (over time)."

Whatever the role of the ominous duo of "fear and trembling," they are clearly to be functioning within the life and for the "work" of the community of faith. Perhaps consistent with the parallel regarding obedience noted above in 2:12 vis-à-vis 2:8 (Paul is to God as the Philippian community is to Christ), Paul writes in 2 Corinthians 7:15: "And [Titus's] heart goes out all the more to you, as he remembers the obedience of all of you, and how you welcomed him with fear and trembling." Notice how Titus (as Paul's representative, who is God's representative) is the recipient of the community's "fear and trembling." And notice how "obedience" is, consistent with the Christ Hymn and this verse which follows it, the key or buzzword for the work of the community. Returning to Philippians, we see that 2:13 squares the circle: regarding the active community of faith, it is, in fact, "God who is at work in you, enabling you both to will and to work. . . ." The sentence recalls for Paul's addressees the (simple) phrase that closes 1:28, while for broader readers of Paul's letters it calls to mind 1 Thessalonians 2:13. Again, Paul's language, with its unambiguously plural use of "you," makes clear that it is the plurality, the community, that is the locus of God's "work."

The next couple of verses recall influential and formative chapters from Scripture. The first is immediately relevant to life together in and as community. Who is it that famously engages in "murmuring"? Again, a plurality: the congregation of children of Israel in the wilderness (see esp. Num. 14:27 [three times]; cf. 14:2 and 36 that in the Septuagint version employ a compound word built on the same root). On one level, Paul (like any number of Jewish and Christian teachers and preachers over the millennia) is saying, don't complain against God and argue among yourselves. But there's far more.

Having brought his addressees (figuratively) into the wilderness in verse 14, he now recasts (in v. 15) a line from the Song of Moses at the close of the book of Deuteronomy in a fascinating and multilayered way. Deuteronomy 32:5 reads, ". . . [God's] degenerate *children* have dealt falsely with him, a *perverse and crooked generation*" (NRSV; italics added to indicate direct parallels with Phil. 2:15. Paul's word order, "crooked and perverse," reflects the Greek of the Septuagint version of this verse). In Moses' song God's "children" are "the perverse and crooked generation." In Paul, the "children" are something else. They find themselves within that broader "crooked and perverse generation." Paul's reworking indicates his eschatological understanding and his ethical framing of Christian life and work within that eschatological context (see, for example, 1 Thess. 4–5, esp. 4:5; 5:1, 4–5; similarly Gal. 1:4).

The two terms that frame verse 15, "stars" and "blameless," suggest other scriptural watersheds, particularly that of the Abraham story. Of the two covenant chapters within the Abraham story, "stars" recalls the first (Gen. 15, esp. 15:5) and "blameless" the second (Gen. 17, esp. 17:1). Clearly for Paul, Abraham is a key figure for Christian formation and proclamation (Gal. 3, Rom. 4) and one could well speculate that Paul had taught this Philippian community something about that patriarch and his relevance to them. But perhaps even more to the point is this verse from Daniel 12:3: "Those who are wise shall shine like the brightness of the sky, and those who lead many to righteousness, like the stars forever and ever." These latter chapters of Daniel are, of course, eschatological in setting and outlook. Further, the call to "lead many to righteousness" in Daniel, to the degree it is active here in Philippians, recalls the "harvest of righteousness" of Philippians 1:11. And that harvest is, of course, an eschatological one—see Philippians 1:10, "day of Christ" (and the comments on the phrase, "the day of Jesus Christ," in 1:6, above).

2:16 picks up broadly on a constellation of matters orbiting around the community's identity and work and its relationship to Paul with its reintroduction of "boasting" into the letter (see 1:25–26). There, as here, the boasting is premised on the ongoing relationship of Paul to the community and to the community's ongoing relationship to its identity and work. We have already seen how Paul's pointed use of "spread" or, better, "progress" ties the work of the community into Paul's circumstance and into the "harvest" associated with "the day of Christ" (1:10–11; see comments on 1:12 and on 1:25–26 above). So here in 2:16, the use of "boasting" and "day of Christ" recalls and affirms all of that. The mutuality motif is reaffirmed and furthered as in 1:26, where it is their ("your") boasting. Here it is Paul's. The crisis and gravity of Paul's current circumstance (see again 1:12 and, esp. 1:19–24), perhaps masked by the creatively used verbs "run" (which prefigures the motif of running a race in ch. 3, esp. v. 12) and "labor" (which recalls the work and production language of 1:22 and 1:11), is again brought front and center in 2:17.

The fascinating and complicated imagery of sacrifice in 2:17 is presented almost in passing. Like the proverbial landmark or turn along a highway it might be said, "blink and you'll miss it." But to do so would be to miss a lot of what is, and isn't, in Philippians. First, many preachers and theologians, beginning within the New Testament, understand Christ's death as one of sacrifice (e.g., Heb. 9:23–26; 10:12 as well as,

within the collection of Paul's letters [see Introduction to the Commentary, above], Eph. 5:2, use the same word that Paul uses here). Neither the Christ Hymn nor the surrounding discussion within Philippians suggests that. The sacrificial imagery in Philippians is consistently in reference to human activity (see also 2:30, "services," which is a translation of the same word used for "offering" here; also 4:18, "sacrifice" and "offering," the latter being a different word than that translated "offering" here). Second, Paul's use of sacrifice imagery underscores the mutuality between himself and the community. It is he that is "poured out as a libation"; it is they, or more particularly their faith, that is "the sacrifice and the offering" over which he, as libation, is poured. Third, we have already seen the nuance and creativity alive within verses 14–15 as Paul draws variously on wilderness (Num. 14), Mosaic (The Song of Moses, esp. Deut. 32:5), Abrahamic (Gen. 15 and 17), and eschatological (esp. Dan. 12:3) motifs. That list is now expanded via the sacrifice language in verse 17 (see esp. Num. 28:3, 9, 19, 31 for repeated identification of sacrificial lambs "without blemish"). Interestingly, and perhaps precisely to the point, the sacrifices outlined in Numbers 28 are "appointed" for use "daily" (Num. 28:3), weekly ("on the Sabbath day," Num. 28:9), monthly (Num. 28:11), and variously on other appointed days throughout the year. The identity and work and "faith" of the community are regular and ongoing. Further underscoring the mutuality, the "libation" or "drink offering" is a regular part of carrying out these sacrifices (see esp. Num. 28:7, 10, 14). No libation, no sacrifice (and vice versa): the community and Paul need each other.

As indicated above, the gravity of Paul's current circumstance is brought back to the fore in verse 17. There are various elements which underscore that—not least the repeated use of "rejoice" language in 2:17–18 (see esp. 1:18), which again underscores the mutuality between him and his addressees. Does the language of "being poured out as a libation" recall and affirm the motif(s) of death and execution found esp. in 1:19–24? Yes. An inscription from the second century ominously suggests a possible understanding of Paul's use herein. In that inscription, the execution of a prophet of the god Apollo is remembered as a "drink offering" (cited in Bauer, 937a). 2 Tim 4:6 appears to use the motif in precisely the same fashion: "I am already being poured out as a libation, and the time of my departure has come." So here. But that said, it is notable that in Philippians 1:24 Paul has arrived at a quite different decision than that coloring 2 Timothy 4:6. At least to the degree Paul can exercise or assume control of the matter, he tells his addressees that he is "convinced" (Phil. 1:25) of ongoing life and, presumably, a stay of execution.

WORK(ERS) OF CHRIST
Philippians 2:19–30

2:19 I hope in the Lord Jesus to send Timothy to you soon, so that I may be cheered by news of you. [20] I have no one like him who will be genuinely concerned for your welfare. [21] All of them are seeking their own interests, not those of Jesus Christ. [22] But Timothy's worth you know, how like a son with a father he has served with me in the work of the gospel. [23] I hope therefore to send him as soon as I see how things go with me; [24] and I trust in the Lord that I will also come soon.

[25] Still, I think it necessary to send to you Epaphroditus—my brother and coworker and fellow soldier, your messenger and minister to my need; [26] for he has been longing for all of you, and has been distressed because you heard that he was ill. [27] He was indeed so ill that he nearly died. But God had mercy on him, and not only on him but on me also, so that I would not have one sorrow after another. [28] I am the more eager to send him, therefore, in order that you may rejoice at seeing him again, and that I may be less anxious. [29] Welcome him then in the Lord with all joy, and honor such people, [30] because he came close to death for the work of Christ, risking his life to make up for those services that you could not give me.

The attention to Paul's current circumstance, raised anew by 2:17, directly informs and colors this section as Paul considers two colleagues. The first, Timothy, is formally coauthor of the letter and is closely aligned and associated with Paul (see comments on 1:1). The second, Epaphroditus, is known among Paul's letters and within the New Testament only in Philippians (see also Phil. 4:18). Beyond taking the opportunity to sort out immediate and longer range plans, Paul is keen to teach something about "genuinely" (v. 20) doing the "work of Christ" (v. 30). These are the next two in a series of models (see comments on 1:7, above) that Paul establishes and considers within Philippians.

One notable characteristic of these verses is the movement from gladness and rejoicing (v. 17–18) to cheer (v. 19). Arguably the word that Paul uses for the potentiality of being "cheered" by news of the Philippians is an uptick from those used in the previous verses. It is unique in his letters and within the New Testament, is built on the word for "soul," and suggests not only "cheer" but what we might call "heart" or "courage." As we've seen so often in this letter, the mutuality between letter writer and addressees is repeatedly affirmed and expanded, and so also here. Further, the gravity of his imprisonment is again at play, both as news of them will mean so much and as his helplessness in visiting them (at least for the time being; see 1:26; 2:24) is again referenced.

The back and forth of positive and negative models in verses 20–22 approximates that which we saw in 1:15–18; indeed the easiest and, perhaps, best reading would be to presume direct congruence with that passage. In that case, the negative models are the same in each passage, while the focus on Timothy being "genuinely concerned" for their "interests" takes particular shape in light of the lead up to the Christ Hymn, especially 2:3. Alternatively, taking Paul's "I have . . ." for all it is worth would seem to indict all the rest of Paul's coworkers and, by extension, all others surrounding him; but it is hard to imagine that he intends that, particularly in light of 1:14 and 2:25–30.

The term translated "like him" is actually far more pointed and, in light of the term used for "cheered" (see discussion immediately above) sets up a catchy word phrase. Like the term for "cheered," the descriptor Paul uses for Timothy is built on the word for "soul." At the risk of engaging in gibberish, one might translate this section of verse 19–20 as follows: ". . . so that I may be good-souled by news of you. I have no one equal-souled. . . ." Paul's descriptions link Timothy very closely with Paul and link Timothy's motives directly with Paul's. Again, mutuality is key: Paul will be cheered by their flourishing; Timothy will have their flourishing to heart (or better, to soul).

Timothy's own "worth" to the mission—or to the spread/progress of the gospel (see comments on 1:12 and 1:25)—is known to the Philippians and is connected, like theirs, to relationship to Paul. That relationship is put in very pronounced imagery as Paul writes that "like a son with a father he has served with me in the work of the gospel." The verb "served" is built on the same root as the title "servants" or "slaves" that Paul and Timothy use at the top of the letter and recalls that title for the reader (see discussion of 1:1, above). The word "son" would be better translated as "child"; the particular word Paul uses has no presumption of gender and is the same as that used of the Philippians (with its attendant biblical allusion) in 2:15. Indeed, Paul uses the same term elsewhere regarding his relationship with Timothy (1 Cor. 4:17) and Onesimus (Phlm. 10; see also 1 Tim. 1:2 and Titus 1:4). The child/father motif is a familiar one to describe what we might call spiritual or moral education within the biblical tradition (Prov., esp. 4:1–2; Sir. 39:13) and is used in Greek philosophical literature with regard to the student/teacher relationship (famously, from the point of view of his students, regarding Socrates: "we felt that he was like a father to us" [Plato, *Phaedo* 116A]; for a contemporary with Paul, see Musonius Rufus, fragment 8, in Lutz).

The popular philosopher and writer, Cicero, who served for a time as governor in the city of Tarsus that is so closely linked with Paul (see esp.

Acts 21:39), wrote, "There are many levels of association among humans:
. . . the same people, tribe, language; . . . it is a still closer bond to be a
member of the same state . . . ; An even closer link of association is that
between kindred" (*On Duties* 1.50.54). It is worth noting that by this point
in the letter, Paul has touched on all three in forming and (re)affirming the
identity and mission of his Philippian addressees—the language of political or state associations ("live as citizens"; see comments on 1:27, above);
the language of people or tribe (with references to the children of Israel
and Abraham, among others, 2:14–15); and the language of kindred or
family ("beloved," 2:12; and "child"/"father" here). Particularly the first,
the language of political or state associations, will loom large later in the
letter (3:20–21).

The family imagery ("brother") continues in verse 25, as does the use
of "co-" or "with" words ("coworker and fellow soldier") that, we have
seen, is so characteristic of this letter (see esp. comments on 1:5, 7, above).
"Brother," of course, reinforces, and is reinforced by, the family imagery within this section (2:12 and 2:22). "Coworker" picks up directly on
the "work" described in verse 22. "Fellow soldier" may have a particular
ring in Philippians' ears as their city had, a few generations prior, been
reconstituted as a military colony (see introduction to Philippians, above).
The two other terms used in reference to Epaphroditus are also notable.
"Messenger" is the NRSV's translation of the word normally translated
as "apostle" (e.g., when used by Paul in reference to Paul, as apostle; see
comments on 1:1, above). At its root, it has the sense of "one sent," or
"ambassador"—that would convey Paul's use here, indicating the importance of Epaphroditus both as a representative of, and link to, the Philippian community.

As "minister" to Paul's need, Epaphroditus is quite literally an embodiment of what Paul was pointing to in 2:17; the word for "minister" and
that for "offering," as in "offering of your faith" are precisely the same.
In order to make the connection clearer, translate the word the same way
here: Epaphroditus is an *offering* to or for Paul's "need." The Greek root
for this word gives us the English word, "liturgy," which is/represents the
work of the community.

Paul's turn from verse 25 to verse 26 is masterful. Anyone familiar with
life in prison (then and now) would have no end of concerns for Paul's
"need," from physical safety to warmth, ventilation, exposure to natural
light, nutrition, exposure (or the hoped and prayed for lack thereof) to
torture and maltreatment, (appropriate) human contact and visitation,
and so on. Yet what does Paul do? He defines and describes his own need

in terms of concern for the Philippians and for Epaphroditus. Indeed the whole of this particular passage is introduced with the statement, "I think it is necessary," which provides a direct link to 1:24: Paul's current state of imprisonment is rendered "necessary" and meaningful by his very relationship to the Philippian community and, by extension, to the spread/progress and work of the gospel (1:25; 2:22; 2:25).

The "work," in this case "of Christ," is referenced again in verse 30 as is/are the "offerings"/ "offering" discussed immediately above. For those keeping score—and it's an important score to keep, as Paul builds for his addressees an understanding of life in community and for the gospel—Paul has used the same word in 2:17 ("offering"), 2:25 ("minister"), and 2:30 ("services"). The direct connection of these three—they're the same Greek word (!)—would not have been lost on the Philippians and should not be lost on any who are privileged to read this letter.

A final nuance to this passage, and to verse 30 in particular, is this: the term translated "life" is the same "soul" word that sits at the root of "cheered" (2:19) and "like" (2:20) as discussed above. That is, via both the meaning of the statement itself, and the word used, Paul ties Epaphroditus and his bold and self-sacrificing action directly into Paul's and Timothy's work; they are all similarly "souled." The charge at the close of verse 29, "honor such people," states what is already clear—these are models for the Christian life of spreading the gospel—and more broadly ties these two, and Paul as well, into that ethic that the Christ Hymn so clearly states.

OUR CITIZENSHIP IS IN HEAVEN
Philippians 3:1–21

3:1 **Finally, my brothers and sisters, rejoice in the Lord. To write the same things to you is not troublesome to me, and for you it is a safeguard.**
    [2] **Beware of the dogs, beware of the evil workers, beware of those who mutilate the flesh!** [3] **For it is we who are the circumcision, who worship in the Spirit of God and boast in Christ Jesus and have no confidence in the flesh—** [4] **even though I, too, have reason for confidence in the flesh.**

If anyone else has reason to be confident in the flesh, I have more: [5] **circumcised on the eighth day, a member of the people of Israel, of the tribe of Benjamin, a Hebrew born of Hebrews; as to the law, a Pharisee;** [6] **as to zeal, a persecutor of the church; as to righteousness under the law, blameless.**
    [7] **Yet whatever gains I had, these I have come to regard as loss because of Christ.** [8] **More than that, I regard everything as loss because of the surpassing value of knowing Christ Jesus my Lord. For his sake I have suffered**

the loss of all things, and I regard them as rubbish, in order that I may gain Christ [9] and be found in him, not having a righteousness of my own that comes from the law, but one that comes through faith in Christ, the righteousness from God based on faith. [10] I want to know Christ and the power of his resurrection and the sharing of his sufferings by becoming like him in his death, [11] if somehow I may attain the resurrection from the dead.

[12] Not that I have already obtained this or have already reached the goal; but I press on to make it my own, because Christ Jesus has made me his own. [13] Beloved, I do not consider that I have made it my own; but this one thing I do: forgetting what lies behind and straining forward to what lies ahead, [14] I press on toward the goal for the prize of the heavenly call of God in Christ Jesus. [15] Let those of us then who are mature be of the same mind; and if you think differently about anything, this too God will reveal to you. [16] Only let us hold fast to what we have attained.

[17] Brothers and sisters, join in imitating me, and observe those who live according to the example you have in us. [18] For many live as enemies of the cross of Christ; I have often told you of them and now I tell you even with tears. [19] Their end is destruction; their god is the belly; and their glory is in their shame; their minds are set on earthly things. [20] But our citizenship is in heaven, and it is from there that we are expecting a Savior, the Lord Jesus Christ. [21] He will transform the body of our humiliation that it may be conformed to the body of his glory, by the power that also enables him to make all things subject to himself.

This section of the letter follows directly on the previous and is very much a continuation of it, providing both negative (vv. 2, 18–19) and positive (vv. 3, 4–14) examples. The positive are dominated by Paul himself. Most important for his addressees and for understanding Philippians, will not be the autobiographical material Paul supplies—interesting and informative as it is—but what he does with it: the modeling of behavior for the whole community and the theological statements contained herein. Following direct, and nuanced, calls for action in verses 15–17 and another round of negative examples (vv. 18–19), Paul's political (1:27) and Christ-based (esp. 2:5–11) ethic of community identity and action reaches its culmination (3:20–21).

The transition verse into this section is a difficult one. First, why begin with "finally" when there is so much of the letter still to come? Second, why "rejoice"—again? Third, to what are the "same things" in the second half of 3:1 referring? Answers to these and related questions provide the opportunity for full and nuanced engagement of this somewhat complex and important section within the whole of the letter.

At its root, the term translated "finally" suggests something like "as for the rest." It can be, and is, used at the close of letters (esp. 2 Cor. 13:11; see also, in this same letter, Phil. 4:8) but can also be used, similarly to here, to introduce a broad set of exhortations (see esp. 1 Thess. 4:1; 2 Thess. 3:1). The call to "rejoice" is nothing new in this letter; quite the opposite, it has been (most recently 2:28 and 2:17–18), and will be even more, used throughout the letter (for discussion of, and references to the verb "rejoice" and the closely related noun form, "joy," throughout the letter, see comments on 1:4, above). The command here includes the important qualifier, "in the Lord." Following the Christ Hymn and preceding the extended section of negative and positive models to come, 3:2–3:14, 3:18–19, which is dominated by Paul himself as model, it appears to be no throwaway phrase. Indeed, the phrase "in the Lord" provides both the problem/challenge and the solution to that problem/challenge.

More so than looking back, the phrase "same things" points ahead to what Paul is about to do in this section. He will put out another warning (v. 2); describe again (see especially 1:15–18, which also included "rejoice") those who threaten Paul's teachings and the identity and mission of community (v. 2); recast "us" as embodying what those opponents claim for themselves (v. 3); set himself—"even though," or perhaps better, *because* he shares essential characteristics with the opponents—as model (v. 4–14); and, finally, put Jesus Christ, as "Lord," in his rightful place and put the community in its rightful place within that cosmic (in terms of both space and time) structure (vv. 20–21). And, along the way, Paul will note again the repetitive nature of his teaching(s) on this matter (see v. 18, "often").

That tension, which has been bubbling (in 1:15–18 and 1:28) at or below the surface throughout the letter, comes closest to erupting in the transition from 3:1 to 3:2. Going over this matter again is not "troublesome" to Paul and is a "safeguard" to them. The latter translates a Greek term that is used to this day in Greece in much the same way that "guarantee" is used in English speaking countries. In contrast to the situation that calls forth Paul's Letter to the Galatians, it would seem that the opponents have not yet directly threatened the community. Paul wants to guarantee that they don't. The repeated command, "beware," underlines the sense of gravity that Paul feels with regard to the threat.

The particular labels used suggest a similar biting irony to that which Paul employs against the rivals in Galatians. Therein, Paul is countering rivals who have, to some significant degree, influenced some among the Gentile Christian communities of Galatia to practice circumcision and other Jewish rites. In Galatians 5:12, Paul writes, "I wish those who unsettle you would castrate themselves!" A few verses later he writes, "if, however, you bite and devour one another, take care that you are not consumed by one another" (Gal. 5:15). Paul's language, edgy as it is, is even more so when one scratches below the surface. For example, though the "wish" of Galatians 5:12 and the statement regarding mutilation in Philippians 3:2 hardly need intensifying, they are given greater force when held up to the prohibition of Deuteronomy 23:1: "No one whose testicles are crushed or whose penis is cut off shall be admitted to the assembly of the LORD." As for the use of "dogs" in Philippians 3:2, does it suggest the same sort of behavior indicated disparagingly in Galatians 5:15? Likely so. And again, the description is given greater depth and irony when held against biblical tradition: dogs play a particular role in the Jezebel story (2 Kgs. 9:36), which may or may not be at play here, along with the generally negative portrait of wild dogs in biblical literature (e.g., 1 Sam. 17:43 and 2 Kgs. 8:13; Matt. 7:6 is of particular interest, as Jesus [a Jew] is addressing a Gentile). That "dogs" refers generally to Gentiles adds particular irony to its usage here.

So, who or what is being referred to in verse 2? Given the language (which, as we've seen, resonates with that in Galatians), the stated concern ("circumcision," v. 3), the sense of threat ("beware . . . beware," v. 2), and the broader context of "rivalry" (1:15) and opposition (esp. 1:28), it is very possible that Paul is countering the same or similar group as that to which he is responding in Galatians. A quick description is difficult for us since we live in such a vastly different religious world, though with labels that might suggest greater similarity than there is. It is easy to presume that these opponents are Jews. Indeed, they are. But that being the case, the opposition between them and Paul has virtually nothing of the sense that Christian versus Jewish religious disagreement might have today. First, Paul, too, is Jewish; directly sharing Scripture, language, and traditions with the opponents. Second, Paul, the Philippian community, and the opponents are all Christian; that is, whatever the tensions and disagreements, they are among those who identify with that movement. Third, the label, "Christian," is not used herein and is not used generally, if at all, by any of those involved. Fourth, at this time, Christianity has no generally recognized existence or status outside of the Jewish fold. Fifth—and as a corollary of the fourth—consideration of how one might welcome/bring/ritualize the entry of Gentile converts into the Christian—and therefore Jewish—fold is an inevitable concern, and one with which Paul is associated directly (for fuller discussion, see Weidmann, *Galatians*). With verse 3, Paul begins the transition through "us" to himself as model—a model pointedly contrasted with those named in verse 2. To the degree that the Philippian community to which Paul writes is made up largely, or even solely, of Gentiles (v. 4 suggests as much), his adoption of the label "circumcision" for them is consistent with the irony exhibited in verse 2.

Beyond irony, he may be making a point about the relative necessity or significance of circumcision for full inclusion in the (Christian) community—for Paul, full membership in the body of Christ does not necessitate or involve circumcision while for the opponents, apparently, it does. The contrast of "Spirit" with "flesh," though it may sound broadly Platonic or gnostic, or perhaps "spiritual" in a popularizing way, is, in Paul's rhetoric, part of the broadside against these opponents (compare Gal., esp. 5:5–6, 5:16–18). As we have seen, for Paul the Spirit is directly associated with Jesus Christ (1:19), as is boasting (1:26, 2:16); and so it is in both cases here. Though it hardly exhausts the nuance and complexity of this verse and the complex situation it reflects, one simple way to update or transition it, and these tensions, into the context of many churches in the United States today would be to ask the question, What practices or assumptions act as a block to acceptance of individuals or groups in the community? What is being asked, required, or presumed? Are those requests, requirements, or presumptions of the Spirit of Jesus Christ, or are they coming from another place? Right or wrong (clearly the opponents thought him wrong), Paul was trying to define and model Christian community across difference and beyond generally accepted religious and cultural practice.

As for Spirit and boasting, so too for "confidence"; the same term (it is actually a verb in Greek) is used three times in verses 3–4. Clearly Paul does not want his addressees to miss it. It recalls 1:14, "confident in the Lord," which captures Paul's non-circumcision position for inclusion of Gentiles in Christian community. But, for the sake of argument, and for the sake of modeling something of the Christian life, Paul considers the alternative (as in the discussion immediately above) that he pegs on the opponents: confidence in the flesh.

Paul's Jewish credentials, so he asserts, are unassailable; and he sets out to prove it. It might be noted again (as was indicated above) that this is not a Christian versus Jewish polemic; such would have made no sense to Paul (a Jew) at a time when Christianity had no status outside the Jewish religious fold. This is a polemic or sustained argument, including some biting irony (as we've seen), against those who promote circumcision among Gentile Christians, a position with which Paul disagrees. First, and relevant to the current concern, Paul was circumcised correctly and properly (Gen. 17:12): if you want to promote circumcision, you could not have a more perfectly practiced model than Paul. Second, Paul holds up the august history of the Jewish people and claims membership in that group. With this language, he also conjures the same biblical record which he did via allusions to the wilderness wandering and the Song of Moses in 2:14–15. What of the tribe of Benjamin? Among other claims to fame, in the blessing of Moses at the close of the book of Deuteronomy, this tribe is called "beloved of the Lord" (Deut. 33:12). The next phrase would seem to affirm all that he has said thus far, while the next three brief, but packed phrases advance Paul's lineage and birthright in a certain (set of) direction(s).

As a Pharisee, with regard "to the law," Paul places himself in that particular Jewish tradition (then) most closely associated with the Judaism practiced by Jews around the world today—rabbinic Judaism. Paul's training and professional identity were based on "the law"—not only the Bible (broadly) or, more particularly, the Torah or the books of Moses, but also what is often called the oral torah—that tradition of teachings going back ostensibly to the revelation to Moses at Sinai and maintained through a chain of legal scholars and teachers. For example, when Paul in Galatians 1:13–14 (a passage exhibiting significant parallels to this) refers to "the traditions of my ancestors," he is very likely speaking specifically about (some form of) the *Pirke Avot*, or *Fathers of Rabbi Nathan*, a foundational tract within rabbinic Judaism that came to be placed at the beginning of the Mishnah, which opens as such: "Moses received the law from Sinai, and he handed it down to Joshua, and Joshua to the elders [the Judges], and the elders to the prophets. . . ." Paul had studied and memorized such material. He knew the Jewish law well, at least as well as anybody (including these opponents) who claimed to base their teachings on understanding Jewish law. Indeed, so zealous was Paul that he even persecuted "the church," *and* so righteous was Paul (at least by the standards he used to measure, then) that he lived up to the very august label for the children of Israel that he alludes to in 2:15, and which he dare only put in the realm of possibility, "may," therein: "blameless."

And "yet," he takes a turn—a turn in his biography, and certainly a turn in his rhetoric and argument herein. For Paul, Christ changed, and Christ changes, everything. That is true (so far as we know) in the life of Paul as an individual (see also Gal. 1:15–16; beside that passage and this within Paul's writings, famous and slightly varying accounts are found in Acts 9:1–22; 22:4–16; and 26:9–18) and it is certainly true for Paul in his mission and letter writing. And notice, the matter is not simply "Christ" but "Christ Jesus" as "Lord." The relevance and multivalence of the term "Lord" does not escape Paul, and he will not have it escape his addressees (see comments on 2:11, above). The colorful language of forfeit or "loss" (twice) and, especially, "rubbish" (v. 8; Martin Luther famously translated the latter with the German equivalent of the word "shit," which captures well the sense of the Greek) establishes, in simple language, what Paul understands, not only for himself but for the whole Christian mission, to be the "gain" (see 1:21) that is in "Christ."

Before moving on to Paul's assessment of the central and foundational relevance of Christ, let us pause for a moment to look back on the sweep of these verses, verses 4–8. Paul had great and central status (v. 5). Indeed, he understood himself to be at the highest level (v. 6). Yet, he gave all that up as "loss" (v. 7). Who does this remind you of? Though Paul constructs no simple and easy correlation between himself and Christ as presented in the Christ Hymn (2:6–8), the loose parallels are there. But Paul is not interested, so much, in the parallel between himself and Christ as much as he is interested in modeling for the community something about life in Christ. And so verses 10–11, which we'll come to shortly, show closer parallels to the Christ Hymn and draws on it in particular ways.

Philippians 3:9 looks like it could be dropped wholesale into the Letter to the Galatians (see, e.g., Gal. 2:16–21). Here, as there, the issue is not one of law versus faith, as such. The question, in context, is one of rival Christian teachings—do Gentile Christians lack anything (such as circumcision or a broader set of laws to be followed including circumcision) in becoming full members of the community? For Paul the answer is, simply, no. And what better example could there be than himself, who had virtually every (physical, genealogical, educational, and experience) marker of one who aspired to be or become Jewish but places no value on those markers relative to his identity in Christ. Was Paul overstating the case vis-à-vis his own (comfort and identity with and within) Judaism? Perhaps Galatians 2:15, where he speaks as an insider with Peter, a fellow Jew, provides some indication for that; but there, as here, the context and intentions are rhetorical. Whatever, Paul's answer is clear—"a righteousness . . . that comes from the law" has no place in determining or deciding Christian identity or the scope of Christian community. But what is determinative?

The answer is not as simple as might first appear. Is it "faith in Christ" (so the NRSV) or "the faith of Christ" (so the NRSV alternative reading) or something else? Paul's Greek phraseology is ambiguous, though the latter NRSV alternative reading is, in fact, the simpler or more natural understanding based on simple rules of Greek grammar. What adds to the complexity and possible nuance is this: the word usually translated "faith" also means "faithfulness" or "trust" or "trustworthiness." Who's "faith" or "faithfulness" is being talked about? Within deep strains of American Protestantism and within much popular preaching, the focus is on the individual's "faith"; it is all about "having faith." It is natural, or common sense, for Americans to read the text that way and were it not for such things as the NRSV alternative reading calling attention to other possibilities, most readers would likely not consider an alternative. What about the "faith of Christ" side of the ledger? Arguably, were "faith of Christ" understood analogously to "faith in Christ," so referring to Christ's "faith" in God, it would make little sense. But, what if we were to understand the word often translated "faith" in its basic sense, in the Greek, of "faithfulness"? Particularly in light of the Christ Hymn, that provides a compelling reading. Therein the narrative of Christ, though being ("in the form of" and having "equality with") God, becoming "emptied" into human life and human death, and then being "exalted" by God and back into God and the divine realm, is told. Christ's faithfulness or trustworthiness is in Christ's actions, including becoming "emptied," "taking the form of a slave," "being born . . . human," being "humbled," and becoming "obedient to the point of death . . . on a cross" (2:7–8). It is that faithfulness which elicited the response from God (2:9) and "should" elicit response from others (2:10–11). To be Christian, to be within Christian community and part of Christian mission, is to be part of, identified with, and *formed by* (see comments on 3:10, below) that faithfulness of Christ (for further discussion, see Weidmann, *Galatians*, 55–56).

Paul's (hoped for, desired) identification with Christ comes front and center in 3:10. Of course, it is no simple parallel between his life's narrative and Christ's. Who would deign to suggest such? Rather, in light of verse 9, Paul's association with Christ is precisely that—association. Or, perhaps it is much more. Paul aspires to "the sharing of [Christ's] sufferings" and to "becoming like him in his death." On the face of it these are deep and arguably unusual and grave aspirations. Further, Paul's words are themselves deep and nuanced in ways that can be lost in translation.

Happily, the NRSV uses "sharing" in verse 10 which signals the direct connection with 1:7 and, by extension, the various places within the letter in which Paul uses the language of "sharing," including the several "with" and "co-" words noted in discussion of 1:7, above. Simply, what Paul wants from and with Christ is akin to that which he (re)affirms in his relationship with the Philippian community. Further, Paul is here serving as a model for the community (via the pattern of positive and negative models that we have observed and via direct commands upcoming in vv. 15 and 17): they, like him, (ought to) aspire to, and do, share in Christ's sufferings (see 1:28–29).

The next phrase, "becoming like him in his death," is much stronger and more pointed in the Greek than the NRSV translation suggests. Three times within the first few lines of the Christ Hymn, including within the very first phrase, the word "form" appears. The first two of these are built on the same Greek word that forms the basis of the verb used here. And, the other part of the verb here is the prefix, "with" or "co-," which Paul has used so often to build and affirm a sense of community with the Philippians around their common identity and mission in Christ (see, again, comments on 1:7, above). Simply, Paul states that he would be "co-formed" in Christ's death. Gruesome on its face, the phrase immediately draws on the important, and repeated, notion of "form" in the Christ Hymn, including, of course, the very first phrase about being in the "form of God" (2:6). In concert with verse 11, the whole sweep of the narrative of the Christ Hymn and participation in that whole sweep is summoned here—including, of course, "resurrection from the dead." The conditional—"if somehow"—is not timid; rather, it opens up the potentiality of creative and suggestive response (see Rom. 6:4–5). Paul proceeds in the next three verses to model and muse on such response.

Verse 12 is among the more fascinating sentences within Paul's letters and one of the more densely, if somewhat awkwardly, crafted. Among the interesting aspects of the sentence is that, as it appears in the Greek, it contains no grammatical objects. That is, using the NRSV translation as the standard, there is no "this" or "the goal" or "it" or "me"—each one of those words, as they appear in the NRSV translation, is a grammatical object and is missing in the Greek. Though it is virtually impossible to render an English sentence from Paul's Greek here, one might attempt it with something along these lines: "Not that I have already taken or have already finished, but I pursue if even I might take hold since I have even been taken hold of by Christ."

Though the whole verse is about taking or seizing—so the first verb, while the last two verb forms are from a compound verb built off the same base—there is no item or state or status that is seized: except, of course, for Paul himself, who has been seized by Christ. One may ask: is this further evidence of Christ's *faithfulness*?

The second verb of verse 12, which the NRSV captures well (though by importing an object) with "reached the goal," suggests an athletic contest or race of some kind. That is indeed what Paul provides in verses 13–14, casting himself as a runner in the midst of a race. First, he (re)focuses his addressees by referring to them as "siblings" (the misleading, grammatically singular, "Beloved" in the NRSV translation). This is the same word that NRSV elsewhere translates "brothers and sisters" and it builds on the family language introduced in 2:22 (see comments, above). Following the first phrase, which is a recapitulation of verse 12, he provides some good coaching technique for maintaining focus: "forgetting what lies behind and straining forward to what lies ahead." Indeed, verse 14 actually begins with the prepositional phrase, "toward the goal," as if to put it, literally, up front. And "the prize" is here, finally, named. Aha, one might think, now Paul, or I, can seize that object; finally! But what is the prize? No thing. Rather, it is "the heavenly call of God in Christ Jesus." How do you grasp that (in any conventional sense of "grasp" or "seize")? You don't; hence the commands that follow in verses 15–17.

Among other noteworthy characteristics of these verses is the consistency of the verb forms. The "forgetting and the straining" are participial forms in the present tense, which is captured well in the NRSV: the actions are not once and done and then the runner can simply go ahead and press on; no, these actions are ongoing and suggest process. Similarly "press on," which is captured well by the NRSV, can be translated, "I am pressing on" to capture the continual sense of the verb form and conveying and affirming ongoing process. Though there is no parallel to the phraseology of this passage among Paul's letters, there is, in 1 Timothy 6:12, this suggestive phrase: "take hold of the eternal life, to which you were called." I wonder if Paul would approve this passage as a mirror for that—such process as is suggested by this passage models the way to "take hold" of something so dear, deep, and cosmic as the "call" of God in Christ Jesus.

Paul is capable of irony not only with regard to opponents (as we saw in 3:2), but also with regard to all who might be among his community of addressees—including himself. The descriptive label that Paul chooses at the top of verse 15, "those of us . . . who are mature," is a noun form built from the second verb of verse 12—"reached the goal" (NRSV) or "finished" (my translation, above). The nuance of that verb is impossible to capture in English because it can mean "finish," or "complete" (as in a race), and can also mean to perfect or reach full maturation. The connection of this label in verse 15 to the verb in verse 12 would have been readily available to Paul's addressees. So, is he setting up an impossibility? After all, none are mature, by his own modeling (so v. 12). Having gained his readers' attention, he then repeats what, as we have already seen, serves as a kind of mantra (and a reaffirmation of the Christ Hymn) throughout the letter, "be of the same mind" (see discussion regarding 2:2, above). The pointed language of revelation—"this too God will reveal to you"— is striking and, arguably, out of place. Paul does not use the term lightly (see Rom. 1:18; 8:18, 1 Cor. 2:10; Gal. 1:16). Perhaps he means it to be taken, simply and at face value, as a possible, or even expected, occurrence when the community is gathered for worship (see 1 Cor. 14:30). Perhaps, too, he is prefiguring the vision of Jesus Christ that he will share in verses 20–21 or the statement of 4:6, "the Lord is near," both of which are apocalyptic in nature.

Verse 16 shares some of the same ironic energy as does verse 15. Though the word for "attained" is different than, and unrelated to, the verb translated "obtained" in verse 12, the sense is, as captured by the NRSV, virtually synonymous.

So, just what is it that "we have attained"? "The heavenly call of God in Christ Jesus" (v. 14) is the short answer. That is hardly something attained, but Paul's readers will excuse him for using that (ironic, knowing) descriptor. That said, what sense are they to make of Paul's call to "hold fast" to that call? Simply considered at face value and certainly when considered in light of the sweep of verses 12–14, that call would suggest movement—"straining forward," pressing on, and the like. Here Paul's rhetoric is ill served by the NRSV translation (and most English translations). The verb that Paul employs suggests not stasis, such as "holding on" but, as we would and should expect, movement.

The verb is actually a technical one, used in military contexts, meaning "to move in battle formation." Given that Paul's addressees are in a city, Philippi, which was reestablished by the Romans as a colony settled by military veterans (see introduction to Philippians, above), and given the "ethic" (to the degree one might refer to it as such) of the Roman phalanx that moving and staying together equals victory, while abandoning or moving separately equals loss, Paul's choice of verb here is quite revealing. As a teacher and rhetorician, Paul knows his audience and uses words, and concepts that will resonate. As a Christian teacher and rhetorician, he understands, and promotes and models here and throughout the letter, the importance of relationship and of community.

With verse 17, Paul brings the extended consideration of himself as model (and, by extension, of Epaphroditus and Timothy) to a close. The simple directive, "observe those who live according to the example you have in us," accomplishes at least three things: (1) it reestablishes Paul (in contrast to the opponents) as model for community and mission; (2) it opens up and establishes others as leaders or potential leaders according "to the example" just laid out; (3) it skillfully uses the best practices of pagan moral philosophy, which are likely familiar to Paul's addressees. For example, the moral philosopher Seneca, a contemporary of Paul and his addressees, writes in one of his letters, "The way is long if one follows precepts, but short and helpful if one follows examples" (*Moral Epistle* 6.6; translation mine). Further, some today might think that Paul is full of himself or egocentric for setting himself up as such an example. Contemporary practices and expectations would indicate otherwise. Seneca continues, in the same section of the same letter, "[The Stoic philosopher] Cleanthes could not have been the express image of Zeno [the founder of Stoicism] if he had merely heard his lectures; he shared in his life, saw into his hidden purposes and watched them to see whether he lived according to his own rules."

In keeping with the pattern we've observed (see, e.g., comments on 3:2, above), Paul moves now to negative examples. Who are these "enemies" and what is their relationship, if any, to those described in 3:2 and, beyond that, 1:28 and 1:15–18? Compounding the question is that, unlike in 3:2, the language herein is even less clear (to us to today) and less resonant with other of Paul's letters. All of that said, Paul's Philippian addressees presumably know well of whom Paul speaks ("I have often told you of them," v. 18) and, if they did not know already, they learn in the letter that Paul is quite concerned about the influence that these enemies might have on the Philippians ("I tell you even with tears," v. 18). Do the Philippians have firsthand experience of these "enemies," or do they know them only through Paul? The latter is quite possible, though the correlation between 3:19 and 1:28 might suggest otherwise. In 1:28 it is "your opponents" who are associated with "destruction"; in 3:19 these "enemies" are similarly tied to "destruction." Does that suggest the "opponents" of 1:28 and the "enemies" of 3:19 are the same? Perhaps.

Lost in the NRSV translation is that the word for "end" is built on the same root word as that for "mature" in verse 15 (see discussion of v. 15, above), which is another nuance, or wrinkle, connecting verse 12, verse 15, and now verse 18. Clearly, the "maturity" or "end" that the enemies display and aspire toward is contraindicated. Another pointed term, of even greater significance within the letter, that Paul uses herein is "minds"—it is actually a verb form in the Greek and is consistent with the usage in 3:15, as well as in 2:2, 2:5, and throughout the letter. Simply put, these enemies are wrongly minded and are therefore minded in contradiction to the Christ Hymn. That they are "enemies," particularly, "of the cross of Christ" (v. 18; cf. discussion of "cross" in 2:8, above) is therefore no surprise and is consistent with their "earthly" mindedness (v. 19).

Are these enemies the same as those in 3:2, who, as discussed above, appear to be consistent with those whom Paul opposes in the Letter to the Galatians? Not necessarily—the descriptions simply do not give us, at this distance of time and space, sufficiently clear evidence—but it is possible and perhaps even likely given the flow of the letter and of this section in particular. It is clear that Paul means to draw a stark contrast between them, on the one hand, and himself and his mission (of which the Philippians are a part) on the other; to say the least, building such a contrast is consistent with his purpose in the Letter to the Galatians (see, e.g., Gal. 4:31; 5:4–6, 16–18). Though different wording is used therein, the heavenly (Phil. 3:14, 20)/earthly (Phil. 3:19) contrast would appear consistent with the Spirit/flesh contrast (Gal. 5:16–18), the God/elemental spirits contrast (Gal. 4:3–4), and, perhaps to a lesser degree, the free/slave contrast (Gal. 4:31). Further, though "shame" is not used of the rivals in Galatians, "pride" is used therein of that which contrasts right behavior (6:4). Given that this whole section (beginning in 3:1) is dominated, at least through 3:9, by the significance (or lack thereof) of circumcision as a marker of Christian identity and given that consideration of these enemies serve as a bridge to Paul's summary vision of Christ Jesus in 3:20–21, it is more likely than not that these enemies are the same as, or similar to, those named in 3:2.

The vision of 3:20–21 is a capstone for this section (3:1–21), draws directly on the Christ Hymn (2:6–11) *and* serves as a culmination of and for the very important directive in 1:27, which, as indicated in discussion of that verse, contains clear and pointed language in the Greek: "Be citizens . . ." or "Live as citizens. . . ." As indicated in discussion above, the NRSV translation of 1:27 simply misses the political sense that the verb form used there carries. Here, however, the translation well indicates that sense in a noun built on the same root word.

The translation of the NRSV is powerful enough. But the term Paul uses is nuanced and had a particular, technical sense of which he, and his addressees, would have been aware. This is no simple "citizenship" but refers to a mandate whereby members of a given group or ethnicity take up residence in a given city. Indeed, this very term could be, and was, used of veterans relocating to colonize—which suggests precisely the reestablishment of Philippi some one hundred years or so prior to Paul's writing (see introduction to Philippians; see also comments on 3:16, above). While some may read these verses and think of the piety captured by the hymn, "I'm but a stranger here, heaven is my home," the language indicates something much more active and, perhaps, subversive or, at least, identity-switching. By the logic of Paul's imagery here, heaven is the mother city from which members of Christian community are sent/mandated to take up residence in (colonial) cities and locales, such as Philippi. In other words, Paul is positing citizenship in an alternative empire.

We have already seen that "Lord," repeated here, was used of the emperor. Similarly, "Savior" resonated in Roman imperial propaganda. For example, in Horace's *Odes* (1.2), Caesar Augustus is portrayed as the "Savior" who came down from heaven. And a monument set up in Ephesus in honor of Julius Caesar, past which Paul might have walked on any number of occasions, decreed that "The cities in Asia [we would say the cities of western Turkey] name Julius Caesar . . . our God Manifest and common Savior of all human life" (Danker 1982, 213–214). Though readers today may roll over such phrases as "the power that also enables him to make all things subject to himself" (see 1 Cor. 15:28, Ps. 8, and discussion of Phil. 2:11, above) one wonders how that may have resonated to those under Roman imperial rule, especially in light of the political phraseology and imagery that Paul presents.

Beyond the compelling understanding of Christ and the identity and mission of the community that Paul presents in verse 20, is the matter of "transformation" in verse 21: "[Lord Jesus Christ] will transform the body of our humiliation." It is noteworthy that "body" is singular, modified by the plural "our." That is captured well by the main reading of NRSV while, in this case, the alternate reading is simply wrong or misleading (with its plural "bodies"). Also noteworthy and not easily caught in English translation is that "humiliation" here, and "humbled" (2:8), are closely related—the one a noun, the other a verb, built on the same root.

Further, "transform" here is built on the same root as the noun "form" in the last line of 2:7. So, this verse ties directly into the Christ Hymn and, in particular, descriptions of Christ's human sojourn. Not to be missed is that Paul is drawing a parallel between "our" corporate "body"—as church or Christian community—and Christ in human form (2:7). The "humiliation" of 3:21, which parallels the work of Christ who "humbles" or "humiliates" himself (3:8), is no reference to "vile" human nature (according to the King James translation) but is a reference to the very work of the Christian community on earth (via its mandate, or "citizenship," 3:20; see discussion, above). The "transformation" and resulting state of being "conformed to the body of [Christ's] glory" (3:21), then, parallels the exaltation of Christ within the Christ Hymn (2:9), in this case enacted not by God on behalf of Christ (so 2:9) but enacted by Christ on behalf of the Christian community. The cosmic vision of 3:20–21 neatly, if in expansive and difficult-to-grasp (at least for us) terms, summarizes the ethical framework within which Paul would have his addressees understand Christ, their identity, and their mission as Christian community.

STAND FIRM IN THE LORD IN THIS WAY
Philippians 4:1–9

4:1 Therefore, my brothers and sisters, whom I love and long for, my joy and crown, stand firm in the Lord in this way, my beloved.

[2] I urge Euodia and I urge Syntyche to be of the same mind in the Lord. [3] Yes, and I ask you also, my loyal companion, help these women, for they have struggled beside me in the work of the gospel, together with Clement and the rest of my co-workers, whose names are in the book of life.

[4] Rejoice in the Lord, always; again I will say, Rejoice. [5] Let your gentleness be known to everyone. The Lord is near. [6] Do not worry about anything, but in everything by prayer and supplication with thanksgiving let your requests be made known to God. [7] And the peace of God, which surpasses all understanding, will guard your hearts and your minds in Christ Jesus.

[8] Finally, beloved, whatever is true, whatever is honorable, whatever is just, whatever is pure, whatever is pleasing, whatever is commendable, if there is any excellence and if there is anything worthy of praise, think about these things. [9] Keep on doing the things you have learned and received and heard and seen in me, and the God of peace will be with you.

As indicated in the formatting of the NRSV, which sets a paragraph break *following* the first verse of this section, 4:1 can also be understood as the final verse of the previous section. The ambiguity or confusion is due to the adverb that Paul uses, which the NRSV translates "in this way." As in English, the term may suggest either of two seemingly opposite things: "in this way" that I have just talked about or "in this way" that I am about to talk about. Or, it can mean both (see, e.g., 1 Cor. 4:1). Perhaps the easiest and best answer (as is further discussed below) is that "in this way" does, indeed, suggest both here. Further, since the first word of 4:1 is a standard term for introducing sentences or whole sections of discourse (as in Phil. 1:12) and since the verse is followed by several commands or directives to the community, it would seem that, on balance, this section of exhortation to the community begins with 4:1.

Verse 1 is clearly transitional. Paul reprises two addresses used previously: (1) "brothers and sisters"—3:1, 13 (see discussion of the NRSV alternative reading, above), 17, as well as 1:12–14 (see discussion of those verses, above); and (2) "beloved" or, better, "beloved ones" (2:12; see discussion above). Perhaps the metaphorical or symbolic kinship suggested by, and very relationship that Paul feels and promotes (e.g., comments on 1:12–14) via, those terms is particularly relevant at this point in the letter. The "joy" Paul expresses is, in Greek, built on the same root as the repeated command to "rejoice" (e.g., 3:1 and, shortly, 4:4). The "crown" recalls the metaphor of the footrace within chapter 3, particularly verses 12–14, for the "crown" here indicated is the standard laurel wreath "prize" (3:14) for which a runner would compete (akin to our "gold medal").

In the comments on 3:16, above, there is much discussion about the apparent disconnect between the seemingly static "hold fast" and the preceding imagery of the footrace, and indeed, as we found, the verb has quite another connotation. What about here? On the face of it, "stand firm" can mean precisely, and simply, that: be or remain in a standing position. That said, this verb can and is used regularly with regard to conviction, belief, or steadfastness. Indeed, as we saw in 1:27, Paul can wonderfully fuse two seemingly opposite concepts: "standing firm" (precisely the same word as that used here) and "striving." In ethical terms, that makes a degree of sense. And here, it takes on particular significance for at least two reasons: (1) the directive to "stand firm" *in the Lord* calls Paul's addressees back to the culmination of the previous section, which is the summary statement of the ethic for identity and mission in/under the Lordship of Christ that Paul has been building throughout the letter; (2) just as "standing firm" in terms of conviction is practiced or enacted by striving *side by side* in 1:27, so here, in 4:2–3, the challenge appears to be a rift or lack of relationship within the community, which calls for greater and deliberate mutuality.

The repeated use of "urge" cannot be, and would not have been, missed. "I'm talkin' to you" has become an often used, and often parodied, phrase in our popular culture around confronting or calling out an individual or group of individuals. Here Paul is—for the first time in this nearly completed letter—directly exhorting individuals within the community *presumably* about a matter which has been brewing under the surface of the letter throughout the whole or, at least, since the beginning of chapter 2 (see "same mind" in 2:2, 5 and any number of the directives included in 2:2–5; see discussion of those verses, above). There are several interesting and frustrating complications regarding verses 3–4. First, are the names of the two colleagues in verse 2 proper names, as indicated in the NRSV, or nicknames? Second, and closely related to that question—is the reference to "my loyal companion" in verse 2 a nickname or descriptor, as in the main text of the NRSV ("my loyal companion"), or is it a proper name, as indicated in the alternative reading. Third, are these individuals simply individuals, or do they suggest or imply groups or parties or house churches?

The NRSV represents a sensible interpretation/translation concerning names. The two pointed out in verse 2 are, indeed, recognizable and otherwise attested names from the ancient world. That they may be nicknames is possible—in that case, their meaning would be "good way" and "common fate," respectively, with the latter being an example of one of the "with" or "co-" words that Paul has favored throughout the letter (the word translated "common" is literally "with"; see discussion of 1:5, above). Consistent with the phrase, "these women," in verse 3, the names are grammatically feminine in form. Meanwhile, the individual at the beginning of verse 3 is referenced with a term nowhere (else) attested as a common name in ancient literature, and so the presumption of a nickname makes sense. It, too, is an example of a "co-" or "with" word: the NRSV's "loyal companion" being, literally, "yoked with." As either a proper name or nickname, based on its grammatical form it would appear to reference a male.

What is going on between these women or, to put the matter differently, what is going on in the community of addressees of which these women are representative? We don't know; and, presumably from our distance of time and space, won't ever know. But there are some hints. First, the direct parallels between 2:1–2 and 4:1–2 are significant. We have already noted "same mind": that is so important as a hallmark of community in 2:2, 5 and is the single matter urged here. Notice too, "joy" in each, 2:1–2 and here (and beyond that, the "progress and joy of faith" in 1:25). And, hidden in the English of the NRSV, is the fact that Paul's words for "urge" (4:2) and "encouragement" (2:1) are built on precisely the same Greek root; their connection would have been readily available to Paul's addressees. Paul would seem to be providing a necessary ingredient, "encouragement," to lead these two to the sort of same-mindedness that he has been describing and calling for throughout chapters 2 and 3.

There are certainly hints of some level of fracture within the community, most notably 2:14. Further, in light of 1:27–28 it is fair to presume that not least of Paul's concerns about (outside) "opponents" is that they might exacerbate fault lines at or below the surface within the community. Is it simply coincidence or is it evidence of a parallel phenomenon in another early Pauline Christian community that amidst the clear divisions among different house churches in Corinth is a certain woman Chloe, with whom a whole group of "people" identify, presumably as a house

church patron or leader (1 Cor. 1:11)? Do these two Philippian women
lead or sponsor (competing) house churches? The description as it develops in verse 3 may well be consistent with such an understanding, but it
may also suggest a much broader level of mission activity and leadership
beyond Philippi with which these women have been linked with regard to
Paul's missionary enterprise (see Rom. 16:1–16).

What connection, if any, do either or both of these leaders have to the
concern for disagreement over circumcision that seems to predominate at
least in the first part of chapter 3? On that we can only speculate though,
in light of 1:27–28, perhaps Paul had some concerns that one or the other
of them may provide a potential foothold for those who would forward a
pro-gentile-circumcision message.

Neither the "loyal companion" nor Clement are otherwise named or,
so far as we can tell, alluded to within the letter. The latter is a familiar
name in early Christian literature and tradition, and it became part of
Christian tradition as far back as the third and fourth centuries to believe
that the Clement named here is Clement of Rome. Though this is possible, there is nothing to indicate it and much contextual and circumstan-
tial evidence to argue against it (the name itself is common, and Clement
of Rome is thriving in the late first and/or early second century in Rome,
while this Clement is thriving fifty years earlier, presumably in and around
Philippi). This name has a clear meaning beyond its use as a proper name:
from the Latin, it means just what an English speaker might presume:
"clement," "calm," "gentle."

The description that Paul gives of Euodia and Syntyche, and of his "co-
workers" more broadly, "they have struggled beside," includes yet another
example of a "with" or "co-" compound word. Indeed, the verb Paul uses
is precisely the one used in 1:27 which, as discussed above, joins "with"
or "together with" with the word for "athlete." And finally, as clearly evident in the English of the NRSV, "co-worker" is also one of Paul's "co-"
words. Consistent with his concern for mutuality, sharing, and struggling
and working together (see, e.g., 1:5, 27) throughout the letter, Paul again
forwards just such an ethic. That whatever divisions are reflected in verses
2–3 are, so to speak, in house, is clearly evident in that Euodia and Syntyche are considered among those "whose names are in the book of life."
Perhaps a curious element here, the inclusion of the book of life is consistent with the interest in apocalyptic that has bubbled up in the latter
chapters of the letter and is about to again in 4:5 (see also 3:20–21, 3:15).
(For other references to the book of life in the New Testament, see Rev.
3:5; 13:8; 17:8; 20:12, 15; see similarly Luke 10:20.)

The call to "rejoice" returns again (see 3:1) in verse 4 (with its own emphasis on "again"), and consistent with 3:1 and the command to "stand firm" in 4:1 (connected to "joy," as it is; see discussion of 4:1), it is again "in the Lord." That placement, "in the Lord," is even more central, of course, than the directed action of rejoicing. It is the defining point of the community's identity and mission (so 1:25 which, as we've seen, in the discussion of 4:1, includes "joy" which is so indicative of this section— "joy," 4:1, "rejoice," here; so the Christ Hymn; so the sweep of ch. 3). As if to underline that centrality of Christ as Lord, Paul writes simply and directly, "the Lord is near." The adverb, here translated "near," is notoriously difficult to interpret and translate, as is the verb derived from the same root word that is found in the summary of Jesus' proclamation in Matthew 4:17 and Mark 1:15. In light of the apocalyptic vision contained in 3:20–21, there can be little doubt that Paul is affirming both the eminence and imminence of the Savior that "we are expecting" (3:20). At the same time, especially in light of what follows in verses 6–7, Psalm 145:18 provides an interesting, while not exact, parallel: "The Lord is near to all who call on him" (the Septuagint version of the text exhibits the same adverb, "near," and a verb for prayer, "call on," which Paul uses elsewhere—e.g., 1 Cor. 1:2—though not here). The two—the vision of Christ as Savior and Lord in 3:20–21 and the notion of God's availability to those who pray—would presumably work well together for Paul as he works to build the community's identity and mission in Christ and with and for each other.

By way of simplistic, but perhaps meaningful, analogy, verse 6 sets me thinking about how many words the people of Hawaii have for the color of the ocean. Paul uses three separate words for prayer in the space of one relatively simple and straightforward sentence. The NRSV captures well the nuances of meaning among the three, especially the latter two which suggest different, major types of prayers—petition and thanksgiving. The term used for "thanksgiving" is that from which Christians derive the term, "eucharist," as exhibited in Paul's presentation of the words of institution in 1 Corinthians 11:24. The NRSV translations, "be known" (v. 5) and "be made known" (v. 6), capture well the closely related verbs that Paul uses and the mutual informing he may have intended for his addressees: the sweep of these verses—relationship toward others, centrality of "the Lord," relationship to God—are consistent with his concern for community identity and mission throughout the letter.

Finally, verse 7 is both comforting and, perhaps, tantalizingly suggestive of an alternative empire (see esp. discussion of 3:20–21, above). What might be lost on our ears but likely not on those of Paul's addressees, is that he is talking here about the "peace of God" and *not* the ubiquitous Pax Romana or Roman peace. In Virgil's *Eclogues*, for example, it is said in reference to Caesar Augustus: "it is a god who made us for this peace" (I.6). Further, what may simply roll over our ears is the final verb, "guard." It, like the verb in 3:16, is a military word (see discussion of 3:16, above; note too that Paul uses "guard," its literal sense, in 2 Cor. 11:32). Indeed, among the words that Seneca offers the emperor Nero, to underline and affirm the power of his office, are reference to "all those many thousands of swords which my [i.e., the emperor's] peace restrains"; after which Seneca, in his own voice, refers to the emperor's "guardianship" (*On Clemency* 1.2, 5). In short, it is the emperor who *guards* the *peace*. Not so for Paul. Also not to be missed, is that Paul is, quite literally, under "imperial guard," within or among "the emperor's household" (see 1:13, 4:20 and discussion esp. of 1:13, above), even as he writes.

The first two words of verse 8 are important. The first is a repetition of that word which begins chapter 3. As indicated in comments on 3:1, it is a somewhat nimble adverbial construction. Here it appears to be suggesting that a whole line of discussion, or even that the letter as a whole, is coming to a close (see 2 Cor. 13:11). Regarding the use of "beloved" here: as discussed regarding 1:12 and 4:1, the NRSV would appear needlessly to cause confusion with its inconsistent use of "beloved" to translate variously Paul's use of a Greek word meaning "beloved" or "beloved ones" and Paul's use of the plural form of the Greek word for brother, which, in the plural, can refer to collective of male and female "brothers and sisters" or "siblings." Adding to the confusion is that the NRSV often—and much more accurately—uses "brothers and sisters" to translate the latter. Here again, as in 1:12, the NRSV uses "beloved" for Paul's "siblings." On some level the two arguably add up to the same thing—Paul's affirmation of close, kindred relationship among those within community that is formed "in the Lord," Jesus Christ; on another level, of course, they are different, and it is good to have a more precise rendering of Paul's language and of the precise metaphor, "siblings," or "brothers and sisters," that he uses repeatedly from 1:12, 14 through this verse and beyond (see 4:21 which exhibits yet another misleading translation of Paul's clear "sibling" language).

The whole of verses 8–9 is captured well in the final directive of verse 8 and the directive that dominates verse 9: "think about these things. Keep on doing the things. . . ." The basic meaning of the first directive is captured better by the NSRV alternative reading, "take account of." That is, indeed, the simple meaning of the verb used, from which we derive our accounting word, "log," as in "keep a log" or "log it in the books." What is even better is the indication of what grammarians call "aspect" in the NRSV translation of the second directive: "keep on doing." Yes! That is precisely the nuance of the participial form that Paul employs. And indeed, the same aspect is evident in Paul's first directive; so, "keep on taking account," or "keep on logging," or perhaps even better, "keep on keeping track." These two directives—"keep on keeping track" and "keep on doing" perfectly balance each other. A further nuance, available to Paul's first addressees, is the connection between the word used for the final directive of verse 8 and the term used for "word" in the phrase "word of life" in 2:16. They are the same—the one (2:16) the noun form, the other (here) the verb form.

That further nuance may be at play within the list of virtues in verse 8. In the Septuagint version of Psalm 12:6 it is not the "promises," but the "sayings" or "words" of the Lord that are "pure." Among the other nuances within the list, is the co-mingling of words with a history in Jewish tradition, including fairly broad early Christian use (such as "pure"; besides the Psalms passage, cf. esp. Prov. 21:8 and, within the New Testament, esp. 2 Cor. 7:11; 11:2; 1 Tim. 5:22; Titus 2:5; Jas. 3:17) and those, based squarely in Greek moral and civic rhetoric, with a much shorter history of Jewish usage and little within early Christian literature (such as "excellence"; used often in Second Temple Jewish literature, such as Wisdom of Solomon and 2, 3, 4 Maccabees, see esp. 4 Macc. 1:2; in the New Testament, only 2 Pet. 1:3, 5 [twice]).

In the discussion of "peace" in verse 7, above, the contrast of Paul's emphasis on community in Christ Jesus with the Pax Romana was noted. In these verses, given the broader consideration of virtues and lack of immediate reference to "Christ Jesus" and "Lord," another sense of "peace" rises, perhaps, to the fore. An interesting verse in biblical tradition that may be providing Paul language and concepts, is Proverbs 12:20: ". . . those who counsel peace have joy." Certainly, "joy" and the closely related "rejoice" are at play throughout the letter and within this section, and "peace" has now been used twice within three verses. Of course, both concepts—the imperial and/or messianic peace of God in Jesus Christ and the peace of God associated with joy—may be at play in both verses 7 and 9. Indeed, to the degree Paul is meaning to set up an alternative empire or ethical base to the one previously available to his addressees—largely or exclusively Gentiles living in a Roman colony founded by military veterans—both of these concepts would be relevant.

GIVING AND RECEIVING
Philippians 4:10–20

> 4:10 I rejoice in the Lord greatly that now at last you have revived your concern for me; indeed, you were concerned for me, but had no opportunity to show it. [11] Not that I am referring to being in need; for I have learned to be content with whatever I have. [12] I know what it is to have little, and I know what it is to have plenty. In any and all circumstances I have learned the secret of being well-fed and of going hungry, of having plenty and of being in need. [13] I can do all things through him who strengthens me. [14] In any case, it was kind of you to share my distress.
>
> [15] You Philippians indeed know that in the early days of the gospel, when I left Macedonia, no church shared with me in the matter of giving and receiving, except you alone. [16] For even when I was in Thessalonica, you sent me help for my needs more than once. [17] Not that I seek the gift, but I seek the profit that accumulates to your account. [18] I have been paid in full and have more than enough; I am fully satisfied, now that I have received from Epaphroditus the gifts you sent, a fragrant offering, a sacrifice acceptable and pleasing to God. [19] And my God will fully satisfy every need of yours according to his riches in glory in Christ Jesus. [20] To our God and Father be glory forever and ever. Amen.

A second major section of exhortation following chapter 3 moves the focus from relationship (among individual leaders [and groups?]) within the community (4:1–9) to the relationship of the community with Paul (4:10–20). Both are familiar concerns from early on in the letter (ch. 1 passim; see, e.g., 1:3–5, 27). As with the previous section, Paul will draw on much that has come before, especially, as we will see, material introducing and flowing immediately from the Christ Hymn of chapter 2.

The familiar language of verse 10 is readily apparent, at least in part. Here Paul reprises again the joy/rejoice theme so familiar, by now, within the letter (see discussions, above, of 4:4; also 3:1). What is lost is the NRSV translation is the vital reprisal of a theme central to the lead-in to the Christ Hymn and to the first section of exhortation in chapter 4 regarding relationships within the community. In verse 10, the NRSV includes the repeated "concern . . . concerned." In Paul's Greek, the word repeated in verse 10 is precisely that with which his addressees have become so familiar in 2:2 [twice], 2:5, 4:2 and elsewhere (see discussion of 2:2, above): "same mind." And his first addressees would have been able to note that connection immediately. What is true on the simplest level is true much more profoundly in terms of establishing and living out the ethic that Paul is building throughout the letter: be minded toward one another, and now (as we read) toward Paul, as Christ was toward humanity. The broad goal and interest is mission for the gospel—that has been clear throughout (see esp. discussion of 1:12 and 1:25, above). But, as Paul focuses first on relationship within community and now on the community's relationship with him, he focuses his gaze, and that mandate of Christ-mindedness, on these specific matters: intra-community relations and relations with Paul.

The twist in verse 11 is noteworthy. On one level, it might play for readers today almost like a scene from a situation comedy in which the two parties know each other, and they know that one of them is about to make an uncomfortable request. If so, the potential implications of 2 Corinthians 11:8–9 are interesting: "I robbed other churches by accepting support from them in order to serve you. And when I was with you and was in need, I did not burden anyone [of you], for my needs were supplied by the friends [literally, 'the siblings'] who came from Macedonia." Notice the colorful language, "robbed," and the reference to "siblings . . . from Macedonia." Now, matters of dating of Paul's Corinthian correspondences, and occurrences addressed within them, are notoriously complicated. That said, given that the founding of Paul's mission work in Corinth clearly predates the writing of Philippians, questions may be asked. Were these "siblings" who traveled in support of Paul's mission Philippians; perhaps including one or more of the leaders named in 4:3? Were the monies "robbed" in order to support Paul's ongoing work in Corinth in part, or in full, donations from the Philippian community? If the answer to any of these questions is "yes," then Paul may be concerned about dipping again into the well. Indeed, via his own testimony to Philippian support, in verses 15–16, he provides precedent both presuming the enthusiastic support of, and some reason for being cautious about presuming more support from, the Philippian community.

But there is also far more going on here that would have been very familiar to many in Paul's and the Philippian addressees' world but not so readily apparent in ours. It is signaled by the explanatory phrase that closes out verse 11 and, in turn, serves a kind of thesis, or topical, statement for the whole of verse 12: ". . . for I have learned to be content with whatever I have." The term here translated "content" is a technical term immediately recognizable as a hallmark of Stoic, and, more broadly, popular moral philosophy. To some degree it parallels the very North American notion of self-sufficiency (though without the consumerist overlay that often accompanies it in our culture). So Paul is establishing his credibility as one who is self-sufficient, thrifty, controlled, and the like—clearly not one who would milk a potential donor for more than is needed for the mission at hand. But, there is more.

Throughout the letter, Paul has been careful to affirm and nurture a strong sense of mutuality on behalf of the mission of the gospel. This is very evident in the "co-" and "with" and "share" words that have been used repeatedly (see discussion of 1:5, 7, above) and that, in 4:14, will be evidenced one last time, via a reprisal of the root word for "co-sharing" which is used in 1:7. The Roman Empire was one in which written and unwritten rules governing relationships were strong. The patron-client relationship, such as that between a teacher and student(s) or between a wealthy patron and that one or group which receives the patron's support, was a time honored, and easily recognized one. So too was the relationship of friendship. Consistent with his affirmation and nurturing of mutuality, Paul is here being careful to avoid the former, and to suggest and promote the latter.

In short, friendship is not cultivated by need. If Paul indicates that he is in "need," he may be establishing a situation wherein he is the client and the Philippians are the patron. Contrariwise, if he—as apostle (which, notice, he does not call himself herein; see discussion of 1:1, above) or teacher, for example—demands assistance, he sets himself up as a patron deserving of some payback from his clients, the Philippians. Paul will have neither here. His rhetoric throughout this section is consistent with that of his contemporary, the popular philosopher Seneca who, in *Moral Epistle* 9, writes that the wise one is content/self-sufficient (that is, as Paul establishes here, has no need) but still seeks and nurtures friendships. That is, true friendship is not cultivated by need, but shared values and interests. Indeed Cicero writes in his famous essay *On Friendship* that when neither party is in need, such help or support as does come from one to other nurtures and strengthens the friendship (51).

Having included a passing reminder of the broader mission on behalf of the gospel, Paul indirectly gets around to asking for a gift in verse 17. The wording here is nuanced and creatively picks up on terms and concepts he has established within the letter. First, the word translated as "profit" in the NRSV is, literally, "fruit." Recall that in chapter 1 Paul establishes both the Philippians' (1:11) and his (1:22) work on behalf of the gospel via such language. Indeed, as discussed above regarding 1:22, both of those verses use precisely the same word that Paul uses here—a fact readily available to Paul's first addressees who could have easily made the connection. So, in verse 17, Paul is providing an opportunity for them to instantiate their "fruit" or "harvest." Further, the word for "account" used herein is precisely that used in verse 8; or, to be precise, it is a noun form of the verb used in 4:8. So, Paul is providing an opportunity for the Philippians to "keep on doing" (4:9) that which they are "keeping on keeping track of," which is in relationship to the "word of life" (2:16).

Indeed, the allusion to 2:16 (through 4:8) that Paul provides in 4:17, is consistent with the shift in imagery that takes place in 4:18, from language of harvest to language of sacrifice. In 2:17 Paul writes of "the sacrifice and the offering of your faith." Here he reprises that by recalling "the gifts you sent, a fragrant offering, a sacrifice acceptable and pleasing to God." The language is similar but different. As the NRSV translation suggests, the word for "sacrifice" is the same in each case. One wonders whether Paul, with this different word, "fragrant offering," is interjecting a term and concept unfamiliar to his addressees, or whether he might in the past have included among his teachings to the Philippians something akin to what he writes in 2 Corinthians 2:14: "But thanks be to God, who in Christ always leads us in triumphal procession, and through us spreads in every place the fragrance that comes from knowing him" (the word translated here "fragrance" is the same as that translated "fragrant offering" in Phil. 4:18; see also 2 Cor. 2:16). Certainly the "spread" discussed in 2 Corinthians 2:14 is consistent with the concern of mission throughout Philippians. The allusions to 2:16 and 2:17 also suggest the consistency of the call to "rejoice" that closes out that section (emphatically and with repetition, vv. 2:17–18) and opens this section (4:10).

If indeed Paul is at pains to promote mutuality via friendship language and tropes, and if indeed it is the case that he will allow neither himself nor the Philippians to be established in any way as benefactor or patron, then who does fill that role? God, of course. And so verse 19 perfectly closes out this section (and v. 13, powerful as it is, simply on the face of it, is a kind of corollary to that understanding of God as patron or benefactor). The language of "in Christ Jesus" recalls that of "in the Lord" that we have seen throughout chapter 4 (see esp. comments on 4:1 and 4:4). And the reprisal of "glory" in both verse 19 and 20 appropriately calls Paul's addressees back to the Christ Hymn (2:11).

FINAL (MUTUAL) GREETINGS
Philippians 4:21–23

4:21 **Greet every saint in Christ Jesus. The friends who are with me greet you.** [22] **All the saints greet you, especially those of the emperor's household.** [23] **The grace of the Lord Jesus Christ be with your spirit.**

It seems especially fitting in this letter, which has so stressed mutuality and relationship, that Paul presents the greetings as he does (three times repeating the same word; once as command, twice by way of report). These short verses, and the greetings they both promote and carry, well sum up much that Paul is after within the letter.

The broken symmetry of the greetings is marvelous. Were Paul able to stop with verse 21, he would have a perfectly balanced statement: (1) you (Philippians) greet each saint; (2) those in the community here greet you. But he can't. He enthuses, it seems, underlining and emphasizing that those present with him—and Timothy—join in the greetings, as do all in the broader community surrounding him in prison (for discussion of Paul's situation and of "the emperor's household," see discussion of 1:12, above). Part of what is notable about these verses is their activeness. These verb forms at the end of verses 21 and 22 are very active—they "do greet," "are greeting" you Philippians via this letter. The mission and the mutuality thereof is not only contained within, but also promoted by, these verses.

Further, and consistent with that, the NRSV has unfortunately, again (with the use of "friends"), engaged in inconsistent translation of Paul's simple, repeated metaphorical and symbolic language (see discussion of 4:8 above). Here Paul effectively uses again the language of family, "brothers and sisters," or perhaps better, "siblings," that he has used throughout (see discussion of 1:12 and 1:14, above). Indeed, this repetition of that simple and profound address calls his addressees back, as does reference to the emperor's household, to his use of the term for the first time in describing his current situation (1:12–14). These are no simple times for Paul and for his mission and for the communities surrounding him—the Philippians included. And these are no cheap, throwaway greetings, but are serious acknowledgment of relationship in and for the mission of the gospel of Jesus Christ; "in Christ Jesus," especially in light of the sweep of this letter, says as much.

Wonderful in Paul's final statement/blessing/promise is the juxtaposition of the singular "spirit" and the plural "your." So easily missed in English, this takes on special meaning in this letter given the parallel juxtaposition of the singular "body" with the plural "our" in the crucial verses of 3:20–21 (see discussion, above). For Paul, it is all about the community, and their identity and mission together, as one, in Christ. Amen.

First Thessalonians

Introduction

The First Letter to the Thessalonians is Paul's earliest extant letter. As such, it is the earliest Christian letter and, for that matter, the earliest Christian document of any kind preserved from antiquity (see above, commentary on Philippians, for consideration of the Christ Hymn found in Phil. 2:6–11 as the earliest extant Christian composition). Is it, then, the first letter that Paul wrote? Perhaps, but there is nothing in the content of the letter, or in any other of Paul's letters, indicating that; he may have written others before this that have been lost.

What we do know is that though 1 Thessalonians is the earliest letter of Paul's that we have, it does *not* come from early in his career as a preacher, teacher, and missionary of and for the gospel. By Paul's own testimony (see Gal. 1:18; 2:1) he had been plying his trade as missionary for many years before heading through Asia Minor (Western Turkey on today's map) and across the Aegean Sea to the northern Greek province of Macedonia (the prefectures of Thessaloniki and Kavala on today's map of Greece; not to be confused with the former Yugoslav Republic of Macedonia, which is further north) to found churches at Philippi, Thessalonica, and elsewhere (see also Acts, beginning with 9:1, for accounts of Paul's call and missionary career; Acts 16:11–17:14 for Paul's activity in the region of Macedonia).

The reconciling of the accounts in Acts with Paul's own testimony in his letters is often no easy matter. So here. There is much in Acts 17–18, which traces Paul's movements from Philippi to Thessalonica and then onto Beroea (a small town within the broader sphere of Thessalonica), Athens, and Corinth, that fits neatly with Paul's own accounts in 1 Thessalonians 2–3 and the letter broadly; not least being those intercity and regional movements. Further, the challenge, difficulty, and even danger that Paul's team is said to encounter in the Acts account (see esp. 17:5–10) appears consistent with Paul's words about "persecution" in 1 Thessalonians 1:6;

2:14–16; 3:3–4 (cf. 1 Thess. 2:18; 2 Thess. 1:4–5). But, on a closer level there seems to be discord between the accounts. Where Acts highlights Paul's activity in "a synagogue of the Jews" and identifies Jews, "devout Greeks" (that is, non-Jews who regularly attend synagogue and are sympathetic toward the [one] God of the Jews), and "not a few leading women" among those who "were persuaded and joined Paul and Silas" (Acts 17:4), 1 Thessalonians leaves no impression that any of these groups are among the letter's addressees. Indeed, the letter's contents strongly suggest (1) a Gentile audience that has only recently converted to belief in [one] God; (2) laborers, not "leading" members of the city (see discussion below); and (3) perhaps even a strictly male group of addressees (see esp. discussion of 1 Thess. 4:4, below)—*if* that is the case, it would make 1 Thessalonians unique among Paul's letters, including that named for the male leader Philemon; or, at the least, it would suggest that the Thessalonian Christians include no women among their leaders. These matters will be taken up in the commentary (see especially 1:3, 6, 9; 4:4, 11).

Like Philippians, 1 Thessalonians is filled with warm, heartfelt, and emotive language bespeaking Paul's particular fondness for the churches of Macedonia, as stated in a later letter to another community: "We want you you to know, brothers and sisters, about the grace of God that has been granted to the churches of Macedonia; . . . their abundant joy . . . for the privilege of sharing in this ministry. . . ." (2 Cor. 8:14). Indeed, early on Paul cites that very "joy" of the Thessalonians as they "received the word" and "became an example to all the believers" in their province and beyond (1 Thess. 1:6–7). Clearly the Thessalonians made the privilege of sharing and extending the gospel Paul preached their own, and just as clearly Paul feels a deep and joyful bond with this community and its response to his mission. The rapid-fire succession of portraits that Paul paints to signify that deep bond, variously describing himself as a nurse, slave, mother, father, and orphan (2:7, 11, 17), are, to say the least, striking.

It is Paul's felt need to be in contact with this community that prompts him to open up renewed communication with the Thessalonians several weeks or a few short months following his and his team's departure from them (3:1–6; see esp. v. 5). Interestingly, the first step in that renewed engagement seems to have come without a letter; Paul simply sends Timothy to them (3:2). On Timothy's return Paul is prompted to write. What it is, precisely, that prompts him he does not say. But, he leaves a clue. At the beginning (1:3) and toward the end (5:8) of the letter, Paul refers to "faith . . . love . . . hope" together. At 3:6 he writes that Timothy has come to him bringing "good news" of the Thessalonians' "faith and love."

What of their "hope"? Perhaps that hope accounts for—or, is a part of—"whatever is lacking in your faith" (1 Thess. 3:10). Certainly we can say that it is Paul's keen desire to "find out about your faith" (3:5) coupled with Timothy's report that prompts this letter to the Thessalonians.

With few exceptions, there is agreement among New Testament scholars that 1 Thessalonians was written in 49 (at the earliest) or the early 50s (at the latest). That is based, to significant degree, on the already mentioned consistency of Acts and 1 Thessalonians around the relative timing and movement of Paul's travels through, and following, his time in Thessalonica. We know with certainty that Paul went to Corinth, and Acts tells us that that followed on the heels of his time in Athens (Acts 18:1), which makes perfect sense in terms of travel routes and Paul's mission expansion as we know it both from Acts and from his own letters. Two external factors then come into play to help set the boundaries for the writing of the letter: (1) the one-year term of Gallio as proconsul based in Corinth, beginning in the late spring or summer of 51, whose time in Corinth overlapped with Paul's (Acts 18:12–17); and (2) the expulsion of the Jews from the city of Rome under Emperor Claudius in 49, which is mentioned in Acts 18:2 by way of introducing Paul's eventual mission partners, Aquila and Priscilla (or, as Paul calls her, Prisca; see also Acts 18:18, 26, Rom. 16:3; 1 Cor. 16:19; 2 Tim. 4:19). Beyond setting a date after which Paul must have been in Corinth (in order to meet Prisca and Aquila), Claudius's edict against the Jews in Rome also plays a possible supporting role in setting the context for Paul's time in Thessalonica. How?

Paul's time in Thessalonica is met with significant pushback—so, as indicated above, Paul's own testimony and the account in Acts agree. All or part of that story lies, very likely, within the context of Thessalonica's connection to Rome. Like Philippi (see introduction to Philippians) the city curried great favor with the empire, in part due to the same worldly wisdom or good fortune displayed by Philippi. Thessalonica ended up supporting the winning side, that of Octavian (later named Caesar Augustus), in the civil wars leading up to the beginning of the Roman Empire; unlike Philippi, however, Thessalonica had deftly to switch sides since it had earlier supported Brutus and Cassius. More so than Philippi, Thessalonica had the good fortune of being a large city with provincial reach, situated on both significant land and sea routes for travel and commerce. Further, it had served as the residence of many Roman senators and knights during the civil war years, even being consecrated as an alternative site for the formal convening of the Roman senate, should such have been deemed necessary. With the ascendancy of Caesar Augustus, Thessalonica minted a coin portraying the head of Julius Caesar, under which was inscribed "god," while the reverse side showed Caesar Augustus. What is more, the city established a temple in the emperor's honor, attended by priests established for the honor of "the Imperator Augustus son of god" and for the goddess Roma and Roman benefactors.

As is seen in his (later) letter to the Philippians, Paul's teachings and descriptions of Christian faith and community life engage the rhetoric of empire (see esp. Phil. 2:11; 3:20) and might be deemed threatening by those who are either informed by, or involved in promoting, Roman imperial propaganda and understandings of Roman peace, power, and prosperity. What were the powers in Thessalonica to think, for example, of teachings that contrasted "idols" with "a living and true God" (1 Thess. 1:9; think of "god" on the coins and temple), that forwarded a separate "kingdom" (2:12; "kingdom" and "empire" are precisely the same word in Greek), and that mocked those who, like good Romans and clients of Rome, said, "There is peace and security" (1 Thess. 5:3; the famous Pax Romana being built on and for imperial notions of peace and security)? One possible set of responses would be to annihilate, exile, or otherwise make life difficult for the proponents of such teachings. And here is where the timing of Paul's ministry in Thessalonica, and the letters which follow, gets really interesting.

For all of its history of honoring Rome, Thessalonica had found itself on the wrong side of a tax revolt in 15 and, under Emperor Tiberius, lost its status as a provincial capital. Almost thirty years later, in 44, Emperor Claudius restored the privilege, to the joy of Thessalonica's political, social, and economic movers and shakers. Five years after that, it is this same Emperor Claudius who expels Jews from the imperial city for purportedly causing trouble. And no more than several months or a year following that, Paul, an itinerant Jew, arrives and begins forming a new faith community. It takes little imagination to see how both the Gentile powers that be and, to the degree such were operative, the Jewish powers that be in this newly reestablished, provincial capital with a long history of honoring the emperor, would want nothing to do with him or his message.

Indeed, the plot might be thickened even further. According to Acts, Paul and his team were charged with "acting contrary to the decrees of the emperor, saying that there is another king named Jesus" (Acts 17:7). A significant amount of material in the final two chapters of the letter concerns the end times (4:14–18; 5:1–11). Interestingly, by Paul's testimony, such is a subject about which "you [Thessalonians] do not need to have anything written to you" (5:1), indicating that Paul, while in Thessalonica, had already taught them, apparently at some length. Emperor Tiberius decreed a ban on predicting the future, here described by Paul's contemporary, the moral philosopher Dio Chrysostom (*Discourses* 57.15.8): "but as for all the other astrologers and magicians and such as practiced divination in any way whatsoever, he put to death those who were foreigners and banished all the citizens that were accused. . . ." Might Paul's teachings about a forthcoming "Lord" (see comments on Phil. 2:11 for the imperial resonance of "Lord") have been perceived as "divination" and flown in the face, at least in some people's estimation, of Tiberius's decree? Further, might such a banishment as called for in Tiberius's decree account for the block on Paul's own return to the city (2:18; see comments below)? Whatever the broad and immediate context, Paul's concern for the Thessalonian community's well-being at a time of "suffering" (1:6) and "persecution" pervades the letter.

Beyond the close ties of care and kinship, including joy in relationship for the spread of the mission, which we have already noted above, the letter is marked by references to thanksgiving (1:2; 2:13; 3:9), prayer (1:2; 3:10–14; 5:23–25), and—interestingly and repeatedly—work and labor (1:3; 2:9; 4:11). Simply at face value, these suggest a basic paradigm that will be reinforced and nuanced in a number of ways within the letter: Paul and his team, on the one hand, and the Thessalonian community, on the other, find their common identity and purpose, and their deep ties to each other, in God and specifically in the gospel of Jesus Christ. The latter set of items, having to do with work and labor, may well also tell us something very directly about Paul and his addressees and their relative place in society—they (Paul included) are indeed workers/laborers, and that sets the context for their meeting and growth together in the form of a faith community (2:9).

To what degree that worldly context forms or influences the contours of the community of faith and its internal leadership will be considered particularly in comments on 4:3–8 and 9–13. All politics is local, it has been said. So is all teaching and preaching, informed by the great, broad, and deep message of gospel. That is most certainly true of this earliest extant letter of Paul.

Commentary

SALUTATION AND ADDRESS
1 Thessalonians 1:1

> 1:1 **Paul, Silvanus, and Timothy,**
> **To the church of the Thessalonians in God the Father and the Lord Jesus Christ:**
> **Grace to you and peace.**

The very first line of this letter might cause pause—here there are several authors named. The two Thessalonian letters are unique among Paul's letters in including two named coauthors. Further, it is notable that no title is presented here for Paul (such as "apostle," as found at the top of Rom., 1 Cor., 2 Cor., Gal.; see below, 1 Thess. 2:7) or for the team of coauthors (such as "servants" or, better, "slaves," Phil. 1:1).

Might the lack of title be consistent with the early date of the letter? Perhaps. By definition, all the other letters of Paul that we have are written later than those to the Thessalonians (presuming the authenticity of 2 Thess.; see introduction to 2 Thess.). Also, and perhaps of even greater relevance, in the case of several of the letters, Paul has clear reason to want to stress (Gal., 1 Cor., 2 Cor.) or convey (Rom.) a sense of apostolic status from the beginning. Herein, other agendas are at play. On the face of it, Paul and his coauthors are perfectly capable of assuming an authoritative role and attendant status (see, e.g., 1:6; 2:7 [wherein "apostle" is used], 2:11) such as an apostolic or other title might convey, but they are also clearly nimble in conveying alternate positions of authority or the seeming lack thereof (2:7, 17). Even more, the lack of any titles at the front of the letter may be both consistent with, and affirming of, the message of mutual reciprocity and parity evident especially in 4:9–12 (see commentary on Philippians, esp. comments on 1:1 and 4:11–12).

Of the two coauthors, Timothy appears as coauthor with Paul in each of the Macedonian correspondences (Phil. and 1 and 2 Thess.) as well as 2 Corinthians and Philemon. Along with Silvanus (who is named as coauthor only here and in 2 Thess.), Timothy accompanied Paul as a member of the inner circle of his mission team. Timothy's role here (3:2, 6) is akin to that projected in Philippians 2:19: visiting the beloved local community and bringing back news to Paul. The close association of Timothy and Paul over years of mission is well attested by the opening addresses of 2 Corinthians, Philippians, 1 and 2 Thessalonians, and Philemon; the references in 1 Thessalonians 3:2, 6 and Philippians 2:19; the praise that Paul bestows in Philippians 2:22; Timothy's appearance as "my coworker" in Romans 16:21; and, of course, by Timothy appearing as the named recipient of two of the Pastoral Epistles (1 and 2 Tim.). Other references in 1 Corinthians 4:17 and 16:10 are consistent with the above, as are the descriptions found in Acts (esp.16:1; 17:14–15; 18:5).

Curiously and somewhat mysteriously, Acts does not mention Timothy as accompanying Paul in his ministry at Philippi and Thessalonica, 16:11–17:10; he simply reappears in 17:14 without any explanation. That apparent absence of Timothy from Thessalonica during the time of Paul's ministry may be relevant to his duties as recounted in 1 Thessalonians 3:2 (see comments below; see also the discussion of the possibility of Paul's banishment in the introduction to this letter, above).

Like Timothy, Silvanus is one of Paul's inner circle. As noted above, he is a coauthor of the two Thessalonian correspondences. Consistent with the accounts of Acts discussed in the introduction to 1 Thessalonians above, he is also named by Paul as one his fellow cofounders, along with Timothy, of the Christian community at Corinth (2 Cor. 1:19). And there the trail runs dry on Silvanus in Paul's letters. Interestingly, that is consistent with Acts, in which this same individual is called Silas, and is last mentioned with Paul at Corinth (Acts 18:5).

The name itself—or perhaps better stated, the names themselves—are somewhat interesting. "Silas" is the Aramaic form of the Hebrew name "Saul." Remember that Paul's Hebrew name is Saul. In other words, if we were to call Saul/Paul by his Aramaic name, we would be calling him by the same name by which Acts calls this individual. What is more, we know them both by their respective Romanized or Latin names. "Paul," based on its Latin root, means "short" and perhaps refers to a physical characteristic of Paul—if so, such stature may have proven convenient when Saul/Paul escaped danger in Damascus by being lowered down though the city wall in a basket (as told by Paul in 2 Cor. 11:32–33; see also Acts 9:25).

"Silvanus," as Saul/Silas is known in these letters to the Thessalonians, is likewise a Latinized or Romanized name, and means, or refers to, "forest" or to the Roman deity associated therewith; what, if anything at all, the name may have to do with some characteristic of Saul/Silas is anybody's guess. Use of the Roman name, as in the case of Paul, does not necessarily suggest or demand, but is certainly consistent with, Roman citizenship, which is something Acts claims for both Silvanus and Paul in 16:37–39 (regarding Paul, see also Acts 22:25–29; 23:27). That Saul/Paul uses the Latinized "Silvanus" to refer to Saul/Silas/Silvanus is perfectly consistent with his use of the Latinized "Paul" for himself.

According to Acts, Silas was one of the "leaders among the brothers" within the Christian community at Jerusalem (15:22). His presence with Paul may be immediately relevant to, or at the very least consistent with, Paul's ongoing concern for collecting and sending support to that Jerusalem community *and* for the Macedonian churches' (which Silas/Silvanus helps to found) own support of that collection (see esp. Rom. 15:26).

Within the New Testament, Silvanus also appears within the First Letter of Peter (5:12). That Silvanus should appear within Peter's sphere is itself consistent with his association with Jerusalem, where Peter is, by Paul's own words, one of "the acknowledged pillars" of the community (Gal. 2:9, wherein Paul uses "Cephas" for Peter; "Cephas" being the Aramaic equivalent of the Greek word "Peter," meaning "rock"). Did Silvanus drop out of Paul's mission enterprise to join Peter or a broader Petrine enterprise? The texts of the New Testament are silent on that. As for Silvanus's influence on the First Letter of Peter, 1 Peter 5:12 is suggestive: "Through Silvanus, whom I consider a faithful brother, I have written this short letter . . ." Taken at face value, the line indicates that Silvanus had a proactive role in producing the letter. Might that account for some similarity in tone between that letter and Paul's letters and this one specifically? Might it, more particularly, account to some degree for choices of vocabulary and topic, perhaps including one of the most difficult-to-understand usages in 1 Thessalonians (the term rendered "body" or, according to the alternative reading, "wife" in 1 Thess. 4:4, NRSV; see comments below), which appears only one other time within the New Testament, at 1 Peter 3:7 (rendered "sex" or, according to the alternative reading, "vessel," NRSV; the occurrence of four different translations for this one term, used in two New Testament texts, is indication of its difficulty).

Paul and his coauthors address the letter "to the church of the Thessalonians." On one level, this is typical among the letters of Paul, which are regularly addressed to "the church" (see 1 Cor., 2 Cor., 2 Thess., and even Phlm. [see Phlm. 1:2]) or "the churches" (Gal.). But within this letter the term resonates in broad and particular ways. In Paul's other letters so addressed (except 2 Thess., which is like 1 Thess.), he writes to "the church in . . ." or, in the case of Galatians, "the churches of. . . ." Either way, the modifier is a locale (Corinth, Galatia, or, in the case of the Letter to Philemon, "your house") and the emphasis is on the broader or universal "church" or "assembly," which is manifested in the given, particular locale. Here, the modifier is the people, "the Thessalonians," which would have been heard by Paul's Gentile addressees in a way quite different from the ways we (variously) hear it now. We will consider first the noun, "church," then the modifier, the people—the "Thessalonians."

The first definition for this noun, translated here as "church," in the standard Greek-English lexicon in use today is "a regularly summoned legislative body" (Bauer, 303b). A close equivalent today might be "town hall meeting"; even within the New Testament, the term is used precisely in that non-Christian, nonsectarian sense regarding the "regular assembly" of the Ephesians in which the citizens of the city would come together to engage in civic governance (Acts 19:39). That sense of the term, and its direct link with the people of the given locale, has deep roots in the Greek democratic tradition; indeed the very term "democracy" is derived from "the assembly of the people" (the word for "people" being *demos*). Is Paul suggesting, or even promoting, an alternative "assembly" of and for the Thessalonians? How interesting. How outrageous.

The very next sentence, which we might be inclined simply to roll over (the way we might be inclined to roll over "church"), is equally, or possibly even more, loaded: "God the Father and the Lord Jesus Christ." Listen to these words of Caesar Augustus, recorded in the ancient funerary inscription, "The Deeds of the Divine Augustus": "The senate and Equestrian order and Roman people all called me father of the country, and voted that the same be inscribed in the vestibule of my temple, in the Julian senate-house, and in the forum of Augustus. . . ." (*Res Gestae* 35). Both literally and figuratively, within the Roman Empire it is inscribed in stone that the emperor is "father." Already noted in the introduction to this letter, above, are the Thessalonian coins and temple that associate the emperor with God. This inscription, found at Philae in Egypt, indicates another way that particular cities could, and did, establish the emperor's associations with divinity: "The emperor . . . divine father among men, who bears the same name as his heavenly father. . . ."

Paul was having none of that Roman propaganda, and was writing to the alternative "town hall meeting" or "assembly" of the Thessalonians in the really divine God and "father." Much is made in many churches today, for good reasons, about the difficulties raised by using male imagery for God. I wonder what Paul would have thought of contemporary discussions and responses to that matter? As indicated in the introduction, above (and in comments on the particular verses, below, esp. 2:7), it would seem that Paul revels in using mixed (gender, age, stature) metaphors regarding authority figures. Given the context of his addressees' social and political position and from the clues and usages within the letter, Paul's pointed use of "father" here would seem to be providing an alternative identity and power base to the pervasive emperor-centered imperial system(s) with which all in the empire were engaged and accountable.

And, Paul ups the ante in the next phrases. Regarding "the Lord," it is fair to say that everyone in the empire knew who "the Lord" was: Caesar, of course (see the discussion of Phil. 2:11 in the commentary on Philippians). Indeed the point is well made within the New Testament itself, but obscured by the translation of the NRSV. In Acts 25:26, where the emperor is referred to as "our sovereign," the Greek word for the NRSV's "sovereign" is actually the same Greek word for "Lord." It is a shame that English readers, because of differing translations of the same word, miss the resonances that Paul's words here carry (Jude 4 makes the same point as Thess. 1:1, even more forcibly).

The greeting itself, "Grace," is quite standard for Paul (Rom. 1:7; 1 Cor. 1:3; 2 Cor. 1:2; Gal. 1:3; Phil. 1:2; 2 Thess. 1:2; Phlm. 3). Its repeated use in the opening of Paul's letters' reflects a simple, but creative, modification of the standard word for "greeting" regularly found at the front of a Greek letter. That modification of Greek salutary convention is balanced by the broadly Semitic or distinctly Jewish idiom, "peace," recalling the *shalom* greeting (see, e.g., Dan. 4:1) standard in epistolary and other addresses. That Paul enjoyed, and found meaningful, this balance of "grace" and "peace" is indicated by the repeated use of the tandem, often within a very few verses of each other (1 Thess. 5:23, 28; see also 2 Thess. 3:16, 18 and Gal. 6:16, 18; Phil. 4:9, 23). But there is more. This "peace" comes on the heels of the identification of a (non-Roman) God, "Father," who is manifest in a (non-Roman) "Lord," all of which is definitive of an alternatively established "assembly of the Thessalonians." Just as so much has already resonated against the Roman Empire and for the gospel that Paul preaches, so this. What is the empire if not promoter and protector of "peace"; so the famous—then, as now—Pax Romana or Roman Peace. Just as it deemed Caesar "Lord," so the Roman senate built an altar to "the peace" of Augustus. Paul is setting his readers up for an alternative "peace." And he delivers, as we will see, especially in 5:23.

Even before that, Paul shows his hand and nurtures his addressees in understanding their Christian community as an alternative (to imperial propaganda) base of identity and service. To return to where this discussion on alternative communities and understandings began, the very word "church" or "assembly" has at its very root the verb "to call" or "call out." As we will see, Paul uses that verb pointedly in 2:12 and 5:24 to call his addressees to God's "kingdom" or "empire" (2:12; these two English words, "kingdom" and "empire," are different translations of the same Greek word) and further to define their God as well as their relationship with that God (5:24). Of course the "you" here, as throughout the letter, is in the plural (like the English "you all" or "y'all"), addressing the plurality of the community.

THANKSGIVING AND REMEMBERING
1 Thessalonians 1:2–10

1:2 **We always give thanks to God for all of you and mention you in our prayers, constantly** [3] **remembering before our God and Father your work of faith and labor of love and steadfastness of hope in our lord Jesus Christ.** [4] **For we know, brothers and sisters beloved by God, that he has chosen you,** [5] **because our message of the gospel came to you not in word only, but also in power and in the Holy Spirit and with full conviction; just as you know what kind of persons we proved to be among you for your sake.** [6] **And you became imitators of us and of the Lord, for in spite of persecution you received the word with joy inspired by the Holy Spirit,** [7] **so that you became an example to all the believers in Macedonia and in Achaia.** [8] **For the word of the Lord has sounded forth from you not only in Macedonia and Achaia, but in every place your faith in God has become known, so that we have no need to speak about it.** [9] **For the people of those regions report about us what kind of welcome we had among you, and how you turned to God from idols, to serve a living and true God,** [10] **and to wait for his Son from heaven, whom he raised from the dead—Jesus, who rescues us from the wrath that is coming.**

The title for this section is neither to be taken for granted—that is, there is more at work here than simply giving thanks and remembering—nor to be presumed as suggesting linear progression—that is, it does not describe two separate actions, one of which finishes before the other begins. This paragraph is masterfully crafted to build and reinforce an ethos within the community and to bring out themes and topics that will be revisited and carried forward in the letter. Not least of those themes is the importance of the members of the community to remember who—and how and why—they are (see esp. 1:9).

Paul is a bit overabundant in his expression of thanks here, which is even more evident in the Greek than in the English of the NRSV. Actually, "we give thanks" (one word in Greek) and "to God" are the first elements in the sentence and serve both as a nice entrée into the letter and as a nice balance to the "grace," which Paul has just offered in the address ("give thanks" [one word] is built on the same root as "grace"). Part of experiencing and expressing God's grace is to be in community with others and to give God thanks for others. Paul and his coauthors knew that dearly and deeply and could not, would not, and did not conceive of the Christian life in any other way. So the letter reinforces that community and relationship right here at the beginning and will soon bring in the work and service with and for others that is integral to the Christian community.

In terms of the sentence structure of Paul's Greek, putting "give thanks" and "God" up front, leaves "always" and "for all" right next to each other. That, in fact, captures well the ethos that the letter works to establish within this young Christian community. As 5:27 reminds the addressees (and us), the letter is to be read aloud to "all" in the community, because its message is for the community.

To "give thanks to God" is to pray (as 1 Cor. 11:24, among any number of other texts in Paul's letters and throughout the New Testament, indicate). In order to be clear—or, is it to add a nuance?—the letter then directly mentions "prayers." This particular word for prayer suggests petitionary prayer—asking God's help or support for someone. In its verb form, this is the sort of prayer meant when someone or some group asks, "Pray for me/us," which is precisely what Paul and his coauthors ask for, using a verbal form of this same word, in 5:25. Such mutuality and reciprocity as these bookending verses indicate (1:2, "to God for all of you"; 5:25, "pray [to God] for us"), are characteristic of the letter as a whole. Though Paul never gets around to making a petition of God here, he has at least suggested, through use of this word, that he does offer such petitionary prayer on behalf of the Thessalonians. And that mutuality will return in considerations of "thanks" (2:13; 5:18) and "prayer" (3:10; see also 3:11–13; 5:17, 23, 25) and elsewhere within the body and at the end of the letter. But first, Paul will establish even further the parameters of prayer.

"Remembering" figures even more strongly in this sentence than is evident in the NRSV. Where the NRSV has the indicative verb, "mention" (v. 2), the letter has a noun form of the word for "remember" coupled with a participle, rendering something along the lines of, "making remembrance of you." So the noun, "remembrance" (v. 2: "mention" in the NRSV) and the verb "remembering" (v. 3) occur in neighboring phrases. And "remember" occurs again at 2:9 leading into the "thanks" of 2:13. And there's more.

"For we know," like "making remembrance," and "remembering," is actually a participle as it occurs in the letter ("knowing"); like the others, it extends from the main verb, "give thanks." That structure strongly indicates that "we know" (or better, "knowing"), like "mention" (or better, "making remembrance") and "remembering," are all forms or aspects of Paul's prayer for the community. And just as "remember" and "thanks" and "prayer" figure in the body of the letter, so too does "know" (2:1, 11; 4:2). As crafted, the letter suggests that its contents are a virtual extension, or acting out, of the thanks that Paul and his coauthors direct to God on behalf of the community. That's not a bad model for mission and ministry—rooted in the relationship to God; acted out in, for, and through the community (see comments on 4:9–12, below).

As noted in the introduction to 1 Thessalonians, above, the triad of "faith . . . love . . . hope" (1:3) is an important element of Paul's message and may, as indicated above, even suggest something about the circumstances which call forth the letter (see 3:5–6, 10).

But here, all seems intact. Their faith, love, and hope are set "in," or on, or (given the Greek grammatical construction) directed toward, "our Lord Jesus Christ" (v. 3) and more, they have been "chosen" by God (v. 4) to carry forward Paul's mission (vv. 6–8), and through that activity their "faith" is itself already storied (v. 8).

This trio of faith, love, and hope occurs elsewhere in Paul's letters; perhaps most well known is 1 Corinthians 13:13, where "love" displaces "hope" as the third, final, and most important (?) item (cf. Rom. 5:1, 4–5 and beyond Paul's letters, 1 Pet. 1:21–22 and Heb. 10:22–24). The list appears in the same order later in this letter, 5:8, and is abridged to exclude "hope" in 3:6 (see also Col. 1:4–5), which may suggest that for Paul, the final item here, "hope," is indeed, on some level, most important.

"Faith" seems always to occur as the first item in these lists and perhaps Paul did conceive of it in some sense as the base or basis. The preaching of the gospel that Paul and his team engage in, according to the testimony of one of his later letters, springs from "faith": "But just as we have the same spirit of faith that is in accordance with the scripture—'I believed, and so I spoke'—we also believe, and so we speak" (2 Cor. 4:13). In the Greek, the noun, "faith," and the verb, "believe," are built on the same root; Paul essentially uses the word "faith" three times in this sentence to explain the basis for his speaking or preaching. So here at the beginning of 1 Thessalonians, the report that "the word of the Lord has sounded forth from you" (1:8) equates with the phrase, "your faith in God has become known"; as in 2 Corinthians 4:13, faith is the basis for, and leads to, proclamation.

Beyond faith, there is "love." According to the well-known rendering of this list of three, "love" is "the greatest" (1 Cor. 13:13). Who would argue? Paul might (since "hope" is yet to come), but let us hold that concern. "Love" is indeed central, as is "faith," to the identity and mission of the community. Interestingly, in Paul's (later) letter to the Thessalonians' neighbors, the Philippians, Paul writes about those who "proclaim Christ out of love" in concert with, and in support of, the imprisoned Paul's own "defense of the gospel" (Phil. 1:16; see discussion in the commentary on Philippians, above). Proclamation stems from "love"; so here, with the Thessalonians (1:3, 6–7). And, consistent with the Philippian passage, the mission work of the Thessalonians is in league with, and in service to, Paul's own proclamation of the gospel.

Paul would seem to give "hope" pride of place in 1 Thessalonians here and even, as we have noted, when its place is null; the very absence of "hope" in 3:6 may suggest that it, in Paul's view, is what is lacking, and therefore what is needed (via this letter) by the Thessalonians (see also 4:13). Further, as we will discuss momentarily, faith and love are paired with a word indicating work. Hope's partnering word is different from the other two. Notice that "steadfastness" and, as the broad and deep meanings of the word also suggest, "patience," "endurance," and "expectation" lend themselves to the longsuffering, steadiness, and anticipation that "hope" both requires and instills. References to "hope" in other letters of Paul suggest something of its place here. In 2 Corinthians 10:15–16, Paul considers "hope" with regard to the proclamation of the good news in, and beyond, the local community. In Romans 5:1–5, it is the "hope" produced by the "character" and "endurance" which circumstances call forth that, in turn, "does not disappoint." As the newly formed alternative community of Thessalonians proclaimed and spread the gospel that they had received from Paul, they met with resistance (1:5, "persecution"). Perhaps that is just the nexus in which hope is, and must be, found.

Of the words linked with "faith" and "love," the one translated "work" is perhaps the more generic, connoting as it can (and does, most likely here), "occupation" or "activity." But that is not to suggest that it is simply flat rhetorically. Its root is included in our word "energy" and, tellingly, is used within a compound verb form in 2:13, stating Paul's understanding that "God's word" is "at work in," or "energizes," "you believers." As we have already seen in the discussion above, "faith" and "believe" share the same root in Greek, and Paul's addressees would have immediately recognized that. So 2:13 stands as a kind of commentary on, corollary to, or affirmation of "work of faith" in 1:3. Just as the Thessalonians are engaged in the work of faith, so God is energizing these faithful ones.

Many readers of this volume will be familiar with the debate in Protestantism broadly, and in Lutheran and Reformed traditions in particular, around the relationship of "faith" and "works." Luther, for example, famously found the Epistle of James wanting for the statement in James 2:17, often translated or paraphrased as "faith without works is dead." For all the good and ill that that debate has engendered through the centuries, it is worth noting that the matter is seemingly always couched in terms of the individual believer. Yet here, and in the letters generally, Paul does not indicate such a concern on the individual level. He is talking first, finally, and throughout about "the assembly" of the people of this city—an assembly alternatively established by God, in Jesus Christ, in mission for the gospel. How might the theological and ecclesiological debate regarding justification and sanctification be influenced were these verses granted weight in setting the terms (the community; not individual believers) and content (mission of and for the gospel) of the debate?

The word translated "labor" just like the English word, indicates that which accompanies work: toil, exertion, and such. It is what a worker engages in "eight hours a day" (a standard—albeit often trespassed—in our society), "from sun to sun" (as I have heard my elders, especially those familiar with agricultural work, say), or "night and day" (as Paul puts in 1 Thess. 2:9). That "work" and "labor" share a common context and close relationship to each other vis-à-vis the workshop and, more broadly, the activity of commerce and production, is indicated in that full verse: "You remember our labor and toil, brothers and sisters; we worked night and day, so that we might not burden any of you while we proclaimed to you the gospel of God" (1 Thess. 2:9; full discussion below). For Paul's Thessalonian addressees, the terms "work" and "labor" draw on what they do in their "day jobs" (another phrase from our society; perhaps "night and day jobs" would better describe the Thessalonians' situation and, for that matter, many within our society as well).

Now, having used terms rooted in, and immediately relevant to, the daily, socioeconomic life of workers (who make up all, or at least a significant portion of, his addressees; see esp. 2:9; 4:9–12) and having established such—in tandem with "faith" and "love"—as foundational to and for their life together as church, Paul changes direction with the word "steadfastness." As discussed above, "steadfastness" moves away from the context of commerce and of the workshop toward that of suffering and persecution of various kinds.

The association of "steadfastness" with "persecution" is easily shown within the New Testament via reference to the beginning of the book of Revelation. Unfortunately, different English translations obscure the correspondence: "I, John, . . . share with you in Jesus the persecution and the kingdom and the patient endurance . . . " (Rev. 1:9; "patient endurance" and "steadfastness" are alternative translations of the same Greek word, while "persecution" is a consistent translation of the same word in Rev. 1:9 and 1 Thess. 1:6). Important to notice is the place of "steadfastness" as a characteristic of the individual (in the case of the revelator, John, referring to himself) and the community (in the case of Paul describing the Thessalonians) in response to persecution (a point made even more simply and strongly in 2 Thess. 1:4).

Once established, via its simple use in 1:3 and then reinforced with the direct mention of "persecution" in 1:5, Paul's inclusion of "steadfastness" in turn suggests another level of meaning to "labor." How? As discussed, "work" and "labor" inform each other to suggest the context of shoptalk, describing what workers, laborers, and craftspeople do. But so also do "steadfastness" and "labor" inform each other to suggest situations of suffering or persecution. In Galatians 6:17, for example, Paul uses this same word, here translated "labor," there translated (in the NRSV) as "trouble": ". . . let no one make trouble for me. . . ." He is, of course, not referencing the toil or exertion associated with work life, but the "trouble" that rival teachers might cause him. So, in light of "steadfastness," that usage of "labor" is now layered with notions of distress, trouble, or difficulty. Which is it, then? Is Paul talking about work or about persecution? The best answer is, "yes!" Such multivalent meaning as is created by this neat, if open-ended, trio of "work," "labor/difficulty," and "steadfastness," linked as they are with "faith," "love," and "hope" establishes well the context(s) in which the community finds itself: faithfully working on behalf of the mission of the gospel, established locally in the context of the workplace, and experiencing some local persecution.

It is a given of the human condition, I suppose, that trouble comes, and it comes in many shapes and sizes. What "persecution" is it that threatens and impacts the nascent Thessalonian community? In the introduction to this letter, above, are discussed some of the broad and particular imperial tenets upon which Paul's preaching, and the community's response and actions, might be infringing. It is possible that there is, has been, or might be some direct action against the community by leading (social, political) citizens or by formal offices, and indeed 1 Thessalonians 2:14–16, on the face of it, suggests as much (see full discussion there). But the word here translated "persecution" itself carries a range of meaning as is evidenced in Paul's (later) letter to the Thessalonians' neighbors in Philippi in which it appears twice (1:17; 4:14); in the first case translated by the NRSV as "suffering," and in the second, "distress." These translations suggest what is indeed the case, which is that the term can refer to direct or indirect action against another or to the particular reaction(s) that an individual or community has in response to some phenomenon. What verse 6 indicates is that some "distress," "suffering," or formal or informal "persecution" accompanied the Thessalonians' acceptance of "the word."

That "word" came via "our message of the gospel"; that is, the proclamation of Paul and his mission team. Paul's language is even more clipped, as there is no word for "message" in the Greek. It is worth pausing to note that given that 1 Thessalonians is Paul's earliest extant letter, and given that the Gospels and all other documents within the New Testament postdate Paul's letters, this is the first and oldest use of the familiar—to us—term, "gospel," within the New Testament. And though it might look innocent, innocuous, and benign to us, as the discussion regarding imperial propaganda in the introduction to this letter and regarding 1:1, above, indicate, Paul appears to choose and use his language carefully and his use of "gospel," here, is no exception.

First, given Paul's own Jewish identity and rabbinical training, he would be familiar with such passages as Isaiah 52:7, which is likewise familiar to many readers of this volume. That passage recalls the movement and arrival of the herald who comes announcing "peace" (see discussion above regarding "peace") and "gospel" or "good news" (different translations of the same word; the Septuagint, ancient Greek, version of the Hebrew bible uses a verb form of the word "gospel") to the people that their God "reigns." That usage in Hebrew Scripture is fully analogous to the use of the term "gospel" in the broadly Greek context, and in the particular context of the political arena: the "good news" has to do with victory, peace, and/or the arrival of a new king.

A great exemplar of this sense of "good news" is found in a very public document that honors Caesar Augustus on the occasion of his birthday. It was published in a number of cities throughout the west coast of Asia Minor (modern day Turkey), through which Paul had traveled on his way to Philippi and then Thessalonica (see introduction to the letter, above). Often cited as the "Priene inscription" (of 9 BCE), because it is the copy from that particular city that has survived, the decree reads in part: "Augustus . . . brought war to an end and set [all things] in peaceful order [and] exceeded the hopes of all those who had received the good news . . . not even [leaving any] hope [of surpassing him] for those who are to come in the future. . . ." The decree then goes on to again reference the "beginning of good news" associated with Augustus's birth.

One can make a short list of immediate connections with Paul's rhetoric at the beginning of 1 Thessalonians: peace, hope, good news. The resonances of imperial propaganda in Paul's usage here, especially in light of 1:1 (see discussions of "church," "Lord," and "peace" above) jump out. Where the imperial "gospel" announces "peace" and "hope," so too does Paul's. And where the gospel decree about Augustus is published around the province in neighboring cities by formal declaration, so is Paul's "sounded forth" by this alternative assembly of Thessalonians not only in their city but also, via their "example" (v. 7) throughout their own province of Macedonia and even beyond (v. 8).

The use of the language of example (v. 7) and imitation ("you became imitators of us"; v. 6) is pointed, as is Paul's association of himself and his team ("us") with none other than "the Lord." He's a bit full of himself, isn't he? Perhaps. However, it is worth noting that all of this language is well established and carries meaning in the Gentile world in which Paul proclaims his message. Paul's contemporary, the Roman philosopher Seneca, writes that "the way is long if one follows precepts, but short and helpful if one follows examples." The Thessalonians spread the gospel via just that vehicle—example. And how did they themselves become such effective models?

Following the line that has just been quoted, Seneca continues by dipping into the august tradition of Greek moral philosophers to construct a fuller description. He continues with reference to Zeno, founder of the Stoic school of moral philosophy, and to Zeno's worthy student and successor: "Cleanthes could not have been the express image of Zeno if he had merely heard his lectures; he shared in his life, saw into his purposes and watched them to see whether he lived according to his own rules" (Seneca, *Moral Epistle* 6.6). As Cleanthes is to Zeno so the Thessalonians are to Paul: the students become imitators of the teacher. Indeed, having established that pattern of "imitation" in 1:6 and "remembering" in 1:2–3, Paul virtually takes a page out of this traditional playbook of moral philosophy by recalling, in chapter 2, one episode or description after another of Paul's actions among the Thessalonians (see also 2 Thess. 3:9, ". . . in order to give you an example to imitate").

And, of course, Paul anchors the whole process in and from God; so the matter of remembering/mentioning in verses 2–3 and beyond, and so also in his citing of "us and the Lord" as the models for imitation. Indeed, Paul and his team draw on resources far greater than themselves: "our message of the gospel came to you . . . in power and in the Holy Spirit." The divine is immediately and intimately involved *and* all of the actions of Paul's team are consistent with that and give testimony to it: "you know what kind of persons we proved to be among you . . ." (1:5).

Another contemporary of Paul's, the moral philosopher Epictetus, anchors his understanding of teaching authority thusly: "the true Cynic [that is, the genuine teacher of moral philosophy] . . . must know that he has been sent by God to human beings" (*Discourse* 3.22). The verb for "sent" is directly related to the noun used by Paul elsewhere for himself and others, "apostle" (see comments on 1 Thess. 2:7, below, and 1:1, above). The notably short and packed, "of us and of the Lord," raises the possibility that Paul's teaching when among the Thessalonians included consideration of the Christ Hymn, or something like it, in establishing the Lord (i.e., Jesus Christ) as one to be imitated (see discussion in commentary on Philippians, above, esp. vv. 2:1–11). Regardless, Paul has established himself according to contemporary Gentile understandings and practices in precisely the position he should be as proclaimer of this unique and special gospel from God. And, he places the Thessalonians, as ones who have adopted and, themselves, forwarded that gospel, exactly where they should be in relationship to both Paul and God (vv. 6–7). Finally, through evoking "God" in 1:4 (cf. "God the Father," 1:1), the "Holy Spirit" in 1:5, and "the Lord" in 1:6 (cf., "Lord Jesus Christ," 1:1) in telling the story of the founding of the community, Paul puts in place the full complement of (what would come to be recognized within developing Christianity as) the Trinity.

Before moving to the final two verses of this section, a word about the label, "brothers and sisters," by which Paul calls his addressees (1:4; cf. 2:1, 9, 14, 17; 3:7; 4:1, 9, 10 ["beloved"], 13; 5:1, 12, 26). Consistent with usage throughout Paul's letters, its formative role here—suggesting and affirming a common familial identity among those who have recently converted from well established (within their own families, city, and broader society) religious practice (see esp. 1:9–10)—is particularly noteworthy. The Greek word can refer either to a plurality of brothers or to a plurality of siblings, including both male and female members. (For the possibility that the term is used to refer specifically to brothers in the context of 1 Thess., see comments on 4:4, 6. For further discussion of the broad and inclusive parameters of the term, see discussion in the commentary on Philippians, above, esp. Phil. 1:12, 14.)

Verses 9 and 10 serve as a kind of spiritual biography of the Thessalonian community. But even as the past is recalled and the future summoned, it is the present which is fully in Paul's sights—indeed, that could be said for the letter as whole. Comparison with Galatians 4:8–9 is fascinating. The two share broad themes (conversion of Gentile communities to the gospel of Jesus Christ) and particular language ("serve/enslaved," "turn"), even as they act as virtual mirrors for each other: here considering the positive and still-fresh conversion to the gospel, there speculating on—and working to stem—the potential turning (a de-conversion, if you will) of the community away from Paul's gospel. The Galatians passage indicates that Paul can use the term, "serve," for service either to God or to the gods of the Gentiles (which he calls "idols" here and "beings that are by nature not gods" there; for further consideration of the verb "serve" see comments on Phil. 2:22). "Idols," here, is a disparaging term, consistent with Paul's Jewish identity and training and with teachings available in contemporary Gentile moral philosophy (e.g., Plutarch, *On Tranquility of Mind*, 477D; for further consideration of the Jewish context, see Weidmann, *Galatians*, 89–91).

Both the disparaging of the Gentile gods and the notion of (the true) God as "living" are evident in the Acts account of Paul's reception and preaching at Lystra: ". . . we bring you good news [a verb form of the word for "gospel"], that you should turn from these worthless things to the living God . . ."(Acts 14:15). This scene, with its misguided "crowds" and "priest," call to mind another writing of Plutarch, *On Superstition*: ". . . superstition is engendered from false reasoning" (165C). One response to such "false reasoning" might be simply to dismiss God or the gods completely (a position considered by certain thoughtful individuals then as now. Plutarch, in the passage just cited, considers that to be "sorry" or "base" judgment. So, of course, would Paul.

Formed and influenced by Jewish notions of that time when Gentiles would "be converted," "abandon their idols," and "worship God in truth" (Tobit 14:6, NRSV; for broader discussion of Paul's mission to the Gentiles, see Weidmann, *Galatians*). Paul offered to the Thessalonians "a living and true God." Such is well-established Jewish language for understanding

God vis-à-vis other gods and vis-à-vis other notions of God or the gods. Among the documents in the so-called Old Testament Apocrypha (readily available in many editions of the NRSV), the aforementioned passage from Tobit includes that notion of "truth," while Sirach 18:1—"[God] who lives forever created the whole universe"—and 3 Maccabees 6:28— ". . . the almighty and living God of heaven . . ."—capture well the notion of the "living" God. Of course, in Paul's preaching this God is known in and through "his Son from heaven, whom he raised from the dead—Jesus, who rescues us from the wrath that is coming" (1 Thess. 1:10).

If John 3:16 is the Gospel in a nutshell, then this statement in 1 Thessalonians 10 might be Paul's gospel in a nutshell. Elsewhere Paul directly ties this "Son," "Jesus," into that notion of God that has predominated in verse 9. For example, in 1 Corinthians 8:6 Paul writes of the "one God, the Father, from whom are all things and for whom we exist." That sounds like the descriptions in verse 9, especially in light of such Jewish texts as are cited in association with verse 9, above. Paul then proceeds, in 1 Corinthians 8:6, to write about "one Lord, Jesus Christ, through whom are all things and through whom we exist." One can speculate that Paul included such description in his preaching and teaching to the Thessalonians; it is certainly consistent with the teaching here (vv. 9–10). But Paul's concerns here are more pointed; this verse prefigures and prepares for eschatological discussions—that is, consideration of the last days of coming times— that will rise up (2:19; 3:13) and eventually come to predominate (4:13–18; 5:1–11) within the body of the letter.

The phrases regarding the expected arrival of God's "Son" from heaven and of the resurrection ("God raised") are consistent with those found in Philippians (3:20–21 and 2:5–11, respectively, though in the latter there is no statement regarding the resurrection per se; see discussion of Phil. 2:8 in commentary on Philippians, above). The second item, regarding the resurrection, is readily available elsewhere in Paul (e.g., Rom. 1:4; 8:11; 1 Cor. 15:15, 20; 2 Cor. 4:14), while the first is less familiar in the letters (Rom. 10:6 and 1 Cor. 15:47 may, or may not, presume it). By way of prefiguring the discussion, below, regarding 4:13–18 one might note what this verse does say ("wait for his Son from heaven") and does not say (anything about going to heaven).

The matter of "wrath" is a recurring theme in this letter (2:16; 5:9; cf. 2 Thess. 1:6–9, though the term is not used therein) as it is in what may be Paul's last extant letter, Romans (1:18; 2:5; 8; 3:5; 5:9; 9:22). The first instance in Romans shares the concept, as found here (though with a different preposition and in varying forms; the plural, "heavens" is actually used in 1 Thess.), "from heaven." That, plus the language of revelation in Romans 1:18 and 2:5 would seem clearly to connect said "wrath" there, as here, to the end times. Romans 5:9 similarly links Christ's salvific act in rescuing "us" ("we" in Rom. 5:9) from that wrath. The final wrath passage in Romans, 9:22, shares Paul's concerns, as here, with "the Gentiles" (Rom. 9:24). The language of "wrath" is familiar from Hebrew Scripture (e.g., Ezra 20:33; Job 20:23; Ps. 78:49; contra Hos. 11:9) and from the apocryphal and pseudepigraphic literature of Judaism more contemporary with Paul when, not coincidentally, Jewish contact with the Greek-speaking Gentile world was on the increase. In *Psalms of Solomon* 2:23, God is called on "to censure" the Gentiles via divine "wrath." Much of the third book of the *Sibylline Oracles* is given over to "that day" (line 55) when "the wrath of the great God" (line 558) is unleashed. Whether in Romans (see esp. 1:16 and 3:21–22) or here, Paul takes care to link this language of "wrath" with the good news of the "gospel."

REMEMBERING CONTINUED:
PAUL WITH THE THESSALONIANS
1 Thessalonians 2:1–12

2:1 You yourselves know, brothers and sisters, that our coming to you was not in vain, [2] but though we had already suffered and been shamefully mistreated at Philippi, as you know, we had courage in our God to declare to you the gospel of God in spite of great opposition. [3] For our appeal does not spring from deceit or impure motives or trickery, [4] but just as we have been approved by God to be entrusted with the message of the gospel, even so we speak, not to please mortals, but to please God who tests our hearts. [5] As you know and as God is our witness, we never came with words of flattery or with a pretext for greed; [6] nor did we seek praise from mortals, whether from you or from others, [7] though we might have made demands as apostles of Christ. But we were gentle among you, like a nurse tenderly caring for her own children. [8] So deeply do we care for you that we are determined to share with you not only the gospel of God but also our own selves, because you have become very dear to us.

[9] You remember our labor and toil, brothers and sisters; we worked night and day, so that we might not burden any of you while we proclaimed to you the gospel of God. [10] You are witnesses and God also, how pure, upright, and blameless our conduct was toward you believers. [11] As you know, we dealt with each one of you like a father with his children, [12] urging and encouraging you and pleading that you lead a life worthy of God, who calls you into his own kingdom and glory.

The active remembering that Paul both models and promotes near the beginning of the letter remains characteristic throughout this section as well. In a sense, the remembering (2:9; cf. 2:1, "you know") seems simply to continue in the same vein as all that follows from 1:2–3. But there is something of a difference. Here the focus switches to Paul and his team and to recalling the content, manner, and effectiveness of "our coming to you" (2:1). What does not switch is Paul's deep sense of relationship with this young community and deep commitment to and for its mission, in concert with Paul, on behalf of the gospel. All would seem to be crafted to meet the needs of affirming and strengthening the addressees' sense of identity and mission with and for each other and for the gospel.

Paul is using technical and pointed language (1) to recall and reestablish the respective roles of himself and his team, on the one hand, and the Thessalonians, on the other, and (2) to (re)orient the community for mission for the foreseeable future. Coming on the heels of that great and impressive rehearsal of the Thessalonians' accomplishments while still in the nascent stages of their formation (1:6–10) and of the core—or, at least, a significant part of it—of Paul's preaching to them, one of Paul's agenda would seem to be to maintain that enthusiasm and progress.

A basic tenet of philosophical advice and teaching is evident in the strategy Paul employs here: remind them what they know (and build on that). Seneca writes, "Advice . . . engages the attention and rouses us, and concentrates the memory" (*Moral Epistle* 94.11). So here and throughout this section ("you know," 2:1, 2, 5, 11; cf. also "remember," v. 9, and "you are witnesses," v. 10) Paul "concentrates the memory" of the Thessalonians, recalling for them that which they already "know" and, in the meantime, (re)instilling those behaviors and characteristics that he would like to see practiced by the community. In a sense, this section (re-)creates a sort of virtual classroom or set of slides consistent with the sort of instruction that Seneca describes Zeno bestowing on Cleanthes (as quoted above in the discussion regarding 1:6): hearing, again, something of Paul's teachings; sharing, again, something of Paul's life and purpose; witnessing, again, the consistency and integrity with which Paul lived and carried out his ministry.

Paul begins at the beginning of the Thessalonians' experience of him and his mission team. Following the first "you know," which is intensified by a reflexive pronoun, captured well by the NRSV's "you yourselves," Paul writes of his team's "coming" (2:1; perhaps better, "entered" or "came in"). The term is a technical one, referring to the first, formal meeting of teacher and student (see Epictetus *Discourse* 1.30.1; 3.1.1). The contrast of "in vain" (v. 1) with "courage" (v. 2) is pointed. Such "courage" (it is, in Paul's Greek, a verb form here) is precisely the same concept and term as is found in Paul's intense rhetoric, while in prison, in chains, in Philippians 1:20. As discussed more fully in the comments on that passage in the commentary on Philippians, above, this courage/boldness indicates a kind of moral courage or willingness to speak frankly in the face of power and draws on a philosophical motif that, within the tradition of Greek moral philosophy, dates back at least to Socrates. It is used to great affect by Paul's contemporary, the moral philosopher Epictetus, who contrasts the "kings [or "emperors"; same word in Greek] and tyrants of this world" who derive their ability to speak and act as they wish *and* squelch the ability of others to do so, through use of "bodyguards and their arms" and such, with the moral exemplar who is "friend and servant to the gods" and has no such power over others, but seizes the right, "if it so pleases the gods" [itself a quote from Plato's *Crito*, 43D], "to speak freely [that is, with "courage"]" (*Discourses* 3.22.94–96). Another contemporary and commentator on moral philosophy, Plutarch, characterizes flatterers as ones who feign a "courage" (or "frankness") which is "in vain" (or "hollow") using precisely the same two words that Paul uses here. Plutarch also uses many other descriptions for what "courage" is not—"false . . . unsound . . . inflated and swollen" (*How to Tell a Flatterer from a Friend*, 59 CD).

One can see how Paul's neatly crafted, interlocking passage unfolds along the lines suggested by these selections from Plutarch and Epictetus. First the Plutarch-like contrasts: Paul's team, the "we," does not engage in "trickery" based on "impure motives," "flattery," or "greed," (vv. 3, 5). But in language akin to that of Epictetus is "approved by God" (see further discussion of this phrase below) and aims to "please God" and not "mortals" (4, 6; cf. Gal. 1:10). Further, as we have already seen (see discussions regarding 1:1, 3, 5, above), Paul's rhetoric in this letter flies, early and often, in the face of imperial propaganda (as it will again at the end of this section, 2:12), rendering Epictetus's contrast of courage/boldness with the "kings and tyrants of this world" quite relevant.

What, precisely, the recollection of shameful mistreatment at Philippi (v. 2) refers to cannot be known for certain. Taking the statement at face value, it is doubtless related to some action(s) taken against Paul and/or the nascent community at Philippi founded by his mission there and, as such, Philippians 1:28–29 may give us some leverage on it. As indicated within the discussion of those verses in the commentary on Philippians, above, there is simply too little evidence to develop a full picture of "the opponents" about whom Paul writes; on balance, they would seem to be non-Jewish, non-Christian, individuals or groups who have some capability of exercising influence or power over the Philippian community—formal governmental officials or, perhaps more likely, those representing social or economic organizations or networks, formal or informal. Either way, the threat was experienced as real and seemingly consistent with the language of "great opposition" of 2:2. Again, the contrast of moral "courage" against worldly power is at play, and Paul's Thessalonian addressees would likely have heard his words in that way.

They would also have heard something else that for us is obscured by English translation. The prominence of "faith" within the letter has been discussed above regarding both 1:3 and 1:7–8. Here in this section, Paul includes the telling phrase translated in the NRSV, "we have been approved by God to be entrusted with the message of the gospel" (v. 4). As in 1:5, there is no "message of" in Paul's Greek; his language is pithy and focused. But more important are the words translated "approved" and "entrusted." The latter translates a passive verb built off the same root word as "faith" and "believe," for which we have no English equivalent. What Paul writes is that he has been "faithed with the gospel." Why is this important? It resonates immediately with 1:5–8 in which Paul's gospel is introduced to the Thessalonians and then spread by them, consistent with their own "faith" (or "faithfulness"). What is more, within 1:5–8 lies verse 6 with its reference to "persecution" (discussed above). The word translated "approved" here is precisely the same as that rendered "tests" later in this same verse, 2:4 (and also at 5:21, "test"). Just as the Thessalonians, as a testimony to their own faith, have spread the gospel through trying conditions (1:5–8), so Paul is *tested* (more so than "approved") by God who "tests our hearts" and Paul has been "faithed" with the gospel. These resonances with 1:5–8 would have been immediately available to Paul's addressees and would have helped to reinforce their close relationship with Paul and his team, their common identity and mission in and for the gospel, and their respect for Paul and his team as models of such faithful stewardship and of the call to mission.

These descriptions and recollections, including the contrasts with broader societal expectations and practices, build toward a quickly proposed and just as quickly rejected proposition: "we might have made demands as apostles of Christ. But. . . ." In comments on the address of 1:1, the presence, or lack thereof, of the title "apostle" within the letters is discussed. Further, comparison with 1 Corinthians 9 indicates that Paul is well able to express an opinion or two on the matter of his apostleship. Here it is less so a matter of argument—indeed there is no argument at all—and more so a rhetorical set-up, something akin to a straight line or a drumroll, prior to the striking portrait he paints in just a few short words at the close of verse 7. What is going on here?

Paul is perfectly capable of using traditional language, as he shows in verse 11: "As you know, we dealt with each one of you like a father with his children. . . ." Such imagery for the teacher vis-à-vis the student or broader community is familiar to readers of this commentary from the biblical Proverbs (3:1; 4:1) and, perhaps more to the point for the Gentile community at Thessalonica, from the Greek moral philosophical standards with which so much of Paul's language in this section and throughout the letter finds resonances. Socrates had a famous student who is not so well known today, Herodes. It is reported that Herodes "regarded [Socrates] as his teacher and father" (Philostratus's *Lives of the Sophists* 490). The sentiment is typical. Plato writes, "we felt that [Socrates] was like a father to us" (*Phaedo* 116A).

Indeed, Paul extends or focuses the image in a rather poignant way—as any parent or teacher or preacher will surely recognize—through the phrase, "each one of you." It is significant on a few levels. First, it is somewhat inconsistent with the thrust of the letter as a whole, which is engaged with the identity and mission of "you" all, as a whole; that is, the whole community of the "church" or "assembly of the Thessalonians." Second, the phrase "each one of you" personalizes the "father" metaphor and not simply in those ways obvious to us on the face of it, but perhaps quite deeply and existentially for these addressees. Among the social and economic organizations or networks (see discussion of 2:2, above) from which and by which members of this nascent Christian community might find themselves alienated would be family (compare Jesus' teachings as recorded in Mark 10:29–30, Luke 12:51–53 as well as the broader story of Jesus' construction of alternative family/community and of alienation—from his own family as recorded in Mark 3:19b–35). Paul is responding to "each" of those (potential) situations. And, as with the broad metaphor Paul's image fits neatly within the moral philosophical tradition: as recorded by Plato, Socrates affirms for his followers that he comes "to each one of you individually like a father. . . ."(*Apology* 31B).

For Paul, at least in one of his later letters, the image suggests a broad range of behaviors and attitudes. In 1 Corinthians 4:14–21 he provides an extended discussion of the relationship that his "beloved children" and he, as "your father through the gospel," share. That said, the passage famously closes with, "Am I to come to you with a stick, or with love in a spirit of gentleness?" (1 Cor. 4:21). That question—whose "stick" is reminiscent, perhaps, of the "rod" of Proverbs (e.g., 13:24) or, more so for Paul's Gentile addressees, the tool of punishment referenced in moral philosophical literature (the same word is used in Plutarch's *Morals* 268D and 693F)—would find a particularly poignant answer if posed regarding the Thessalonians, and Paul appears to veer significantly from traditional language and expectations in order to respond to it.

Paul closes verse 7 with an extraordinarily poignant metaphor, with complexities on several levels: "But we were gentle among you, like a nurse tenderly caring for her own children." Simply on the face of it, even in our world, the gender-switching image is striking: Paul, a male, comparing himself and his male counterpart(s), Silvanus (and perhaps Timothy as well) to a female caregiver. That Paul is capable of and willing to compare himself both to metaphorical females and to actual females is evident virtually throughout his letter-writing career. In Galatians 4:19, Paul assumes the role of one who is giving, and has already given, birth: "My little children, for whom I am again in the pain of childbirth. . . ." In 1 Corinthians 7:39–40 in a somewhat ambiguous statement, Paul appears to put himself squarely in the place of the widows whose condition he is addressing: "A wife is bound as long as her husband lives. But if the husband dies, she is free to marry. . . . But in my judgment she is more blessed if she remains as she is. And I think that I too have the Spirit of God."

But, there is more here than a simple, if compelling, association with a female nurse. What appears to be referenced is not just any nurse, but a wet nurse. And, interestingly, that too is an image Paul would hold onto throughout, or at least well into, his letter-writing career. First Corinthians 3:1–2 is a revisiting of this very same metaphor: ". . . as infants in Christ. I fed you with milk. . . ." Within the world in which Paul writes, who feeds infants milk if not wet nurse or mother? The station of wet nurses within society was clear—they were slaves. And as with any commodity (as horrible as the notion of commodifying a human being is, that is how slave-based societies treat those who are enslaved), there were opinions about when and how to choose a wet nurse. The first-century physician Soranus advises that the way to pick a wet nurse is to find a candidate whose own child was still an infant—that is, one who had not been lactating for too long (Soranus, *Gynaecology* 2.18–20). What would that mean for the enslaved wet nurse? She was either separated from her own children completely or, at best, would be available to her own only after the children for which she was forced to care had their fill. Consider, then, the human emotion, pathos, and depth of compassion behind Paul's words, "like a nurse tenderly caring for her own children." Tenderly indeed! As is so with the phrase added to the father metaphor, "with *his* children" (v. 11; italics added), even more so, with the addition of the phrase, "*her* own children" (v. 7; italics added) here. Paul is both constructing and reinforcing the sense of kinship and common identity among those within the community and between the community and his team (so v. 8). What is more, he is also modeling for teachers and preachers of all eras and circumstances how to locate the human where the powers that be either ignore or work against that very humanity.

Paul then moves from clear metaphor—Paul is neither woman nor nurse nor is he father to any of these addressees—to simple reality. In verse 9 Paul seems to return to the sort of modeling and recalling of virtuous behavior in which he engages in verses 3–7, but with a concreteness not found there. Here Paul brings his addressees right back into the immediate and very real workshop setting in which their (Christian) community with each other and with Paul was formed. That simple and profound point should not be missed—Paul links his manual, technical labor side-by-side with members of this community with his proclamation of the gospel to them; this "church" or "assembly" was formed in the workplace.

I remember learning as a child that the Inuit people had many words for snow. The reason for adults sharing with me (and every other kid I knew) this tidbit of knowledge apparently was to teach us that experience leads to knowledge, and the ability to perceive and express that knowledge in increasingly nuanced ways increases the opportunity and ability to thrive. Just so, Paul would seem to have a lot of knowledge about the workplace: the NRSV captures well the three different terms for manual labor, all with overlapping but distinct meanings, which Paul employs one after another in this one sentence.

According to Acts 18:3, Paul was a tentmaker (or leather-worker; perhaps, specifically, he made awnings for urban shopkeepers). Consistent with that passage, which ties Paul's profession directly to that of the city-hopping husband and wife team, Priscilla and Aquila, Paul would appear on the testimony of his own letters and Acts to have indeed gravitated toward urban centers. Beyond verse 9 here, Paul writes of his work especially in 2 Thessalonians 3:7–8 and 1 Corinthians 4:12. It appears clear, on the basis of those passages and others (e.g., 2 Cor. 6:5; 11:23, 27), that Paul did not romanticize his work (in the manner that any number of preachers, politicians and other public figures do today). Nor does he simply mean to model virtuous behavior, though that may well be part of his agenda (and the passages from 2 Thess. and 1 Cor., cited above, lean in that direction). Here, access and opportunity are being remembered, as is mission-sustaining behavior. A comparison with another contemporary of Paul's among moral philosophers (beyond Plutarch and Epictetus cited above), Musonius Rufus, is helpful. It was among Musonius's beliefs and standards that the teacher "should endure hardships, and suffer the pains of labor with his own body, rather than depend upon another for sustenance" (fragment 11, in Lutz). Paul would surely have agreed; more so, he extended such teaching and practice into a community ethic (see esp. 4:11–12; 5:11–15; also 2 Thess. 2:6–13) and, in particular, a community leadership ethic.

The section ends with 2:12, which mixes emotive and directive language with a revisiting of empire-tinged rhetoric. Lost in the English of the NRSV is that "appeal" at the top of this section, 2:3, and "urging" here are built from the same root word. The root word itself, like so many other terms and concepts that Paul uses herein, has a broad and deep presence within the moral philosophical tradition as well as within the New Testament. As for the latter, many will be familiar with the term with which Jesus introduces the Holy Spirit in John 14:16. "Paraclete" [a transliteration of the Greek], which the NRSV translates as "Advocate," is a noun from the same root. As for the broader meanings and uses of the word, it is no coincidence that in John 14:26, among the activities of this Advocate is to "remind"—as Paul does so often in this section that is demarcated by appearances of this word (2:3, 12). The same connection is found in contemporaneous moral philosophical literature. For example, in *Moral Epistle* 94.21, Seneca introduces the importance of urging/encouraging immediately following the assertion that it is important to "refresh the memory" (see also 94.11, 25). Another thing that the Advocate does is "testify" (John 15:26), which translates yet another root word that is used in 1 Thessalonians 2:12, there translated by the NRSV as "pleading" (see also 1 Thess. 4:6, which contains an intensified form of this same word, "solemnly warned"). "Urging" is serious business, having to do with a range of teachings and activities—comforting, warning, exhorting—that focus and support individuals and communities in understanding and acting on their identity and mission.

The very next phrase in verse 12 affirms precisely that: "lead a life worthy of God." That which the NRSV translates "lead a life" is also a stock term and concept—which is by no means to suggest it is unimportant! Literally meaning "walk," it resonated in the Greek language as a concept akin to "walking the walk" or even "just do it" in today's common English usage. For example, Epictetus's simple command to students who would act on or live by their principles even in the face of great adversity: "walk" (*Discourses* 1.18.20; see also comments on 4:12 for a possible allusion to Gen. 17:1).

Interestingly, for Epictetus, among the reasons for the adversity being discussed is that an unnamed "tyrant" might imprison, or even "cut off" the neck of, the would-be philosopher. Such actions are, after all, among what tyrants—for example, the emperor and imperial bureau-crats—did to perceived troublemakers. Paul's own imprisonment—see commentary on Philippians, above—may well attest to that (for a narra-tive of Paul's beheading which, according to tradition, was his fate, see the second-century *Acts of Paul*). In comments on 1:1 and 1:2–10 above, time and again we have seen how Paul's language resonates with—and more pointedly, against—imperial propaganda and presumptions. So as verse 12 draws to a close Paul affirms and extends the community's very formation and identity as an alternative assembly "called out" for mis-sion of the gospel (see above, esp. comments on 1:1). The language of "call" here is even more colorful than indicated in the NRSV, though the nuance of Paul's Greek, which employs a participle here, is not eas-ily captured in standard English: "presently calling" or "actively calling" might get at it.

The NRSV captures Paul's use of the intensifying reflexive pronoun attached to "kingdom": "[God's] own." What is so important about that? In league with so much of the language in chapter 1, it amounts to a not-so-veiled swipe at the empire. "Kingdom" and "empire" are different English renderings of one Greek word, so whether hearing the words of Jesus read from the Gospels or the words of Paul read from his letters, Greek-speakers would have heard "empire" where we English speakers hear "kingdom." That puts us at a great disadvantage in perceiving the resonances of the pointed language. Indeed recognizing that simple and direct connection—kingdom = empire—goes a long way toward helping us understand both Jesus' and Paul's earthly fates. In terms of this letter, this final phrase of verse 12 contains much that Paul has established thus far: the active calling (2:12) of the living, active God (1:9–10), and the dynamism of that God's gospel and of the communities associated with, and defined by, it (1:5–7). Just as Paul's own descriptions of himself and his team are both jarring (wet nurse, 2:7) and deeply meaningful and personal ("her own," 2:7; "his," 2:11), so his descriptions of God and kingdom/empire are jarring and suggest a personal and community attachment to God's call and to God's "own" kingdom/empire.

THANKSGIVING CONTINUED AND IMITATION EXTENDED
1 Thessalonians 2:13–16

2:13 **We also constantly give thanks to God for this, that when you received the word of God that you heard from us, you accepted it not as a human word but as what it really is, God's word, which is also at work in you believers.** [14] **For you, brothers and sisters, became imitators of the churches of God in Christ Jesus that are in Judea, for you suffered the same things from your own compatriots as they did from the Jews,** [15] **who killed both the Lord Jesus and the prophets, and drove us out; they displease God and oppose everyone** [16] **by hindering us from speaking to the Gentiles so that they may be saved. Thus they have constantly been filling up the measure of their sins; but God's wrath has overtaken them at last.**

The letter's content continues to unfold via yet another return to language and themes that Paul has already established and through which he continues to construct and affirm the strong bonds between his addressees and himself and—not coincidentally—to prepare them for the advice and teachings forthcoming in chapters 4 and 5. Here, it is the action and theme of thanksgiving (1:2) that Paul revisits, soon developing yet other themes, including that of imitation beyond what Paul had recalled earlier (1:6–7). In so doing, Paul introduces a whole area of discussion more characteristic of Romans (see esp. chs. 9–11), which is likely his latest letter that we have, than it is of his earliest extant letter. Indeed, many scholars have argued that these seemingly uncharacteristic verses regarding "the Jews" (more on the precise meaning of the use of that term, below) are, in fact, an interpolation. That is, they were added later by a student of Paul's or some other interested party. That notion is not entertained herein because there is no textual or manuscript evidence for it and because these verses, if difficult on some level, do indeed fit neatly into the content, sweep, and language of the letter as well as into the context from which and for which Paul writes. Here Paul, through the theme of imitation, extends for his addressees the bonds of community with and among those in gospel mission beyond the bipartite paradigm of the Thessalonians' partnership with Paul and Paul's team and also sets the stage for extending the bonds of their common experience beyond that which has been recalled and into the present circumstance (2:17–18).

The first sentence of this section, verse 13, is packed with elements that draw on, and extend, themes already introduced in the letter. The matter of extending toward something new is signaled, in a manner lost in the English of the NRSV, by the placing of the phrase translated, "for this," at the beginning of the sentence. Something along this line captures the structure of the sentence as written: "About this we also constantly give thanks. . . ." "About what?," is the obvious question to ask. Paul has their/ our ear, and he responds in verse 14. But first he includes a recapitulation of some important themes.

Both the naming/action of giving thanks and the inclusion of the adverb "constantly" draw directly on 1:2. As discussed above in the comments on that verse and those following it, Paul's introduction of thanksgivings itself leads to a "remembering" (1:3; and, as discussed above, the remembering language actually begins itself in 1:2), which carries Paul into and through the discussion of the founding of the community and its impressive work already on behalf of the mission of the gospel (1:5–10).

Central to that verse, 1:5, is the coming of the gospel message to the Thessalonians "not in words only. . . ." While the word, "word," takes on something of a disparaging hue in 1:5, here it enjoys something of a resuscitation both in terms of quantity and quality: it is used three times in one sentence, and associated clearly with "God." The NRSV captures well the sense of its second use (consistent with 1:5) and third use (closely and directly connected to God). Its first appearance is slightly more complicated than the NRSV indicates, and it is worth pausing briefly to take notice.

Paul the missionary, teacher, preacher, and letter writer knows that there is an art—even a dance (to extend the metaphor)—to communication. He honors that, and honors his addressees, by drawing out the first description of "word" in this verse. Where the NRSV has "you received the word of God that you heard from us" Paul writes something more akin to: "accepting a word of hearing from us you received it as God's." Paul is recognizing something of the real-world and real-time nature of the work of the gospel, and the roles of all involved—proclaimer/community founder and listener/convert/community member. This little phrase brings him, them, and us right back into the workshop where Paul did his proclaiming and they did their accepting/converting/forming (2:9). They heard Paul's message and determined that they were hearing God's message. Paul is acknowledging that, and acknowledging their role. There are theological as well as pastoral implications to this understanding.

For example, what about 1:5? There the Thessalonians get no credit, so to speak. The message "came," it wasn't "accepted" or "received," and there the Holy Spirit is the actor, with no indication of agency on the part of Thessalonians. Who is the real actor here and who should get the credit? God/Holy Spirit or the Thessalonians? Paul's answer is a resounding yes. He has no interest in a theological debate. He has direct interest in honoring the Thessalonians and their openness and efforts, as well as, of course, and not to be missed, recognizing the role and agency of the divine (the Holy Spirit is not named here as in 1:5). In doing that, Paul marvelously draws on the theme/reality of work discussed and recalled in 2:9. There is no indication at all that any of the three words used for different aspects of "work" in 2:9 indicate anything but manual and/or professional labor. Here the "work" of God's word is indicated by way of a compound verb built on precisely the same root, "worked," used in 2:9—again a nod to that workplace setting where the Thessalonians accepted, and the Holy Spirit came with, the word. The compound verb here amounts to a somewhat intensified form of "work"; from it we derive our word "energize," which would serve as a nice translation (though the NRSV's "at work" rightly maintains the direct connection with "worked" in 2:9).

Finally, a consideration of the final word in 2:13 will move us into the next verse and the rest of this section: "believers." The use of this term here brings the discussion of 2:4 (which draws on 1:5–8; see comments, above) full circle. As noted above, the words "entrusted" in 2:4 and "faith" in 1:8 share the same root. We can now add to that list, "believers"—again, built on the same root. So, from 1:8 through 2:4 and now here, Paul has affirmed and extended the association of the Thessalonian community with faith/trustworthiness/believing and, not coincidentally, provided a kind of lesson indicating something of the breadth and depth of the word and concept "faith." More, Paul has tied in the Thessalonians' faith/belief directly to his God-approved trustworthiness (2:4). On that very score, we have already observed how the themes of persecution (1:6) and testing/approval (2:4; see discussion above) are linked. It is precisely that avenue that Paul will explore next, in 2:14–16. This section, perhaps more than any other, suggests that on some level the letter is a kind of commentary on, and promoting of, the notion of "work of faith" that Paul introduced in 1:3.

We know and, more to the immediate point, the Thessalonians know from their own experience and from the discussion of chapter 1, especially 1:6, that they are imitators of Paul. Here Paul introduces a rather new and expanded concept: "you . . . became imitators of the churches of God in Christ Jesus that are in Judea. . . ." Paul radically alters the pattern set in 1:6: ". . . you became imitators of us and of the Lord . . ." (see discussion, above). Now neither the Lord, nor their teacher, but another community, quite removed by ethnicity and geography becomes the model for what "you," the Thessalonian community, has already accomplished. One wonders if the Thessalonians knew they were "imitators" of these Judeans at

the point in time in which Paul says they were; it appears a retrospective announcement/understanding—and a rather world-shattering one.

Based on the text of the letter as we have it, there are few allusions to Scripture—what has been traditionally called by Christians, the "Old Testament." Of course, there was no New Testament at the time of Paul's writing, and so no Old Testament. In terms of this letter, there are few indications that Paul has taught this community of Gentiles much about Jewish practice or Jewish communities. (Here Galatians serves as an interesting contrast, for its many references and allusion to the Scripture and Jewish religious practice is written in reaction to the Gentile community's exposure to Christian teachers promoting Jewish practice.) Further, though there are clear references and allusions to imperial practice and propaganda, there has been little reference to peoples or communities of any kinds beyond the local, or regional (1:8) sphere. Even the exciting report of 1:8 includes nothing more foreign or distant than the Thessalonians' own province of Macedonia and the southern Greek, Greek speaking, region in which the major cities of Athens and Corinth are located. Here Paul shatters such boundaries.

At the very least Paul is modeling a kind of ecumenism; perhaps a handy equivalent would be the "sister synod" or "partner" programs that many churches and denominations promote, which link individual congregations or regional bodies on one continent to those in another. On another level, he is reinforcing what is suggested by the report of 1:5–8, that one church community can and does fulfill the role of teacher and model for others. On yet another, he offers some sense of pride of place to the Judean Christian community (consistent with what he writes in Gal. 1:17–2:10). All of that said, the very proposition raises the question, How?

Here the plot thickens and becomes thorny for many readers today, whose own traditions trace through a millennia-old Christian bias that includes formal and informal, and direct and indirect, acts of persecution against Judaism and Jewish peoples. That Paul could or would have had any of that history or bias available to him or would have had any interest in inciting such is impossible. A footnote in the NRSV would be handy at the end of verse 14 indicating that "Jews" could be or should be understood as "Judeans"; even better would be placing "Judeans" in the main text. Even on its face, that renders a clearer, more succinct reading. Paul is keeping it simple and so should we. Paul is drawing a direct comparison between this Thessalonian community and the persecution it has experienced at the hands of its "compatriots" (a helpful translation for Paul's word here that indicates member of the same tribe or national/

ethnic group) with the Judean Christian community and the persecution it has experienced at the hand of its "compatriots." The Judean Christian community was clearly Jewish, as were its compatriots. There were clearly Jews living elsewhere than Judea—Paul is living proof of that—but he clearly does not have them in view, nor does he have any Jews of any other time or place in mind.

But there is more, or perhaps better stated, less. Paul is not talking about all Judeans. He is speaking of those leaders among the people who were involved in killing "both the Lord Jesus and the prophets, and drove us out; they displease God and oppose everyone by hindering us from speaking to Gentiles so that they may be saved." Now it is getting personal.

Paul lumps a lot into this part (vv. 15–16) of the sentence which has started back in verse 14. It is important to separate out some of the elements and their relevance. Beginning with the latter phrases, one can see immediately that Paul is including his very mission, "us," in the mix; indeed, this very letter itself is indication of Paul's sense of call to reach out "to Gentiles so that they may be saved." He has a personal stake in the matter and so does "everyone," Jew and Greek, which goes without saying given Paul's understanding of God and God's relationship to humanity. Further, given a (then) traditional Jewish worldview that separates the world's population into "Jew" and "Gentile"—a worldview that Paul shares or, at the very least, is well versed in and willing to use (see Gal. 2:15)—the content of verses 15–16 involves "everyone." And that begins to bring us to the earlier phrase regarding Jesus and the prophets.

Going back to the first phrases of verse 15 we see that Paul lumps the killing of Jesus and the prophets with driving "us" out. Though in Hebrew Scripture there is no killing of a major, or even minor, prophet recorded, there is evident a tradition about persecuting and killing the prophets (1 Kgs. 19:10–14; 2; Chr. 36:11–17). The emotional words of Jesus recorded in Luke 13:34 (see also Matt. 23:37) appear to draw directly on this tradition, as do the pointed and graphic words Jesus speaks to the lawyer at Luke 11:47–52. Paul may be drawing to some degree directly on the words of Jesus, though that is not necessary given the availability of this tradition in Scripture and more broadly. (The tradition reaches a kind of high point with the so-called *Martyrdom of Isaiah*, which depicts the prophet being sawed in half; interestingly, that document gained its final form at about the time that Paul is writing, mid-first century.) Clearly Paul, like Jesus as recorded in Luke (and, to a lesser degree, Matt.), is linking the tradition with Jesus' own death. He is also linking it directly to his mission.

For Paul, of course, Jesus' death and resurrection ushers in the new age. That understanding provides the glue that holds together the lumping of Paul's mission with the killing of Jesus and the prophets with the eschatological pronouncement that closes out the letter. Paul's statement here at the close of the section is harsh; it is clearly judgment, and just as clearly based on an end-time scenario. For a broader discussion about God's "wrath," see discussion of 1:10, above. For the notion of a "measure" of sin and God's punishment, 2 Maccabees 6:12–17 provides an interesting foil for Paul's statement here,

> Now I urge those who read this book . . . to recognize that these punishments were designed not to destroy but to discipline our people. In fact, it is a sign of great kindness not to let the impious alone for long, but to punish them immediately. For in the case of the other nations the Lord waits patiently to punish them until they have reached the full measure of their sins; but he does not deal in this way with us. . . . his own people.

Paul here is turning a Jewish tradition back on the leaders in Judea (consistent with Dan. 8:23); he is also opening out that tradition to "the other nations" (i.e., the "Gentiles," which translates the same Greek word as does "nations"). That is the good news, presumably, that he wishes his Gentile audience to be aware of—the God-blessed mission out to the nations/Gentiles of which he understands his proclamation of the gospel to be a part. And, that is the good news that connects these Gentile Thessalonians to their Jewish, or Judean, models and "compatriots."

AS FOR US: PAUL'S TEAM
1 Thessalonians 2:17–3:9

2:17 **As for us, brothers and sisters, when, for a short time, we were made orphans by being separated from you—in person, not in heart—we longed with great eagerness to see you face to face.** [18] **For we wanted to come to you—certainly I, Paul, wanted to again and again—but Satan blocked our way.** [19] **For what is our hope or joy or crown of boasting before our Lord Jesus at his coming? Is it not you?** [20] **Yes, you are our glory and joy!**
    [3:1] **Therefore when we could bear it no longer, we decided to be left alone in Athens;** [2] **and we sent Timothy, our brother and co-worker for God in proclaiming the gospel of Christ, to strengthen and encourage you for the sake of your faith,** [3] **so that no one would be shaken by these persecutions. Indeed, you yourselves know that this is what we are destined for.** [4] **In fact,**

when we were with you, we told you beforehand that we were to suffer persecution; so it turned out, as you know. [5] For this reason, when I could bear
it no longer, I sent to find out about your faith; I was afraid that somehow
the tempter had tempted you and that our labor had been in vain.

[6] But Timothy has just now come to us from you, and has brought us
the good news of your faith and love. He has told us also that you always
remember us kindly and long to see us—just as we long to see you. [7] For this
reason, brothers and sisters, during all our distress and persecution we have
been encouraged about you through your faith. [8] For we now live, if you
continue to stand firm in the Lord. [9] How can we thank God enough for you
in return for all the joy that we feel before our God because of you?

The focus now turns, again, away from the Thessalonians to Paul and his
team (as it had in 2:1–12). This time, however, it is not remembrance that
carries the narrative, descriptions, and teachings that are provided but
something of an update that bridges the time from Paul's departure from
Thessalonica to the occasion of writing the letter. It is no surprise, given
what we have seen thus far, that the rhetoric and descriptions remain heartfelt and emotive—even strikingly so (esp. 2:17). The sense of struggle and
challenge remains on the scene (2:18; 3:3–4, 7), and faith and faithfulness
merit yet another revisiting (3:5; see also 6, 8). And though remembrance of
the founding and first wave of activity of the community does not carry the
content of the section, it returns as a motif (3:6), as does thanksgiving (3:9).

The section starts with a flourish of sorts, that picks up on the metaphorical language for the relationship of teacher-student, community
founder-community that has been used already in this chapter—namely,
the strikingly complex image of the wet nurse/mother in 2:7 and that of the
father in 2:11. Here the image of choice is orphan. And what a choice it is.

A stock image within the moral philosophical tradition is that of the student or community being "orphaned" by the death or departure of the great
teacher or leader. In the comments on 2:7, above, Socrates' student Herodes,
who himself became a popular teacher, is mentioned. It is recorded that
Herodes' own students, on his death, were like "children bereft of an excel-
lent father" (Philostratus's *Lives of the Sophists*, 566). In the passage from
Plato cited above, in that same discussion ("we felt that [Socrates] was like a
father to us"), the sentiment continues, ". . . and that when bereft of him we
should pass the rest of our lives as orphans" (*Phaedo* 116A).

Paul's team turns the table on that stock image, putting themselves ("us")
in the place of "orphans" and putting the "(alternative) assembly" (see
comments on 1:1, above) of Thessalonians in the role of teacher or leader.
We can imagine that the rhetorical move would have been unexpected

(though, following 2:7, perhaps the addressees would have come to expect the unexpected) and elicit a reaction along these lines: they must be mistaken; is it not we who are orphaned by them? But the letter continues, consistently maintaining the focus of this section on the desire to connect with the Thessalonians. In so doing, this section affirms and increases the sense of warmth and mutual regard between Paul and his team and the Thessalonians and models shared leadership in and for the gospel.

Verse 18 continues in the same vein as verse 17, affirming the closeness and sense of mutuality: "we wanted to come to you." Then, two things happen back-to-back: (1) the voice of Paul, for the first time overtly, steps out front and center; (2) a third party—beyond Paul and Paul's team, on the one hand, and the Thessalonians on the other—is introduced. What does "Satan" have to do with this situation?

There are at least two related answers to that question. Paul has already given a hint in 1:10 ("wait for . . . [God's] Son from heaven . . . who rescues us from the wrath that is coming") and 2:16 ("Gentiles . . . saved"; "God's wrath . . . at last"), and will do so again in 2:19 ("our Lord Jesus at his coming"), that consideration of the end times is of concern within the letter (to which a good bit of chs. 4 and 5 will be given). Satan certainly has something to do with the end times (as is treated directly in Paul's second letter to the Thessalonians, esp. 2 Thess. 2:9; see also comments on "air" in 1 Thess. 4:17, below). On a related note, Satan has something to do with obstructing or turning aside God's agents from carrying out their missions. This is shown brilliantly in the Gospel account of Jesus rebuking Peter as both "Satan" and "stumbling block"; remember, it is Peter who, in reaction to Jesus' prediction of the coming passion, takes Jesus "aside" in an attempt to prevent Jesus' from continuing on toward Jerusalem (Matt. 16:21–23, cf. Mark 8:31–33; see also the temptation accounts in Matt. 4 and Luke 4). And so here, Paul's concern extends from himself and his team (2:18) to the Thessalonians (3:5, "tempter")—that is, he is concerned that mission of and for the gospel not be knocked off course.

How, in earthly terms, was the way "blocked"? Apparently, either Paul is not concerned with answering that or the answer would have been so obvious that it needed no ink. In the introduction to the letter, above, is discussion about one possible governmental/bureaucratic explanation: Paul was formally blocked from return to the city due to his teaching, in particular that having to do with the end times (see 5:1). Were that the case, it might explain, or affirm, the congruence of eschatological components in this section of the letter: Satan, Lord Jesus' coming and, as we will see, the mention of "boasting" and a "crown." It might also explain the designation of Timothy (3:2) as the one sent to the Thessalonians; were Paul formally banished from the city it is certainly possible that Silvanus would have been as well, whereas Timothy (at least if the account in Acts 16–17 is to be believed) was apparently not present in Thessalonica at the founding of the community there and so would have been free to enter the city (see discussion of 1:1, above).

Another consideration might be Paul's own health. He would famously write in 2 Corinthians 12:7 of a "thorn" in his side. What that "thorn" was is a subject of endless speculation. What is clear is that Paul associates its placement with Satan or, to be more precise, "a messenger of Satan" (2 Cor. 12:7). Three times in two verses, Paul identifies "weakness" or "weaknesses" in association with the placing of that "thorn." Has Satan "blocked" Paul here via some physical illness, weakness, or malady?

The language of 2:19—"joy," "crown," "boasting"—is similar to that Paul would later use in his letter to the Thessalonians' Macedonian neighbors at Philippi. There, as here, the context of the end times stands out: "It is by your holding fast to the word of life that I can boast on the day of Christ that I did not run in vain" (Phil. 2:16). The running metaphor links directly with that of "crown"—a knot which Paul ties in Philippians via the footrace imagery of Philippians 3:12–14 and the naming of the "crown" in Philippians 4:1. At Philippians 4:1 also, "joy" is identified, as it is throughout Philippians in association with the community (Phil. 1:3, 25; 2:2, 29; see also the use of the related verb, "rejoice," in 1:18; 2:17, 18, 28; 3:1; 4:1, 10). The theme of boasting on the day of the Lord is perhaps most succinctly put within Paul's letters at 2 Corinthians 1:14 ("on the day of the Lord Jesus we are your boast even as you are our boast"). Presumably his addressees are well aware of these connections since they have heard Paul, to a significant degree, discuss the end times (5:1–2).

One final note before moving to chapter 3 is that recurring matter of "hope." As we have already seen, it looms large in the letter and indeed may, on some level, provide occasion for the writing of the letter itself (see introduction to the letter, above; also 1:3). Before 3:6, where "hope" is conspicuous in its absence, and 3:10 wherein the absent "hope" of 3:6 may account for that which is "lacking" in the Thessalonians' faith, Paul makes this statement: "for what is our hope or joy or crown of boasting before our Lord Jesus at his coming? Is it not you?" The sentiment is directly analogous to that of 2 Corinthians 1:4, and is, as we have seen, perfectly consistent with Paul's letter to the Philippians. But, found in none of those verses is the emphasis on, or even presence of, "hope." How relevant is it for this community, which is lacking "hope" of some sort on some level, to hear and know that they indeed are "hope" for their mentor and his team and indeed stand as a personification or embodiment of "hope" at the "coming" of "our Lord?" If their lack of "hope" has something to do with their reckoning of death or of expectations of the end times (as 4:13–5:11 would suggest) then this eschatologically and imperially tinged language takes on even more depth of meaning and purpose. It is the "coming" not of the "Lord" emperor from Rome, but of Jesus Christ, that sets both the identity and mission of this alternative "assembly of the Thessalonians " (see esp. 1:1; for discussion of this particular word for "coming," see discussion of 4:15–17 below).

The travelogue or diary of sorts that begins chapter 3 serves to update the addressees on Paul's situation and the context for the writing of the letter and to affirm and underline much that has already been written in the letter. Noted in comments on the previous section, above, is the direct verbal connection between the noun, "appeal," in 2:3 and the verb, "urging," in 2:12. They are built on the same root word, which would have been immediately evident to Paul's addressees. So too the verb "encourage" here. Paul again dips into the deep well of that root word, with its range of meanings including comforting, warning, exhorting, as well as the meanings suggested by the three NRSV translations encountered here.

The needs and the responses are deep and pastoral as is affirmed by the final phrase of verse 2, "for the sake of your faith." On one level, the phrase needs no commentary; all or most readers of this volume will have some direct, existential sense of what it might, does, or can mean. Can we get further leverage on the phrase from the letter itself? Timothy, who is sent to do the appealing/urging/encouraging is described here as "co-worker . . . in proclaiming the gospel of Christ." The Thessalonians own faith is first introduced in direct association with "work" (1:3) and is established as that which "has become known" through their missionary efforts in their own and neighboring regions (1:5–8). This is a robust, active, "working" faith. And indeed, when the term recurs in this same section, at 3:5, it is in association with Paul's "labor" (a term that recalls 2:9 and is directly associated with "work"). The Thessalonians' "faith" has to do not—or certainly not only —with their own individual, personal confessions but with their faithful commitment to their corporate identity as an "assembly" defined by and for the mission of the gospel of Jesus Christ. There is a lot of "work" and "labor" associated with such an identity and such a commitment. And, a lot of room for losing that sense of mission, which explains Paul's revisiting of Satan/the tempter, this time in conjunction with the Thessalonians.

Persecution, of most any shape and size, can be a motivator for losing sense of identity and mission. Whatever the persecution(s) is (are) that Paul has in mind in verses 3–4, he is doubtless rightfully concerned about the impact on the community. The NRSV captures well the repetition of this root word in the two verses. What may not be evident is the alternative use of the noun (v. 3) and the verb (v. 4) forms: "suffer persecution" is one word in the Greek. The possibilities range from informal social or economic harassment and shunning to formal government action and threat to life and/or limb (the Acts account of Paul's time at Thessalonica names both "city authorities" and "some ruffians in the marketplaces" as involved in countering him and his teaching; Acts 17:5–6). Presumably, since there is no indication of any formal charges or punishments brought, what the Thessalonians are up against is more so harassment and shunning, whether by family, friends, and associates, or broader social and economic networks, etc. One example of what they might have been up against can be gleaned, in a handy way, by a reading of 1 Corinthians 8; if the equivalent of the chamber of commerce says that we ought to be meeting and eating at a local temple, and given our newfound identity in, and commitment to, this gospel we are not comfortable doing so, the consequences to our business, and various other dealings may be significant. Of course, more pointed or harsher implications are possible, especially in light of the critical orientation that much of Paul's language (see esp. 1:1; 2:12, and, below, 5:3) seems to take vis-à-vis the empire.

The language at the close of verse 3 is fairly well served by the NRSV translation, though neither a *Star Wars*'s Luke Skywalker-like "destiny" nor a Calvinist "predestination" are suggested. Paul's word, which is nontechnical, broad, and simple, means "to be set" or "to be placed." The NRSV translation captures well the proactive orientation of Paul's statement: it is "for," or even "into," "this" messy, real-life, precarious context that "we"—in the Thessalonians' case as a formed community, an alternative "assembly," "called out" by God—"have been set." There is a sense of destiny in that!

We might simply pass over Paul's wonderful statement at verse 6, aided and abetted by the NRSV translation, but it is genuinely creative, even playful, and worthy of noticing. Paul has already established, early and often, the importance and relevance of "the gospel" (1:5; 2:2, 4, 8, 9; 3:2) as a technical term for his proclamation and, more broadly, mission. Here he uses precisely that same language: The NRSV's "brought us good news" is a translation of the verb form of the noun translated "gospel" elsewhere. To capture something of the wit of Paul's language, we might say that Timothy "evangelizes" to Paul about the Thessalonians. Why is this important? Beyond the simple, and presumably flattering and affirming, equation of the Thessalonian community's "good news" with the "good news" of *the* gospel, is the broader theological and ecclesiastical implication: the health and well-being, the identity and mission, of this "assembly" is indeed part and parcel of *the* gospel. Those are high stakes.

The revisiting of "faith and love" at the close of verse 6 call's Paul's addressees back to the "work of faith and labor of love and steadfastness of hope" that Paul introduced at the beginning of the letter (1:3) and, despite the affirmation of "hope" that Paul and his team posit for the Thessalonians (2:19), raises the question of why there is no "hope" stated in this verse. But there is no time for dwelling on that here. Paul continues by completing the circle he had begun to draw also at the beginning (1:2–3) and reaffirmed in 2:9: the Thessalonians do indeed remember, and their mutual affection and yearning for renewed truck with Paul and his team matches and mirrors theirs. And, by way of completing another circle, just as Timothy was sent to "encourage" them (3:2), so their "faith(fullness)" (see discussion of 3:5, above), which Paul has acknowledged via Timothy's report (3:6), has "encouraged" Paul and his team (3:7; see comments on 3:2 for broader use of this root word throughout the letter). Finally, herein, Paul revisits the language of "persecution" (see comments on 3:3–4) forming another connection between the Thessalonians and himself and his team.

The language and context of 3:8–9 recall 2:19. There it was "joy," "crown," and "boasting," here it is "joy," and "stand firm." Of the particular passages in Philippians discussed regarding 2:19, Philippians 1:25 was cited only in passing (in a list of references to "joy"). Paul does indeed name "joy" at Philippians 1:25, along with "boasting" in Philippians 1:26, and "standing firm" in 1:27. All of these interlocking terms and concepts, and their similar uses with and around each other in these Macedonian correspondences, suggests that Paul may have included these very terms in his formative preaching within each of the these communities. Stated here perhaps even more simply and profoundly than in Philippians is the mutuality and up building shared between the addressees and Paul and his team: "For we now live, if you continue to stand firm in the Lord." And just as the prominent themes of "remembering" and "encouraging" are brought to some sort of climax in 3:6–7, so here does giving "thanks" reemerge. Where Paul's initial thanksgiving leads him to remember and recall how "you" Thessalonians "received the word with joy . . ." (1:2, 6), here in 3:9 it is "you" Thessalonians that bring Paul "joy." Paul is, in a sense, acting out what he has announced in 3:6, directly connecting the "gospel" of Jesus Christ with the "gospel" of the Thessalonians (see comments on 3:6, above). Because of their status as an "assembly" "called out" and formed by God, they are indeed an integral part of the gospel message and their "standing firm" is well worthy of providing Paul with such "joy" as they had initially felt with and from the Holy Spirit.

PRAYER REVISITED
1 Thessalonians 3:10–13

> 3:10 **Night and day we pray most earnestly that we may see you face to face and restore whatever is lacking in your faith.**
> [11] **Now may our God and Father himself and our Lord Jesus direct our way to you.** [12] **And may the Lord make you increase and abound in love for one another and for all, just as we abound in love for you.** [13] **And may he so strengthen your hearts in holiness that you may be blameless before our God and Father at the coming our Lord Jesus with all his saints.**

Prayer is introduced into the letter in 1:2, where it is intimately associated with thanksgiving and remembering (1:2–3), which themselves have been revisited throughout the letter thus far (as previous section titles and discussion indicate). As recently as 3:6 remembering is treated, and as recently as the previous verse, 3:9, "thanks" again appears. Now Paul returns to prayer as a kind of bookend (1:2–3:10) on all this treatment of thanksgiving and remembrance. Importantly, the letter is coming to a transitional point in terms of type or quality of content, moving from a kind of reportage or narrative of what has happened and is happening to teaching or exhorting (beginning with 4:1). Of course, as the comments thus far have indicated, there is much teaching and formation in, with, and under such reporting as Paul has included in these first three chapters of the letter, and that will continue to influence the whole of the letter. Paul will pray again at the close of the letter, at 5:23–24, following the directive to "pray without ceasing" (5:17). So, in punctuating these major parts of the letter with prayer, and bookending these deep and creative discussions and examples of thanksgiving and remembrances with prayer, Paul is modeling something of the regularity, discipline, and relevance of prayer; perhaps, too, he is suggesting something about the "work" of prayer.

The phrase "night and day" immediately call Paul's addressees back to 2:9, with its multiple words for "work" and its evoking of the workshop setting in which he and they worked side by side and in which he proclaimed to them the gospel. Is it not marvelous and relevant that Paul turns precisely the same phrase in establishing the boundaries and practice of prayer? In light of 2:9, prayer is clearly something that involves (to use the words from 2:9) "labor" and "toil" and is "worked" at. Even without that rich base that Paul has provided for experiencing prayer, "night and day" leaves little wiggle room—prayer is a constant activity of and for the mission of the gospel, which means that it involves engagement with and for others.

Evident in the letter thus far are the importance of work (as just discussed above) and faith (see comments on 3:5 above, for references also to earlier discussions). When Paul introduces prayer at 1:2, it leads him into a recounting of the Thessalonians' "work of faith" (1:3, 5–8). Here it leads to a stated concern, and more importantly to the stated goal, to "restore whatever is lacking in your faith." As discussed, that lack may have something to do with hope (3:6; 4:13) and, if 4:13 is further indication, it has something to do with grief and concern for those who have died. Paul intends an active response. This same word used here, "restore" or "put in order," is used by the moral philosopher Epictetus to draw an analogy regarding preparation for the moral life: "But the one who lays hold of my neck and puts my loins and my shoulders into proper order helps me" (Epictetus *Discourses* 3.20.10, my trans). Like a chiropractor, to use the Epictetus's analogy, Paul looks toward active engagement to put the body of the Thessalonian community into shape. If "face to face" is not possible at the moment, so then this letter.

For the first time now (1:2–3 simply recalls and reports on "prayers"), Paul engages directly in prayer. The first sentence is deceptively simple. In the comments on 2:18, above, 2 Corinthians 12:7 is referenced as another passage in which Satan, or more particularly, "a messenger of Satan," is credited with holding Paul back in some fashion. There he describes how he "appealed to the Lord" repeatedly, but the response was no (recognizable) change in circumstance. How about here? Paul does not consider what God's response might be or if and when Paul might accept a negative response.

That said Paul does engage in this letter itself as an active response in light of the current "blocked" circumstance (2:19). What's more, he creatively and suggestively seems to key his petitions to "our God and Father himself and our Lord Jesus" (for discussion of these descriptions, see comments on 1:1, above) to the concerns that he will engage and teachings he will forward in the coming chapters. For example, the petition that "you increase and abound in love for one another and for all" (3:12) fits neatly with Paul's words in 4:9–12, while the prayer for "holiness" (3:13) jibes with Paul's teaching in 4:3–8 (indeed, the word translated "sanctification" in 4:3 is very closely related to, and built from the same root as the word for "holiness in 3:13). Another word association within 3:13 and extending into the next section of the letter, begins with "blameless." The occurrences of "please God" and "behave properly" (literally, "walk") together suggest an allusion to Genesis 17:1 (see further discussion in comments on 4:1 and 4:12, below). Finally, the "coming of Lord" (3:13) is treated at some length in 4:13–5:11 (for discussion of this particular word for "coming," see comments on 4:15).

A word about the final phrase of chapter 3 is in order, especially in light of the discussion that will take place at 4:13–17. The word translated "saints" can indeed mean, and refer to, saints. Now, what Paul means by "saints" is itself worth asking. It is clear from the beginning and end of Philippians (1:1; 4:22; see commentary on Philippians, above) that Paul uses the term to refer to living, active members of communities formed around the gospel; in other words, people we might simply call "Christians" (which is a term he never uses; see also Rom. 8:27, 1 Cor. 1:2; 6:1–2). Of course, using "saints" in this context (3:13) would appear to indicate that it refers to those who have already died and are then returning, in a sense, with "Lord Jesus."

But, there is a significant problem with that understanding even though it may make "common sense" to Christians and others today who understand those who have died to have "gone to heaven." In 1 Thessalonians 4:15–17, Paul rehearses the "coming of the Lord" in some detail; therein he states that "the dead in Christ will rise" at that time—not sooner. In other words, there are no "saints" descending from heaven, for they will be rising up from the ground (see discussion below). Further, Paul's language here is consistent with biblical literature and, as such, is better rendered "holy ones" (which would be a direct, literal translation of the word) or even "angels." In Daniel 7:18, in a similar context, there is reference to the "holy ones" with the "Most High." In Zechariah 14:5, it is stated plainly, "the Lord your God will come, and all the holy ones with him." Interesting, by way of comparison, is that Jesus' words, as recorded in Matthew 25:31, seem to borrow from this very passage in Zechariah, and, among other changes, is the switch from "holy ones" to "angels." Paul himself uses "angels" in a similar context in 2 Thessalonians 1:7 and even references "the archangel's call" in 1 Thessalonians 4:16. So, based on the broader context of 1 Thessalonians (esp. 4:15–17) and on the scriptural literature in and with which he has been formed, it would seem that Paul here means heavenly "holy ones"; that is, angels or heavenly host. "Saints" is misleading.

LIFE IN COMMUNITY
1 Thessalonians 4:1–12

4:1 **Finally, brothers and sisters, we ask and urge you in the Lord Jesus that, as you learned from us how you ought to live and to please God (as, in fact, you are doing), you should do so more and more. ² For you know what instructions we gave you through the Lord Jesus. ³ For this is the will of God, your sanctification: that you abstain from fornication; ⁴ that each one of you know how to control your own body in holiness and honor, ⁵ not with lustful passion, like the Gentiles who do not know God; ⁶ that no one wrong or exploit a brother or sister in this matter, because the Lord is an avenger in all these things, just as we have already told you beforehand and solemnly warned you. ⁷ For God did not call us to impurity but in holiness. ⁸ Therefore whoever rejects this rejects not human authority but God, who also gives his Holy Spirit to you.**

⁹ Now concerning love of the brothers and sisters, you do not need to have anyone write to you, for you yourselves have been taught by God to love one another; ¹⁰ and indeed you do love all the brothers and sisters throughout Macedonia. But we urge you, beloved, to do so more and more, ¹¹ to aspire to live quietly, to mind your own affairs, and to work with your hands, as we directed you, ¹² so that you may behave properly toward outsiders and be dependent on no one.

As discussed in comments on the previous section of prayer that closes out chapter 3, we are at a major transition point in the letter. The transition here is directly into teaching and exhortation, marked very clearly in the first sentence (4:1): "we ask and urge. . . ." And that said, the very use of "urge"—which connects directly with verses 2:3, 12; and 3:2—is clear indication that this asking and encouraging will build on what has come before (for more on "ask," see comments on 5:12, below). In that same vein, Paul also brings back the word that literally means "walk" (see comments on 2:12, above) twice in this verse, here translated "to live" and "you are doing." These two words, along with a third ("instructions"; v. 2) help set both the front end (4:1–2) and the close (4:10–12) of this section (a rhetorical bookend that is lost in the English of the NRSV): "urge" in 4:10 is closely followed by "directed" (a verb form of the noun, "instructions") in 4:11, and at the beginning of 4:12, "behave properly" translates the same word as walk/live/doing. Adding to this rhetorical pattern is the fact that "urge" and "instructions"/ "directed" are related, as compound terms that share a common first word. For more on the particular language Paul uses in 4:1, and possible associations with "blameless" in 3:13, see comments on 4:1, below.

As for the major themes or concerns to be considered in this section and beyond, as noted in the comments on the prayer section, they are laid out well in 3:12–13: Holy living (4:3–8) and love for one another (4:9–12), having to do with personal and community morality and life together, which is revisited in 5:12–22, and concerns regarding the end times (4:13–5:11).

Yet another sign to Paul's addressees that they have entered into a new part of the letter is the use of the word "finally" here. As discussed in comments on Philippians 3:1 (see commentary on Philippians, above) this word, which at its root means something along the lines of "as for the rest," can indeed mean "finally" and so bring a letter to a close (so 2 Cor. 13:11). Consistently in his letters to the Macedonian churches, Paul uses it to introduce discussions that involve exhortation (see also Phil. 3:1 and 2 Thess. 3:1). The dual verbs, "ask" and "urge," clearly indicate as much— exhortation is coming.

There is another set of verbs in 4:1 that would appear to give this verse a particular resonance both with the previous section and with the Abraham narrative in Scripture and which suggests something of the interlocking worlds of which Paul is a part and through which he works to navigate on behalf of his gospel. Though not evident (at least not overtly) in either of the Thessalonian letters, Paul's debt to the scriptural narratives on Abraham clearly goes deep (see Rom. 4 and Gal. 3:6–18). In 3:13 he has introduced the concept/term "blameless." The word he uses is the same word used in the Septuagint in the following verse: "When Abram was ninety-nine years old, the Lord appeared to Abram, and said to him, 'I am God Almighty; walk before me, and be blameless'" (Gen. 17:1). That alone is of some interest. But the matter gets far more interesting.

Note the word, "walk," in this important verse on Abram/Abraham. Recalling the discussions in the overview to this section and in the comments on 2:12, above, we know that Paul uses in 4:1 ("to live"; "doing") and 4:12 ("behave properly") a word that literally means "walk." So, we see another direct connection with Genesis 17:1 regarding Abraham. But there is a wrinkle. The ancient Greek version of Genesis 17:1 uses no such word at all; rather, where the word "walk" is found in Hebrew (all standard English translations are based on the Hebrew text of Hebrew Scripture), the Septuagint includes a Greek word meaning "please." Look now, again, at 4:1—both "walk" *and* "please" are there (an even further wrinkle is that Paul's word for "please" here is not the same as that found in the Septuagint, but shares, broadly, its meaning). Has Paul, in 3:13–4:1, provided a multilingual pastiche of, or a complex allusion to, Genesis 17:1, including "blameless" as well as both "walk" (via a Greek translation of the word found in the Hebrew version) and "please" (via a synonym of the word found in the Greek version)? If so, 1 Thessalonians 3:13–4:1 offers something of a window onto Paul's fertile and complex mind at work, linking his exhortation to this developing Gentile Christian community to a foundational text regarding the foundational figure of Abraham, as known variously via the Hebrew and Greek versions of Scripture. Further, these two verses may privilege its readers with the earliest evidence available that Paul has begun to associate Gentile converts to the "gospel" with Abraham (an association that serves as a major linchpin of this argument in Galatians, esp. 3:6–10).

As discussed in the comments on 2:1, above, a basic tenet of philosophical advice and teaching is to remind addressees what they already know and build on that. As is evident throughout chapter 2, so here in 4:2: "you know. . . ." Another, and arguably related, tenet evident in 4:1 is to assume the orientation that the individual or group addressed is already engaging in the desired behavior. So Paul's contemporary Seneca, in the very first words of *Moral Epistle* 1—"Continue to act thusly . . ."—which then goes on to give advice and present teachings.

In verse 3 Paul moves to a discussion of "sanctification" via a word, which, as indicated in the comments on the prayer of 3:11–13, is the same as that translated, "holiness" (3:13). This same word is used throughout this section: "sanctification (v. 3), "holiness" (v. 4), "holiness" (v. 7), and, via a very closely related word, built from the same root, in the first part, "holy," of the reference to "[God's] Holy Spirit" (v. 8). Worthy of note is that the content and framing of the section thus far has been set up by the introduction of sanctification/holiness: verse 1 recalls what the Thessalonians had already "learned" and were already "doing," and verse 2 affirms that the Thessalonians already "know" the "instructions." Fair enough. So, why all this instruction and doing? The answer: "For" (NRSV) or "because" "your sanctification" is "the will of God."

And that "you" (see comments on 1:1), and in this case the "your," is plural, referring to the whole community. That should not be missed by those interested in ecclesiology (understanding of "church") or in the place/context/role of morality. Paul has established the context *not* as one of personal morality—which is what has dominated American discussion of morality in churches and in the broader popular culture—but as one of morality in and among "you all," the alternative "assembly" "called out" by God. With that base and within that framework, the general thrust and particular teachings of 4:3–12 take on added meaning.

The directive at the close of verse 3 is even more general in the Greek than the NRSV's "fornication" suggests. The Greek word, from which derives the English word "pornography," has a range of meaning captured well by the phrase, "sexual immorality." It serves here as a kind of heading, or broad statement, following which the teachings become more specific.

The difficulty in understanding 4:4 has already been mentioned in discussion of Silvanus, above (see comments on 1:1). The word translated in the NRSV text as "body" is used only here and in one other place in the New Testament, 1 Peter 3:7. Between those two verses, the NRSV provides no less than four different translations for the same word, including both primary and alternative (i.e., footnoted) readings: "body" or, according to the alternative reading, "wife" (1 Thess. 4:4); "sex" or, according to the alternative reading, "vessel" (1 Pet. 3:7). Well, which is it?

Actually, there is a fairly easy answer which is well represented by the alternative reading for 1 Peter 3:7. This word means, simply, "vessel" or container, jar, dish—something we, like Paul's Thessalonian addressees, would have around our homes and encounter every day. But, that is decidedly not the meaning projected onto it in this context here, as both the lead-in statement regarding "fornication" or, better, "sexual morality" in verse 3, and the extended explanation of verse 5 make clear. We are dealing here in metaphor and, perhaps better stated, slang. On that score, the primary reading of 1 Peter 3:7 captures the broad context well—this is a teaching about "sex." But, what is it particularly that Paul is teaching about or with reference to?

The NRSV primary and alternative readings for this verse capture well two possibilities: "body" and "wife." For most readers of this volume and of the NRSV, the former is likely the more comfortable and the more readily usable for current contexts of preaching and teaching. But, particularly given the verb with which it is linked, translated by the NRSV "control," it is the less likely. That verb, which Paul does not use elsewhere, actually has a rather narrow range meanings and usages, captured well in its uses, and the attendant NRSV translations, in the book of Acts: 1:18 ("acquire"), 8:20 ("obtain"), 22:28 ("get"). The NRSV's "control" here, simply based on meaning and usage of the verb itself, would seem unwarranted. So, where does that leave us with this verse? On the face of it, as in the NRSV text, the alternative reading for the noun is the better one, and the verb translation is misleading. Where the NRSV reads, "control your own body" the more accurate, if more uncomfortable (for most readers of this volume and of the NRSV) reading, is "acquire" or "possess your own wife."

And that gender-specific reading brings us to 4:6, which raises a matter flagged in comments regarding "brothers and sisters" in 1:4. If the reading of 4:4 indicated here is correct, then the directive in 4:6, "that no one wrong or exploit a brother or sister" (alternative reading: "brother") would refer to only "a brother" (i.e., male—and for that matter, adult— member of the community). And that, then, would raise the question of whether throughout the letter Paul has in view a readership of only male "brothers" or a full complement of "brothers and sisters," or better "siblings" (i.e., all male and female members of the community; see comments on 1:4, above), as is typical of his letters. And all of that raises the question, is Paul in 1 Thessalonians showing his male chauvinist colors and being blind to the needs, desires, or even presence of women?

The question is vitally important on its face and fascinating in terms of the sweep of this very letter. As we have already seen, the image in 2:7 suggests a keen ability to empathize across gender differences and experiences to a degree which would arguably be impressive for a writer or teacher today and even more then. Moving beyond that, Paul shows further ability to empathize across other significant difference by assuming the role of "orphan" in 2:17. So, what is going on here? Beyond ability, is it plausible to suggest that Paul exercises an interest in assuming these unexpected roles? And if so, what might that interest be in service to?

What if we (as eavesdroppers, of a sort, onto this ancient letter) understand Paul to be writing to an all-male club? I *don't* use the phrase "all-male club" loosely. As we have seen, the physical setting and context of Paul's original proclamation to these Thessalonians was the workshop (see comments on 1:3 and 2:9, above), and that remains the understood setting of these particular teachings (4:11–12; see comments below). Paul is addressing them where they are, both literally and figuratively, *and* is challenging them with imagery and associations that expand significantly beyond where they are, literally and figuratively, by bringing in other— and others'—perspectives and experiences.

So, how does or how can all of this preach? Firstly, bringing in other— and others'—perspectives and experiences is itself not a bad recipe for preaching and teaching. *Every* community, like *every* individual, is limited in its viewpoints, perspectives, and experiences. Being observant of those and addressing them is something modeled by Paul throughout 1 Thessalonians.

On another level, there is the broader and perhaps even more basic question of how, and for what purpose, to "translate." I have attempted to indicate the "more accurate" translation of the text, above, based on historical, social, and linguistic data. The goal of any translation, finally, is to make meaning of, and with, the text. Put in the vernacular, a good and worthy question about Paul's teaching in 4:4–6 is "how does it translate?" Though it bypasses the social and economic reality of the gender-specific workshop setting and the social and linguistic reality of the gender-specific language, the NRSV text as it stands arguably translates well overall. Presuming my arguments above are correct, students, preachers, and teachers are left with the challenge of making meaning of that text for a given Christian community, or for the Christian community broadly, today. Consistent with that, the NRSV primary reading orients Paul's reading to and for a fully male and female audience. Further, even acknowledging that Paul drafted this particular teaching with a gender-specific audience in mind, evidence from Paul's own Macedonian correspondences suggests that he would have approved that broader goal. So Philippians 4:8–9, which shares similar language regarding teaching and practice as is found here, is clearly addressed to a wide audience of "brothers and sisters" or "siblings," including women (see Phil. 4:2).

Interlocking with, and bringing to a close, the teachings of 4:4–6, are explanations and directives that draw on earlier elements within the letter. 1 Thessalonians 4:5 offers a nod to 1:9–10 and with it an implicit reminder to Paul's addressees of their newfound identity with God, their forward-looking orientation and identity as defined by Jesus, and their break with a past defined by "idols." Consistent with that is the close use of "know" in verses 4 and 5 in what may seem, at first blush, very different contexts. In American popular culture, everyone from Sunday school children to stand-up comedians knows what it means to "know" someone in the biblical sense. But, Paul's usage here does not reflect that biblical sense of "know"; he is after something very different which the NRSV captures well. In 4:4 Paul's concern is that "you know how . . ."; using precisely the same word, in 4:5 his affirmation is that his addressees do "know God." In terms of moral behavior within, and as a member of, the community, the one equates to the other—at least so God would have it (4:3): knowing God is consistent with knowing how to behave with and toward others. Philosophers and ethicists can—and have, and will—debate that matter endlessly; it, too, may be worthy of a sermon. But, for Paul the point is

not to be missed, as stated in verse 7, "God did not call us to impurity but in holiness." That is, holiness is the state or condition in/within which the community is called to be.

The next sentence, along with its nod to 2:4 and 1:15 (it is God, via the Holy Spirit, not mortals or human authority, who founds and defines the community) underlines the all-pervasiveness of the holy vis-à-vis Christian community. That God's will is your sanctification/holiness (4:3; see discussion above regarding these being two different translations of the same word), that active and responsible knowledge regarding holiness is expected of the community (4:4), and that holiness is that to and for which God calls the community (4:7; cf. 1:1 and 2:12 for comments on "call" language) is summed up in a kind of concrete way in the final phrase of verse 8. The word translated "also" can also serve as a simple intensifier, which is the more likely, and meaningful, sense here: "God . . . even gives his Holy Spirit to you."

Before moving to verses 9–12, a closer look at verse 6 is in order. On one level, the passing and somewhat unusual reference to God as "avenger" (Paul uses the term only one other time, Rom. 13:4, where it refers to an earthly authority) would appear as a kind of moralistic warning: do as I say or God will get you. In fact, the word resonates in a particular way, deeply relevant to the letter as a whole, to Paul's initial proclamation to the Thessalonians, and, perhaps, to the broader external context from which and within which Paul writes. This label of "avenger" for God or, in this case, "the Lord" (which, for Paul, is Jesus: see esp. 1:1, 3; 2:15, 19; 3:11, 13; 4:1, 2) is familiar from Scripture (besides the Micah passages discussed here, see esp. Deut. 32:35, 36, 39; Pss. 94:1, 99:8). Micah 5:10–15 shares a lot of language and broader context with 1 Thessalonians 1:9–10: the coming "day" of judgment (v. 10), idols (vv. 13–14), "wrath," (v. 15), and "nations" or Gentiles (v. 15). Also found in Micah 5:15 is "vengeance." The Greek word for "vengeance" used in the Septuagint version of Micah is built from the same root as is "avenger." So, particular language and broader context suggest these verses from Micah as background for Paul's use of "avenger" here. Telling, too, is the passing comment of Paul in 1 Thessalonians 4:6, "just as we have already told you beforehand . . . ," which rings true to the comment at 5:1: "Now concerning the times and the seasons . . . you do not need to have anything written to you." It is very likely that discussion of the "avenger" and the content of 4:4–8 more broadly is consistent with Paul's initial teaching to the Thessalonians, marked as it was by discussion of the end times (for further discussion, see comments on 2:19, below, and introduction; see also discussion of 2 Thess. 1:5, 8).

Finally in verse 6 is the somewhat emphatic close to the phrase just discussed, which reads, "and [as we] solemnly warned you." As noted in comments on 2:12, the words for "pleading" there, and "solemnly warned" here, share the same root (the latter, which is one word in Greek, is simply a compound verb built on the same verb as "pleading"). Worthy of note is that the appeal of 2:12, "pleading that you lead a life worthy of God," is perfectly consistent with Paul's treatment of God-willed holiness in and for the community here (4:3–8).

Having established the centrality of "holiness" from God's will to God's own Spirit, Paul now turns to "love of brothers and sisters" (see the NRSV note, "brothers"; for discussion of the possibility of the gender-specific "brothers" in this letter, and particularly this section, see discussion of 4:4, 6 above). The Greek word here is the one from which the city, Philadelphia, takes its name. As that city's nickname, "city of brotherly love," suggests, the word is used regarding love within families and for family members (see Plutarch, *On Brotherly Love*, 478A–492B). Its use here resonates both with what has been written, especially in Paul's use of family language (see comments above, esp. 1:4; 2:7, 12, 17), and with what is shortly to come. (Though lost in English translation, "aspire," 4:11 and this word are both compound words beginning with the same, immediately noticeable, term for "love"; see comments on 4:11, below).

"Taught by God" is a unique term, used only here in Paul's letters and within the whole New Testament, and used rarely throughout later literature (probably in each of those few cases directly borrowing from this). Whatever else it might mean for Paul and his addressees, in the context of such direct family language it certainly affirms and builds on Paul's use of family/parental language for God (see 1:1). More specifically, it calls his addressees back to 1:4–6 in suggestive ways. There, 1:4, God "has chosen you," the Holy Spirit is on the scene in association with "power" and "full conviction" (1:5), and Paul and his team ("us") are in the role of teacher, along with "the Lord" (1:6; presumably Jesus). Here, simply and profoundly, God is teacher (see comments on 1:4–6, above).

The rhetorical pattern of suggesting that there is no "need" for this particular teaching (4:9) because "you" are already acting accordingly (presumed in 4:10) is familiar from 4:1 and 2:1 (see comments above). That said, the sweep of these three verses is striking, as Paul moves the scope and focus from "one another" within the local community (4:9), through Christian communities "throughout" the region" (4:10) and then "toward outsiders" broadly (4:12). The reintroduction in 4:10 of "urge" language (see esp. comments on 4:1 and 2:12) in concert with yet another direct use of family language (see alternative, far more accurate reading for "beloved"—"brothers") puts particular focus on the directives that follow in verse 11. Further, the directives in verse 11 are organized under the main verb, "aspire," which, as indicated above, is related to the organizing verb for this set of verses (4:9–12), "love of brothers and sisters," through the first term, "love" (it means literally, "love of honor"). Now, Paul will take such aspiration for "love of honor" in a particular direction via the ethos of family love.

Each of the three directives in verse 11 brings the addressees back to the context of the workshop. In 1:3 that language is used metaphorically; in 2:9, its use is largely or fully nonmetaphorical (see esp. comments on 1:3 and 2:9, above). Here, there is a deep and meaningful marriage of those metaphorical and nonmetaphorical precedents as Paul, following a nod to the founding of the community (see above, comments regarding "taught by God"), speaks directly to actions and a broader ethos regarding relating to another and to others *as God's assembly* within the workshop setting. Recall that from the first verse of the letter onward, Paul has been affirming and (re)constructing this community as an alternative "assembly of the Thessalonians" with an alternative "Lord" and alternative understanding of "peace" (see esp. comments on 1:1 and 2:12). Here, building to significant degree on the reports of the founding of community in both 1:4–6 and 2:9, Paul puts the focus directly on how to relate to one another and to the broader mission of the community.

The notion that one is "to aspire," in other words, to love and pursue honor for oneself and family, was as much a part of the Gentile world within which and for which Paul was writing as was the air that was breathed. School children are still taught today about the Roman *cursus honorum*, literally the "course of honor," by which one progressed through public and political life to fame and fortune. That "course of honor" is the ultimate example, in the Roman imperial context, of the very aspiring that this very word suggests. On another societal level, the word was used among trade associations and within workshop settings regarding such rivalry and competition as would attend the pursuit of power and honor. The verbs that follow directly upon "aspire" could not be less expected. Aspire "to live eagerly, in the broader public eye, competing with 'brothers' in your own workshop or from your same trade to gain a higher position"—such would have been the expected directives following "aspire." Paul presents virtual opposites or, at the very least, alternatives, akin to the alternative understanding of "assembly," "Lord," "peace," and "kingdom/empire" already presented (in 1:1 and 2:12).

In terms of what we might call church polity, Paul is presenting what some today would call a "flattened structure"—it is decidedly not top-down ("be dependent of no one," 4:12), depends on all being engaged ("work with your hands," 4:11), and shuns currying favor with constituents or power-brokers ("live quietly," "mind your own affairs," 4:11). The measure of an alternative assembly which has been "taught by God" is "to please God" not others. So, again, the call for dependence from any patrons or systems that bring their own agenda (4:12). As noted above, that "outsiders" are evoked at the end of these verses gives them quite a sweep (from internal to external concern). The "proper behavior" (literally, "good form") called for is suggested by all that has preceded and by the final phrase of the section that follows.

To say the very least, within the alternative "assembly of God" there is no need for "honor" such as is given or expected in the broader "outside" society; that said, there is need for all to be engaged. Those characteristics fit well the second term that Paul uses for "love," following "taught by God," in 4:9. Many readers of this volume will have read about or heard sermons or bible study descriptions of "agape love"; that is the term Paul uses here. A terse and helpful definition of such "agape" is found in 2 Corinthians 8:8, in which Paul confesses to his addressees that "I am testing the genuineness of your love against the earnestness of others." Notice that the definition is, in grammatical terms, a negative one; it tells the reader what agape love is not. Immediately relevant to this discussion is that that "earnestness" against which this God-taught love of the Christian assembly stands is precisely the societally-expected standard. Indeed, 2 Corinthians 8:8, written years later than this, stands as a kind of summation of 1 Thessalonians 4:9–12.

MEET THE LORD: THE FUTURE AND NOW
1 Thessalonians 4:13–18

4:13 **But we do not want you to be uninformed, brothers and sisters, about those who have died, so that you may not grieve as others do who have no hope.** [14] **For since we believe that Jesus died and rose again, even so, through Jesus, God will bring with him those who have died.** [15] **For this we declare to you by the word of the Lord, that we who are alive, who are left until the coming of the Lord, will by no means precede those who have died.** [16] **For the Lord himself, with a cry of command, with the archangel's call and with the sound of God's trumpet, will descend from heaven, and the dead in Christ** will rise first. [17] Then we who are alive, who are left, will be caught up in the clouds together with them to meet the Lord in the air; and so we will be with the Lord forever. [18] Therefore encourage one another with these words.

We have seen repeatedly how Paul employs the rhetorical move of introducing teachings with the reassurance and affirmation that his addressees already "know," are already "doing," or "do not need" to receive that which he is about to present (see esp. comments on 2:1; 4:1–2, and 4:9; see also 5:1). But not here. Paul makes no hint of such a move. On the contrary he underlines the importance of the teaching through the phrase, "we do not want," which uses a verb form of the noun, "will," used in 4:3, "for this is the will of God." From God's "will" to Paul's "want." The importance of the teaching that follows is highlighted, and layered by that link with 4:3 as well as by the reintroduction here of "hope." The vision that follows is extraordinary both for what it does, and does not, say.

Another link, beyond "want," to the previous section is the reference in 4:13 to "others . . . who have no hope." Both the context and content of this phrase recall 4:5, "Gentiles who do not know God." This is insider/outsider language, as is shown by Paul's use of the same term, "others," in 5:6 (see also Rev. 9:20, where the NRSV translates the same word as "the rest"). Does Paul use it to exclude? Perhaps one could make a strong case for such an understanding. However, it is important to recall that Paul is here forming community; and in particular, he is forming a community of converts within a society that marginalizes and persecutes them, whether through such imperial propaganda as has been discussed in 1:1 and 2:12 and elsewhere or through social, economic, or even legal means, (see especially 1:6; 2:3; and 2:14). Pointing to what the "Gentiles" or "the others" do is a simple, effective way of defining and describing what "you" don't do.

The importance of "hope" within the letter has been discussed already (esp. in the introduction to the letter, above, and in comments on 1:3; see also 3:6, 10). Here "hope" or—more to the point—"no hope" is given something of a definition: it is directly associated with grieving. Is "hope," then, the opposite of grieving? As one who has grieved great loss and as a pastor who has sat with, comforted, counseled, and worshiped with those who "grieve," I want to be clear that there is no inverse correlation between grieving and hope; the hopeful do indeed grieve (and for all the right reasons).

As it turns out, Paul would agree—and profoundly so. He never commands or asks that the Thessalonians cease to grieve in the face of death of loved ones, though such is a move familiar in the moral philosophy of the day. Among those contemporaries who have been regularly cited above, Plutarch captures the broadly accepted approach when he counsels a friend not to grieve his own son's death since, on reasoned reflection, one must realize that all are mortal and all die (*Letter to Apollonius* 103F–104A). Others promote that same understanding via gender-specific descriptions or stereotypes. Seneca, for example, offers, "You are like a woman in the way you take your son's death" (*Moral Epistle* 99.2). On the flip side of that (gender stereotyped) coin, Epictetus cites the posited standard that soldiers (who were all male in Epictetus's frame of reference) do not grieve their own fallen (*Discourses* 1.11.31). If Paul's immediate addressees are indeed gender-specific (i.e., male; see comments on 4:4, 6) his shunning of such an approach is all the more noteworthy.

Not only does Paul not instruct against grieving, but grieving in the face of the death of loved ones is precisely what he expects—and honors—in preparing the community to support one another. After first establishing what the community gathered around Christ does not do—the Greek of the second half of verse 13 is a bit clearer than the NRSV's English, "lest you grieve just as others do . . ."—Paul closes the section, "Therefore encourage one another . . ." (4:18). As noted especially in comments on 2:12 and 2:3 (see also 3:3, 7), and as is lost in the varying English translations of the NRSV ("appeal," "urge," and "encourage"), this one nuanced Greek root word that Paul repeatedly uses includes the sense of "comfort." What Paul writes, and concludes ("therefore"), is that the community encourage/comfort each other in their time of grieving. How?

A comparison with Paul's later, masterful letter to the Romans sheds some light. There he directly and compellingly links the community to Jesus, particularly to Jesus' death and resurrection: "Do you not know that all of us who have been baptized into Christ Jesus were baptized into his death? Therefore we have been buried with him . . . so that, just as Christ was raised from the dead . . . so too we might walk in newness of life" (Rom. 6:3–4; cf. Rom. 8:29–30). Here, Paul starts in a very similar place, with a rehearsal of Jesus' death and resurrection (v. 14). The repeated use of "fallen asleep" (see the NRSV alternative readings for vv. 13 and 14) might be a circumlocution for the harsher "died" (in the Gentile world of the first century as in ours, just such language was often used to soften the blow) but it also sets up well the narrative to follow, within which, profoundly, Paul uses the stark and direct "dead [ones]" in verse 16.

The suggestive beginning of verse 15 raises more questions (for us) than it answers, though its immediate intention is relatively clear. The

Greek words for "declare" and "word" are built from the same root—from "the Lord" to Paul's lips and then to the Thessalonians' ears: this is direct teaching that can be relied on. The problem for us is that there is no extant teaching of Jesus that parallels that which Paul relates in verses 15–17. So, is Paul suggesting that he is aware of a direct saying of (the earthly) Jesus which is otherwise unknown in the form Paul has it here? (For possible, partial antecedents, see Matt. 24:30–31; 26:64; Mark 9:1; John 6:39–40.) Or is he intimating that he has received a teaching from (the heavenly) Jesus via a vision or other revelation (cf. Gal. 1:16; 2:2; 2 Cor. 12:1–7a; 13:3; and esp. 1 Cor. 15:51)? Is he adopting a stance of prophetic inspiration (cf. Sir. 48:3)? Whatever ambiguity remains is not Paul's concern. Rather, it is the authenticity of this teaching from God of which Paul is assured, and which he passes along as such.

What has been percolating throughout the letter now comes to the fore, the "coming" of the Lord (2:19; 3:13, see comments above; see also 1:10). Via 2:19; 3:6, and, more immediately, 4:13 the letter's addressees have been set up to expect here a word of hope. And so Paul delivers on two levels: (1) by directly addressing the (complex set of the) Thessalonians' concerns and (2) by affirming and defining the identity of this alternative community called out by God (see comments on 1:1, above). The driving question that Paul has received, likely via Timothy bringing the concern from the Thessalonians back with him (3:6), seems to be fairly pointed: not only, if at all, what will happen to those who die (4:14) but, more specifically, what is the juxtaposition or relationship of those "who are alive" with those who have died/are asleep (4:15)? It is in responding to that concern that Paul furthers for the Thessalonians their unique and newfound identity in Christ.

As far as storytelling and histrionics go, Paul would appear to have a lot to learn from the writer/recorder of the Apocalypse or even from Jesus himself (see the so-called "mini-apocalypse," Mark 13:3–27 and parallels). That is, for all the imagery packed into these few, extraordinary verses, Paul seems to have something of a tin ear for narrative description. To be sure, there is the "archangel's call" and "God's trumpet"—impressive enough—but Paul does little with them, and he keeps such description to a minimum. There is something far different going on here than what we find in such extended narratives as are included in Revelation, in Jesus' mini-apocalypse, and in such apocalyptic texts as *1 Enoch*, for example, with their fantastic imagery. Paul's goal, in keeping with the two-point agenda indicated above, appears to dictate the narrow—and profound—limits of his description.

Paul affirms that "the dead in Christ will rise first" (4:16). That is, hardly forgotten or relegated to some secondary status, those who have died (and will die in the future; life—and death—after all, go on) will enjoy honored status on Christ's return. "Not to worry," one can almost hear Paul saying to his addressees. But, in and around that response to a pastoral concern, Paul uses pointed language to (re)establish the identity of the Thessalonian community and remind them of the basis upon which their hope is built. In particular, "coming" (4:15) and "meet" (4:17), which bookend the action described in these verses, would have resonated to suggest a particular context for Paul's Thessalonian addressees.

Though "coming" would come to have a technical meaning in Christianity as reference to the expected, eschatological return of Christ (see, for example Matt. 24:27; Jas. 5:7; 1 Pet. 1:16; 3:3; 1 John 2:28)—indeed Paul's usage herein marks the earliest such usage in the New Testament—the letters' addressees would doubtless have been familiar with its then-technical sense of marking the arrival of an emperor, king, or other dignitary. That is what these verses presume, especially in yoking the term with "meet," which is also a technical term. It was traditional for a greeting party to throw open the city gates and proceed outside the city at some distance to meet the arriving dignitary. In *Jewish Antiquities* 11.327 Josephus describes just such an event, involving the arrival of Alexander the Great at Jerusalem, using precisely these two words that Paul uses here. Paul takes that basic movement and gives it a cosmic scope.

The arriving dignitary is, of course, none other than "the Lord" Jesus whose description vis-à-vis the generally recognized "Lord," the Roman emperor, has been operative in the letter since 1:1 (see comments on those verses, above). The movement of this "Lord" is consistent with that which Paul relates in Philippians 3:20 and one wonders whether such a teaching, and the recitation of the Christ Hymn (Phil. 2:6–11) which it presumes, were part of Paul's original teaching to the Thessalonian community. Regardless, the Lord "will descend from heaven" and do so in a fashion appropriate both to the Jewish apocalyptic genre on which Paul draws for the descriptions herein (see Dan. 7:13; 10:6; *1 Enoch* 14:8; 20:1–8; cf. Mark 14:62; Rev. 1:10; 14:2; 19:6; see also comments on 3:13, below) and to the "cry of command" and trumpet sounding of imperial armies and royal processions. Among the scriptural allusions, of which there are many, Joel 2 rises for its use of "blow the trumpet" at the head of the chapter as well as verse 15, and its language of "assembly" in verses 15–16 (see "congregation" in Joel 2:16 NRSV) which, in the Septuagint version, uses the same term that Paul uses for church or assembly in 1 Thessalonians 1:1 (the word for trumpet in the Septuagint is also that which Paul uses).

The word that the NRSV translates "caught up" is, to say the least, colorful. Already in these verses Paul has switched from a soft indicator of death ("fallen asleep"; see the NRSV alternative reading for vv. 14 and 15) to a simpler, more direct statement ("the dead [ones]," v. 16). Now in verse 17 he employs a standard term used in reference to the death of a loved one. Translated in the NRSV as "caught up," this Greek word's meaning is better captured by such English terms as "snatch" or "take away" since they suggest the contexts of thievery or capture with regard to which the word was often used, as well as the emotional baggage accompanying its use with regard to death. Poignantly, many ancient Greek inscriptions employ the term to indicate the survivors' sense of having their loved ones taken away. Among contemporaneous philosophers cited above (see comments on 4:13 regarding grieving) Plutach also uses this same term (e.g., *Letter to Apollonius* 111D, 117BD). What does Paul do? He turns the term on its head. Herein, it is not Fate or the gods that "take away" loved ones to be with the dead. Rather, those who are already dead "will be caught up . . . to meet the Lord in the air." The contrast with the Thessalonians' former gods and beliefs (see 1:9) could not be greater. But there is more.

It is often presumed, whether broadly in popular culture or more specifically in church settings, that the resurrection of the dead has to do with "being with Jesus in heaven." A quick reading of this passage might suggest as much. But what is not said is just as important as what is. Paul nowhere states or suggests that the Lord, having descended from heaven, will return there. That in itself is notable. Further, and significantly, as has already been discussed, Paul's language is clear—those who are alive and those who have already died and will be raised up, will together form a greeting party to "meet" the Lord who is "coming." Those two words, "meet" and "coming," indicate in no uncertain terms that the coming Lord who is met is coming to the very place from which the greeters have come; it would make no sense for the emperor or other dignitary, on approaching the welcoming party sent out from the city, to do an about face and retreat or, even more bizarrely, take that greeting party away from the city.

Moreover, the meeting place is "the air." That, of course, adds to the cosmic scope of this passage and does so in a pointed way. The greeting party is not—notice, this is important—"caught up" into heaven. The Lord has already descended from heaven; no part of the action of these verses takes place in heaven. According to the way the cosmos was understood in the Greek world to and for which Paul wrote, the realm of the air was that where spirits, good and evil, lived. This sense of things is captured very well within the collection of Paul's letters in the New Testament by Ephesians 2:2, which describes the character that we would call the devil or Satan thusly: ". . . the ruler of the power of the air, the spirit that is now at work among those who are disobedient." As a final, symbolic gesture, the "coming" Lord pauses "in the air," with the community formed in his name, indicating that God is indeed triumphant. And, indeed, once the "power" associated with "the air" is defeated, how much more so will such relatively insignificant powers as the earthly empire of Rome and such like domineering institutions fall. And so, as is indicated at the close of verse 17, surely "we will be with the Lord forever." Finally, where will that posited and "forever" presence with the Lord be? Surely, the language and imagery suggest not heaven but earth. As such, this passage is consistent with the great vision that closes the book of Revelation (see esp. 21:2–3).

Paul's dense, efficient language here should not be missed. In a deceptively easy merging of the genres of Jewish apocalyptic and pagan visitation literature, he has not only answered the pastoral call to offer hope to the fledgling community, but he has also established for them in cosmic terms their identity as God's own community.

PUT ON FAITH, LOVE, AND HOPE
1 Thessalonians 5:1–11

> 5:1 Now concerning the times and the seasons, brothers and sisters, you do not need to have anything written to you. [2] For you yourselves know very well that the day of the Lord will come like a thief in the night. [3] When they say, "There is peace and security," then sudden destruction will come upon them, as labor pains come upon a pregnant woman, and there will be no escape! [4] But you, beloved, are not in darkness, for that day to surprise you like a thief; [5] for you are all children of light and children of the day; we are not of the night or of darkness. [6] So then let us not fall asleep as others do, but let us keep awake and be sober; [7] for those who sleep sleep at night, and those who are drunk get drunk at night. [8] But since we belong to the day, let us be sober, and put on the breastplate of faith and love, and for a helmet the hope of salvation. [9] For God has destined us not for wrath but for obtaining salvation through our Lord Jesus Christ, [10] who died for us, so that whether we are awake or asleep we may live with him. [11] Therefore encourage one another and build up each other, as indeed you are doing.

This section continues in a similar vein to that which precedes it. Having established the defining actions that are to come and the community's identity in light of that, Paul proceeds with consideration of the end times (esp. 5:1–3), the current context (5:3), and the mission and identity of the community in light of both (5:4–11). The section ends as does the previous section—"encourage one another" (5:11; cf. comments on 4:18 and on 4:1, above).

The first three verses serve as introduction and orientation to the teachings of 5:4–11. The phrases, "you do not need to have anything written to you" (v. 1) and "you yourselves know well" (v. 2), are akin to the rhetorical move exercised repeatedly throughout chapters 4 and 5 (see esp. 4:2, 9), wherein Paul reminds his readers of what they already know. Further, as discussion in the introduction to this letter indicates, such teaching was very likely foundational and formative for this community and may account both for Paul's reticence (or even legal inability) to return to Thessalonica (see comments on 2:18, above) and even, in some manner, for the persecution that the community feels (see comments on 3:3, above).

The teaching in verse 2 regarding "the day of the Lord" is familiar from material in the Gospels and the New Testament more broadly (Matt. 24:43 and Luke 12:39; Mark 13:32–37; see also 2 Pet. 3:10; Rev. 3:3; 16:15). Of these, only the passage from 2 Peter shares, with the teaching here, "the day of the Lord," and none specifically mention "night" though such can be assumed in the Gospel passages. As in the previous section, Paul's language is both efficient and well chosen. The clear indication of "night" prefigures that which will come in verses 4–10.

The wording of verse 3 is likewise reminiscent of the Gospel passages cited immediately above, perhaps especially the broader sweep of the "mini-apocalypse" in Mark 13, beginning in verse 14, "flee" (see v. 17 regarding "those who are pregnant . . ."; see also Luke 21:34). Perhaps more immediately relevant to the overall message of 1 Thessalonians is the beginning of the verse, "When they say, 'There is peace and security,' then. . . ." Here, on the heels of that great description of the alternative (to the emperor) Lord Jesus "coming" from heaven, greeted by the alternative (to the imperially-recognized) community of Thessalonians—that is the dead (who are now raised) in Christ along with those who are left— Paul calls his readers right back to his initial address, "Grace to you and peace," which ends, of course, in "peace" (see comments on 1:1, above). Paul proclaims that the "living and true God" is about "true" "peace and security." "Peace" and "security," especially "peace," were regularly used to tout the great Pax Romana (see comments on 1:1, above). The Roman historian, Velleius Paterculus, a younger contemporary of Paul, uses two equivalent Latin terms in tandem to describe the "assurance of safety, order, peace and tranquility" associated with the ascendancy of Rome (*Compendium of Roman History* II, 103.5; cf. Tacitus *Histories* 2.12.1 and 4.73). Also contemporary with Paul is Epictetus who, in a manner similar to Paul herein, cites imperial "security" (using the same word as Paul does here), with contempt, in favor of God (*Discourses* 1.9.7). Consistent with 1 Thessalonians 4:15–17, 5:3 holds up and promotes an alternative to imperially proclaimed "peace and security."

Paul's contrastive strategy is clear as he begins verse 4 with an emphasis on "you," the alternative community who has been called by God (see comments on 1:1), and a simple, but profound, "but." It is "others" (v. 6) who are caught up in that false sense of "peace and security" and who are "in darkness" (v. 4), "of the night or of darkness" (v. 5), and variously "fall asleep" and "get drunk" (v. 7). "You," by way of contrast, are "children of light and children of the day" (v. 5) who are to "keep awake and be sober" (v. 6). These descriptions in verses 4–7 are broadly reminiscent (for us) of the Gospel texts cited above, as they contrast the readiness or preparedness of the community with the lack thereof that is associated with others. Even more familiar to many readers of this volume is the Johannine imagery of light and darkness (John 1:5, 8–9; 12:35, 46; see also Rev. 8:12). Paul would have had a deep well from which to draw available to him through his life and training in Judaism (e.g., in the Hebrew Bible, Job 22:11; 29:2–3; Pss. 74; 82:5; in later apocalyptic texts, *1 Enoch* 41:8, 4; Ezra 14:20; and, among the Dead Sea Scroll texts, see *The Community Rule*, esp. 1QS 3.13–4.23). Paul's Thessalonian addressees are far more likely to have been familiar with these tropes through their use in contemporary moral philosophy. For example, Plutarch similarly uses the "keep awake" and "sober" in tandem (*To an Uneducated Ruler* 781D). A stock character in both contemporary Greek and Latin moral philosophy was a certain "Polemo," who was converted from his former life into the sobriety of wisdom (Horace, *Satire* 2.3.253–257; for a fuller portrait, see the second-century writer Lucian, *The Double Indictment* 17). Beyond the insider/outsider-"you"/"others" sensibility (though see below, comments on 5:10), for Paul's original addressees these descriptions would reinforce their own before/after stories, from their life before to their life in community in Jesus Christ now.

Parallel to the beginning of verse 4, "But you," is the opening of verse 8, "But we." This parallel is lost in the NRSV translation which adds a "since" not found in the Greek of the letter. With verse 8, the teaching moves beyond the contrastive language, as Paul introduces a new trope, that of military garb, while revisiting the familiar threesome of "faith," "love," and "hope," so important to characterizing the identity and mission of the community (1:3 and 3:6, 10; see comments on 3:10, above). Paul uses the language of military imagery with some frequency in his letters (see esp. Rom. 13:12–14, which includes parallels to language of "drunkenness" found here in verse 7; also Rom. 6:13, alternative reading, and 2 Cor. 6:7; 10:3–5; Phil. 2:25 [see also Phil. 3:16 and 4:7, and discussion of those verses in commentary on Philippians, above]; Phlm. 2). The closest parallel to these verses within the Pauline corpus is Ephesians 6:10–18 and those who are familiar with that passage have a tendency to read 1 Thessalonians 5:8 in light of it. Among the many notable differences between these two passages is the presence of the "the sword" in Ephesians; there is no weapon or held instrument of any kind in 1 Thessalonians. The imagery here includes simply the two items that are put on (more on that below). Consistent, presumably, between the two is the context of cosmic evil (see comments on 1 Thess. 4:16, "air," above, which references Eph. 2:2; see also Eph. 6:12). While Ephesians 6:10–18 considers the struggle at some length, including graphic imagery (e.g., "flaming arrows," 6:16), 1 Thessalonians simply does not consider any battle activity.

The most direct antecedent in Hebrew Scripture for Paul's metaphor here, and its likely source (at least on the level of scriptural referent), is Isaiah 59:17. Therein it is God who "puts on righteousness like a breastplate, and a helmet of salvation on his head. . . ." The resonances with our text are immediately evident: "breastplate . . . helmet . . . salvation." (For further resonances between the texts, see more broadly the "light"/"darkness" imagery of Isaiah 60:1–3 [and 19–20] and 1 Thess. 5:4–5; see also the "build up" language of Isaiah 60:10 and 1 Thess. 5:12.) Interestingly, what accompanies the breastplate is *not* "righteousness" but "faith and love." Why? Internal to 1 Thessalonians we can find an answer with reference to 1:3 (see below). What may also be worthy of note is the resonance between these verses and Philippians 1:10–11, particularly in light of the eschatological context of both. There the community's mission in anticipation of "the day of Christ" (Phil. 1:10) will have been realized by its "having produced the harvest of righteousness" (see above, commentary on Philippians, comments on 1:10–11 and 2:16). Paul does not use "righteousness" in 1 Thessalonians. He does, however, use strong language at the beginning of the letter to describe the community's identity and work (1:3, and more broadly 1:3–10). And, that is precisely what shows up here in 5:8: ("faith and love"; see 1:3, also 3:6). The helmet here, just like Isaiah 59:17, is yoked with "salvation" but, of course, there is a difference. And the difference is "hope." What is realized in the narrative of Isaiah 59 (God's final appearance) is anticipated here. Consistent with that it is indeed "hope," and more broadly described "the steadfastness of hope" (1:3) which will carry the community in its mission of faith and love and hold it in its identity as God's "assembly" (1:1).

And what could make that point clearer than putting the community in God's place, which is precisely what Paul has done here. In the great vision and narrative of Isaiah 59–60, it is God who wears the armor. To overstate the case, there is no God here—of course, that is far from true, as verse 9 makes clear. Nevertheless, it is the community that—to switch the metaphor—is in God's shoes. What about that? The NRSV does a disservice with its translation of verse 8. The direct exhortation within verse 8 is simply, and pointedly, "let us be sober." The rest of the verse, as is clear in Paul's Greek, describes matters and states of being that already are: "We, being of the day . . . having been clothed with a breastplate of faith and love and as a breastplate, hope of salvation." The protective gear of "faith and love" and "hope of salvation" have already been given (presumably by God; notice the passive voice of the verb, "having been clothed" [the NRSV translates the same word thusly in the famous passage of Luke 24:49, "until you have been clothed with power from on high"]); these are the community's birthright by virtue of its being "called out" (see comments on 1:1) as God's own. No level of sobriety or training or wit can gain them. The community is God's and *because of that* it enjoys such protective gear.

Important for North American ears, given the tendency of popular Protestantism to focus on the individual and to interpret the Bible through that individualistic lens, is the message of verse 9, which affirms all that has come before. It is about "us," the "assembly of Thessalonians" called out by God. And in particular, what the community is all about is "obtaining salvation through our Lord Jesus Christ." The resonance with 1:10 is clear, especially since "wrath" occurs in both verses. But this verse, and its broader context, informs and builds on 1:10 mightily. First, it puts a very active spin on the notion of "wait" in 1:10. Second, it puts the "us" of 1:10 into creative tension.

Just how broadly can that "us" be understood? For the past several verses (5:4–8) Paul would seem to have been separating "us" from a presumed "them" who "sleep" and are "drunk." Yet previously, in 4:12 and 3:12, Paul clearly has his sights on "outsiders" and "all" (see also 5:15). And here, after specifically taking pains to separate "us" from those who are "asleep" (5:6; "sleep," 5:7), Paul allows, "so that whether we are awake or asleep we may live with [Lord Jesus Christ]," using precisely the same word for "asleep" in 5:10 as he had for "asleep"/"sleep" in 5:6, 7 (and though, as discussed above, the word the NRSV translates "died" in 4:13 and 4:14 literally means "sleep," Paul uses a separate word there; 5:10 does *not* refer back to 4:13, 14). To say the least, then, boundaries would appear to be porous! Further, it is the orientation to "encourage" and "build up" that defines the community and allows it to thrive in its mission. Notably, "judgment" (which many attuned to popular notions of Christianity today presume to be a Christian prerogative as regards "the day of the Lord," 5:2, which is often referred to in popular parlance—notice—as "judgment day") is nowhere to be found in the community's identity or mission. Such judgment suggests or affirms separation; here the lines between *in* ("awake") and *out* ("asleep") are blurred while community purpose is very clear: "encourage one another and build up each other."

AN APPEAL: LIFE IN COMMUNITY REVISITED
1 Thessalonians 5:12–22

5:12 **But we appeal to you, brothers and sisters, to respect those who labor among you, and have charge of you in the Lord and admonish you;** [13] **esteem them very highly in love because of their work. Be at peace among yourselves.** [14] **And we urge you, beloved, to admonish the idlers, encourage the fainthearted, help the weak, be patient with all of them.** [15] **See that none of you repays evil for evil, but always seek to do good to one another and to all.** [16] **Rejoice always,** [17] **pray without ceasing,** [18] **give thanks in all circumstances; for this is the will of God in Christ Jesus for you.** [19] **Do not quench the Spirit.** [20] **Do no despise the words of prophets,** [21] **but test everything; hold fast to what is good;** [22] **abstain from every form of evil.**

With verse 12, the gears switch again, moving ostensibly from consideration of matters relating to the context of the end times (4:13–5:10) back to the concerns of life and work in community (5:12–22). Of course, those areas of consideration are not unrelated, as the direct overlap of the language of "encouragement" (4:18; 5:11; cf. 5:14 and, earlier, 4:1, 9) indicates. Indeed the very structure of the exhortations sections in chapters 4 and 5 (in which the two sections on life in community bookend those regarding the end times) suggest such a relationship. The matter of "work" (see "labor," 5:12) recalls 4:11 and earlier discussions of work (see discussion below). That tie to earlier discussions goes far deeper than simple vocabulary for labor and raises again in earnest the matter of the immediate context of the Thessalonian community's structure and life. Finally Paul revisits prayer and "thanks" (5:17, 18), which together have marked the letter from the beginning (1:2); indeed here the prominence of "thanks," in concert with prayer and rejoicing, is stated in no uncertain terms: "the will of God . . . for you" (5:18; cf 4:3). Following a final flurry of directives (5:19–22), Paul will be ready to begin closing out the letter.

Paul opens the section with a direct "appeal." It is a verb that is likewise used to open the first section on community exhortation (4:1, "ask") where it appears in tandem with the more frequently used appeal/urge/ encourage (see esp. comments on 4:1 and 3:2). The parallel occurrences in 4:1 and here affirm the relationship of the two sections on community exhortation. They also suggest something else—that Paul's more limited use of this verb is quite deliberate. Paul's only other uses of the term, which are both in letters closely related to this, are on occasions when the close relationship of Paul to the immediate addressee(s) and the urgency of the appeal are of utmost importance: in 2 Thessalonians 2:1 the NRSV translation captures just that spirit through the use of "beg"; in Philippians 4:3 it is with deep concern for community leadership that Paul chooses to "ask" a particular identified colleague to "help" the situation that is deteriorating due to rivalry among two named colleagues.

Here it is indeed leadership and concern for community life that rise to the fore. The appeal "to respect those who labor among, and have charge of you" recalls previous discussions of work in 1:3, 2:9, and 3:5, perhaps especially 2:9 with its direct description of Paul's leadership pattern: "we worked . . . while we proclaimed to you. . . ." As discussed especially in comments especially on 2:9 and 4:4, 6, and 4:9–12 it is the workshop, the place where manual labor and technical skill are practiced, that provides the immediate context for the development and formation of the Thessalonian community. These verses would appear to pick up where 4:9–12 left off.

Had Paul put a period after "labor among you" the message might be almost synonymous with the last phrase of 4:9, "love one another," for, almost by definition, the "brothers and sisters" (or at least the immediate core thereof) are fellow workers (for further discussion, see esp. comments on 4:4, 6, above). But here "labor" clearly extends beyond immediate, literal meaning of labor associated with manufacturing and beyond the "work" and "labor" generally on behalf of the gospel (1:3). The particular "labor" under discussion is clearly on behalf of the Christian "assembly" ("in the Lord") and involves some level of leadership and oversight: "have charge of you . . . and admonish you."

In comments on 4:9–12, especially verse 11, it is noted that the directives therein are counter to what would be expected in the broader culture and present what corporate management specialists today might refer to as "flattened structure"—that is, not top-down ("be dependent on no one," 4:12), expects the engagement of all ("work with your hands," 4:11), and shuns the establishment of power bases with or among constituents and power brokers ("live quietly," "mind your own affairs," 4:11). There is much consistent with those directives here: "Be at peace among yourselves . . . admonish the idlers, encourage the fainthearted, help the weak, be patient with all of them. See that none of you repays evil for evil, but always seek to do good to one another and to all." A closer look may get us even closer to the context and message here.

Much has been made of the "idlers" in verse 14 and, indeed, the NRSV translation itself provides a strong sense of the generally prevailing understanding among interpreters of this passage that these are members of the community who, for whatever reason, are somehow lazy. (Perhaps there is an overanxious expectation of the end times [5:1]; after all, if the Lord is coming tomorrow or the next day, why bother getting up and going to work?) But such an interpretation neglects both the nuanced, multivalent way that Paul has used "work" language from 1:3 through 2:9 to 4:9–12, and here; it is indicative both of the workshop setting *and* of the identity and mission of the "assembly" called by God. Such an understanding of "idlers" also neglects to take into account the context of life in and among the workshops as the trades were variously managed and organized in the cities around the Mediterranean at the time Paul writes.

The same word translated here "idlers" also carries the sense of "disorderly conduct" or, in our parlance," "troublemakers." When understood thusly, the resonance of this verse with 4:11 begins to come into focus. Then as now, trade guilds and other such associations were governed by bylaws. The directives here, such as are quoted above ("peace . . . help . . . be patient," etc.) would seem to stand such bylaws on their head. For example, monetary fines were instituted and exacted; even expulsion was a stated punishment for those causing disturbance. Not here in this alternative assembly. Consistent with the porous community boundaries of 5:10 (see discussion above) no such activity is directed or suggested. Quite the opposite—members of the community are to go out of their way to maintain all within the community and to look to support each other, not to exact punishment or pronounce banishment.

And then there is the matter of leadership. As discussed in 4:11–12 the management suggested would appear to be rather nonhierarchical. That said, the directives of 5:12 would seem clearly to indicate that there are particular individuals who hold leadership roles. What is worth noting, however, is the repetition of "admonish" in 5:12 and 14. At the very least, this suggests that all members of the community can and should take on the role and responsibility of leadership. Further, the lack of any names of individuals or offices, along with the repeated references to the "labor" or "work" of leadership, particularly in light of 4:9–12, may even suggest that such leadership was a shared, perhaps rotating, function.

And that said, within those striking and tender images recalling the leadership of Paul's team at the time of the founding of the Thessalonian community (2:7–12), there may lie a telling clue as to how the act of admonishing might be practiced. Acts 20:31, the nuances of which the NRSV translation ("I did not cease . . . to warn everyone") does not fully capture, indicates something important about the practice of admonishment. Therein this same word, (translated not "admonish" but "warn" in the NRSV) is used along with the very pointed language, "each one of you." Though that language is not used here, it may be presumed by the Thessalonians based on Paul's own dealings with them (as recalled in 2:11, "each one of you"). Further, the overall ethic is clear: "always seek to do good to one another and to all."

With the triad of "rejoice . . . pray . . . thanks" (5:16–18) and the bringing in of "the Spirit" (v. 19), Paul returns to themes and practices described at the top of the letter regarding the founding of the Thessalonian community and its identity and mission. The first ("rejoice") and last ("Spirit") of these elements recall directly 1:5–6. Therein it was "joy inspired by the Holy Spirit" that characterized the manner in which the Thessalonians "received" (v. 6) and acted on (v. 7) the word. The verb "rejoice," here, and "joy" are built on the same root and immediately recognizable as related terms. In 1:5–6 "the gospel came to you [Thessalonians] . . . in power and in the Holy Spirit . . ." and though it was, to be sure, the Thessalonians who "received" it, their "joy" (noun) is "inspired by" the Spirit. Here that noun, "joy," has become an active verb as the Thessalonians are not only to "rejoice" but to do so "always" (recalling the manner in which Paul and his team "give thanks" in 1:2 and prefiguring the directive to come, "pray without ceasing" (5:17). Further, it is the Thessalonians who are commanded by way of imperative regarding the Spirit, "Do not quench." As the community has matured from the first wave of formation recalled in 1:6, so Paul is laying responsibility for continued growth squarely on it.

Precisely in that vein, Paul continues in verse 20, "Do not despise the words of prophets," or better, as the NRSV alternative reading, "Do

not despise prophecies." Prophecy is, of course, directly related to the Spirit. To a later church under different circumstances, Paul will famously indicate the many "varieties of gifts" of the Spirit, including, of course, "prophecy" (1 Cor. 12:10). There is no question that verse 20 is to be read directly in light of what immediately precedes it. A standard sociologically influenced way of reading New Testament and other Scriptures is to distinguish between a time of "charismatic" growth and leadership followed by a time of institutionalization. One can interpret many sorts of movements—religious, political, musical—through such a lens. To the degree that such an interpretative lens is reflective of actual development, it is interesting to note here that the Thessalonian community is, by definition, making some initial moves from its exciting inception of growth and spread (1:6–7) to a time of settling down and formation (so the exhortations of chs. 4–5). While the Spirit and prophecy are more characteristic of initial charismatic reception and growth, concerns for community governance, management, and life together are more characteristic of institutionalization. Here, following several statements directly having to do with possible complications regarding leadership and the managing of those who might variously disturb, or require extra attention from, the community (5:12–15), Paul turns to a reconsideration and recasting (via "prophecies") of the (continuing) place of the "Spirit."

Along with "everything" (v. 21) else that is involved in community life and that demands attention from the community, are "prophecies," *and*, along with everything else, they are to be considered and tested. The word for "test" that Paul chooses here is directly associated with "spirits" in the later statement in 1 John 4:1: ". . . but test the spirits to see whether they are from God; for many false prophets have gone out into the world." There is every reason to believe that Paul's purposes are quite analogous—clearly any purported word of the Spirit, or prophecy, is to be tested by the community (a truism that has stood the test of time). That said, let God's assembly, whether in first-century Thessalonica or in any locale in any century, not despise outright any word that may be indeed be prophecy consistent with, and ultimately from, the Spirit.

Between "rejoice" (5:16) and "Spirit" (5:19), which call the addressees back to the top of the letter, particularly 1:5–6, there lies "pray" and "give thanks" (1:17–18), which likewise recalls the top of the letter, particularly 1:2–3. These two recur throughout the letter ("thanks," 2:13; "prayer," 3:10, 11–13 and, shortly, 5:23, 25) cementing the close relationship and sense of reciprocity that Paul feels for, and expects from, the Thessalonians. As we have seen (in comments on 1:2, above) this particular term for prayer has the sense of petitionary prayer: that is, asking for God's help. Such is certainly consistent with the "thanks" passage herein with its somewhat ominous—or, is it hopeful (?)—"give thanks in all circumstances." Paul writes similarly to the Philippians, "Do not worry about anything, but in everything by prayer and supplication with thanksgiving let your requests be made known to God" (Phil. 4:6). That passage would almost seem a commentary on 1 Thessalonians 5:17–18, especially with final statement of 5:18: "for this is the will of God in Christ Jesus for you." Prayer and thanksgiving are centering in practice—and they are to be practiced—and it is from them, in a real sense, that the mission and identity of community, rooted in relationship to God and each other, are acted out (see comments on 1:2–3, above, and comments on Phil. 4:6 in commentary on Philippians, above).

Regarding the statement, "this is the will of God," which closes 5:18, Paul apparently was never taught the maxim that "you can't have it both ways." He does, with this phrase. Having already established "your [i.e., the Thessalonian community's] sanctification" (4:3) as God's "will" for his addressees, Paul now labels another practice in the same manner. But what is the antecedent of "this"? An argument can be made for either (1) "give thanks in all circumstances" (5:18) and, perhaps, the directives to "Rejoice" (5:16) and "pray" (5:17) that immediately precede it, or (2) the act of not quenching the Spirit (5:20) and, perhaps, the balance of 5:21–22 as well. 4:3 is, in fact, Paul's only other use of the phrase, "this is the will of God," throughout his letters, and there the "this" is clearly forward pointing, as the NRSV translation indicates well: that is, "this" clearly refers to content that follows. The only other uses within the New Testament are found in John 6:39–40, and in both of those cases the "this" also points forward. So, in every other instance of this phrase, whether by Paul or Jesus, the content of the "this" that is marked as "the will of God" *follows*. Taking that pattern and laying it over the case here, it is, then, number 2 above, the act of not quenching the Spirit (5:20) and perhaps the balance of 5:21–22 that fall out from it, that equals "the will of God" for the Thessalonians. That said, the NRSV translation, given its punctuation, clearly suggests number 1, and indeed the force of the initial (1:2–3) and subsequent (2:13; 3:10; 5:25; see also the prayers of 3:11–13, and 5:23) considerations of thanksgiving and prayer earlier in the letter may affirm that that choice is consistent with Paul's understanding. A final possibility is that Paul would favor the ambiguity that allows either choice to account for the "this." Whatever the case may be, Paul is not yet done with the notion of sanctification, as the prayer of 5:23 indicates.

FINAL PRAYERS, COMMANDS, AND GREETINGS
1 Thessalonians 5:23–27

> 5:23 **May the God of peace himself sanctify you entirely; and may your spirit and soul and body be kept sound and blameless at the coming of our Lord Jesus Christ.** [24] **The one who calls you is faithful, and he will do this.**
>
> [25] **Beloved, pray for us.**
>
> [26] **Greet all the brothers and sisters with a holy kiss. I solemnly command you by the Lord that this letter be read to all of them.**
>
> [27] **The grace of our Lord Jesus Christ be with you.**

As discussed in comments on the preceding section, prayer is a recurring theme and action throughout the letter at the beginning (1:2–3), middle (3:10, 11–13), and end (5:17–18, 23–24, 25). As discussed in the comments on 1:2–3, the very crafting of the letter suggests that it, and beyond it, the whole ongoing relationship of Paul and the Thessalonians and the whole ongoing mission and enterprise of the community are a virtual extension or acting out of the prayer that Paul and his team "constantly" offer to God on the community's behalf. There has been at least the hint of reciprocity and mutual forbearance at points throughout the letter (e.g., 2:19–20; 3:6). Here, with the direct appeal to the Thessalonians to "pray for us," end (5:25) and beginning (1:2) are directly, and prayerfully, linked. So too is affirmed the communal nature both of the letter and its message and of the community's identity and mission. These have been clear and consistent throughout, through the command to "read" aloud "the letter to all . . ." and with the prayer that posits the community, together, as (one) "spirit and soul and body."

The beginning of the prayers at 3:11 and 5:23 are precisely the same, stressing the very "selfness" (if there is such a phrase in English) of God's action on the community's behalf; these are not anchorless wishes, nor are they left to abstract fate or to human design. God, God's self, is directly invoked. Here in 5:23 there is the further stress on "entirely," which, as Paul wrote it, is not an adverb but a plural adjective, rendering, "May . . . God . . . sanctify you as complete ones. . . ." The sanctification language draws the addressees back to 4:3, which is itself recalled in the "will of God" phrase in verse 18 as discussed above. The prayer, then, is particularly fitting at the close of the exhortation section of this letter (beginning at 4:1), which includes near the beginning (4:3) the statement about God's will being "your sanctification," and closes with another summoning of God's will (5:18). Responsibility is laid squarely on the community (see esp. comments on 5:19–20) to carry out its mission as the called assembly of God, while the completion of sanctification is appropriated to God.

In Paul's Greek it is literally the case that where the first phrase of 5:23 ends the next one picks up. "Entirely" (as per the NRSV) or "complete ones" (as discussed above) closes out the first phrase (as it does in the NRSV) while "sound" begins the next. This second phrase is, in effect, a comment on the first. What is easily—and often—missed by those who are used to reading with popular American notions of individuality is the collective "your" as used herein. As he has throughout the entire letter, Paul is addressing the whole community regarding the whole community. That "your" is plural is crystal clear in the Greek. Meanwhile, "spirit . . . soul . . . body" are all clearly single (that is, the letter is not talking about bodies, souls, and spirits) and there are also clearly no particles or modifiers indicating something along the lines of "each" or "each one" (as occurs in 2:11, for example). That is, the letter is not addressing *each* of "your" bodies, souls, and spirits.

Something akin to this collective sense occurs in Paul's other Macedonian correspondence, regarding "you" Philippians "standing firm in one spirit . . . with one mind" (Phil. 1:27). The narrator of Acts uses a similar trope regarding the early Jerusalem community: "Now the whole group of those who believed were of one heart and soul" (4:32). Clearly early Christians, Paul foremost among them, use the comparison of the whole community to a human being in order to relate an ethic of corporate mutuality, responsibility, and relationship with and among each other and God. That said, this is the only time that Paul employs a tripartite anthropology, divided into body, soul, and spirit (the twofold, body/spirit occurs repeatedly in later letters; Rom. 8:10, 13; 1 Cor. 5:3; 7:34).

The identification of God as "the God of peace" and the use of the adverbial "at the coming of our Lord Jesus Christ" recall earlier mentions and considerations of "peace" (see esp. 1:1; 5:3, and attendant comments, above) and the "coming" of "the Lord" (see esp. 2:19; 4:15, and attendant comments, above). Together, these are deeply and profoundly definitive of the community and its particular identity and mission. The addition of "our" here to "Lord," not found in earlier iterations of the phrase within the letter, is affirmation of that. Putting a period or exclamation on the earlier passages mentioned above, these phrases serve as a final reminder and charge to the community that not the Roman emperor, but God, brings genuine "peace," and not the Roman emperor, but "our Lord," will triumph.

The simple, indicative statements of 5:24 work in tandem with the prayer of 5:23 to remind and charge the community for their continued life and growth together. "The one who calls" brings the addressees back to 1:1, with affirmation of their designation as an alternative "assembly" shaped and called by God (see esp. comments on 1:1, above). "Faith" language has not been central to this letter as it is elsewhere in Paul's correspondence (for further discussion see Weidmann, *Galatians*, esp. regarding Gal. 2:16; 3:6–9, 26), but how fitting and telling this statement is here. For so many familiar with American Protestantism, it goes without saying that our faith is all about, well, "faith." Here Paul would seem to agree, but with a twist—it is not "your" or "our" faith that Paul highlights, but God's. It is God who is "faithful" and God who "will do." The Thessalonians can bank on that. And indeed the very language, "calls" (see 1:1) and grammatical tense "will" (see esp. 4:15–17 on the "coming") provide, respectively, both the foundation for, and ultimate goal of, their identity and mission together as God's alternative "assembly."

The mutuality within the community and among community members has been considered at length in the exhortation of chapters 4–5, especially 4:1–12, and 5:12–15; see also 5:10. The scope of community practice and concern, of course, extends even beyond any hard and fast community boundary (see 4:12; 5:15; see also 5:10, and comments above) and nowhere is that more intimately the case than in relationship to Paul and his team (see esp. 2:19 and 3:6). The simple command/petition in 5:25, "pray for us" is a fitting, poignant, and knowing close to the recurrence of prayer throughout the letter (see discussion, above, in the introduction to this section). What Paul and his team do "constantly" for the Thessalonians, so also he would have them do.

The address, "beloved," is rendered more accurately in the alternative NRSV reading "brothers" (see esp. comments on 4:4, 6, above, for consideration of the gender-specific, "brothers," v. "brothers and sisters"). It affirms the close sense of kinship within the community. So too the address in 5:26, which uses precisely the same word. The direct kinship language and "kiss" go hand in hand, as comparison with 1 Corinthians 16:20 and 2 Corinthians 13:11–12 (in which "brothers" or "brothers and sisters" is also present) indicates (see also 1 Pet. 5:14, in the context of the family language of 1 Pet. 5:12–13). Such an act expressing kinship, with its attendant scriptural and theological meaning (see Gen. 2:7, and recall that "breath" and "spirit" are precisely the same words in both Hebrew and Greek; see also the "Spirit" that precedes this injunction, 5:19), became standard in many early Christian communities around the Mediterranean.

The command "that this letter be read to all" underlines, again, the familial nature of community identity, life, and mission, as the alternative reading of the NRSV indicates; here again the word for "brothers" is used in Paul's Greek. The "all" speaks for itself; no one in the community is to be left out because, anticipating a later discourse of Paul's on the integrity of the whole community (1 Cor. 12:12–31), if any are forgotten or ignored, then the "body" is, by definition, not "sound" (5:23). The sudden switch again to the first person "I" here (see 2:18; 3:5), especially when read in light of 2 Thessalonians 3:17 may transport us back to the actual physical writing of the letter: perhaps Paul has grabbed the pen.

The word for "solemnly command" could hardly be stronger. It is a compound word not used elsewhere in the New Testament. A shorter, noncompound version of the same word is used in both Mark (5:7) and Acts (19:13) in the context of exorcism narratives, in both cases translated in the NRSV, "adjure." The word, at its root, carries the sense of an "oath." Perhaps Paul is stressing deeply the full sharing with and for the whole community that is the basis of identity and mission.

The final greeting or benediction is familiar from Paul's letters generally (Rom. 16:20; 1 Cor. 16:23; 2 Cor. 13:13; Gal. 6:18; Phil. 4:23; Phlm. 15), which is not to say that it has no immediate relevance and depth here. Just as "Grace . . . and peace" to "you," the full community, marks the beginning of the letter, so too does the statement that the "peace" and "grace" that are "with you" in "our Lord Jesus Christ" end the letter and carry the community onward.

Second Thessalonians

Introduction

Paul's Second Letter to the Thessalonians is a unique and fascinating letter. It is unique among the letters in this volume because it is the only one whose authorship is questioned seriously within modern scholarship. Among its many fascinating characteristics is the degree to which the contents of this short letter—a little over half the length of 1 Thessalonians—both resonate with and differ from 1 Thessalonians. Who wrote it? When? Why? And what does it say?

The first and best answer to the question of authorship is that which the letter itself provides, "Paul, Silvanus, and Timothy"; that is, precisely the same team that produced 1 Thessalonians. As with 1 Thessalonians, Paul's voice is clearest and most prominent (see 2:5; 3:17, "I"). The letter was written very shortly after 1 Thessalonians—likely a matter of months and, therefore, likely from Corinth (for Paul's movements following his time in Thessalonica, see the introduction to 1 Thessalonians, above). It was written in response (3:11) to a deteriorating situation within the Christian community at Thessalonica that was likely caused, at least in part, by 1 Thessalonians itself—or, more particularly, misinterpretations of it and of Paul's teachings more broadly (2:2). Given that 1 Thessalonians is Paul's first extant letter, 2 Thessalonians is the second oldest letter of Paul's that we have. So, what's the problem within modern scholarship?

Beginning in earnest in the early twentieth century, New Testament scholars have questioned the authorship of the document in part because of its similarities to 1 Thessalonians. Why? Some of the correlations appear ham-handed (e.g., see the repetition of "our Father and the Lord Jesus Christ" in 1:1–2). The argument goes that whoever wrote 2 Thessalonians appears to be trying a bit too hard to mimic, and perhaps replace, 1 Thessalonians; were it Paul himself or Paul's team who authored it, the repetitions and similarities would appear less forced and more natural.

Consistent with such an understanding are the stylistic and content differences that are notable vis-à-vis 1 Thessalonians. Fans of Hemingway may like the short, pointed phrases and sentences which are, arguably, characteristic of 1 Thessalonians (see esp. 1 Thessalonians 5:16–18). In contrast, 2 Thessalonians is characterized by longer, more complex sentences (e.g., in the Greek, 2 Thessalonians 3–10 is one sentence). Too, the overall tone of 2 Thessalonians seems to have shifted significantly away from the closeness and warmth of 1 Thessalonians (see esp. 2:7–3:10) to a more rigid, authoritarian tone (e.g., 3:6, "we command," and 2:15, citing "the traditions" taught by Paul). And then, there is the lack of any reference to the death and resurrection of Jesus Christ, which is such a hallmark of Paul's preaching (see 1 Thess. 1:10; 4:14; 5:9–10) and the excessive—so the argument goes—focus on judgment and vengeance (e.g., 2 Thess. 1:8–9). Why somebody would write such a letter, to whom, and in response to—and under—what circumstances, are matters of discussion. There is some consensus among those who argue that the letter was not written by Paul that it was written by a student or circle of students of Paul toward the end of the first century—which is about the time that the book of Revelation was likely composed—and that it reflects something of the same heightening of persecution against early Christian communities that that book does. The letter's internal focus on authenticity (2:2; 3:17) is noteworthy on its face; were it, in fact, a pseudonymous composition, those verses become all the more extraordinary (see further consideration of 2:2 within this introduction, below). Handy summaries and considerations of the arguments for pseudonymity are available in Krentz (6:519b–522b), and Furnish, (127–42); Malherbe (2000, 349–75) argues in favor of Paul's authorship.

Consideration of the arguments both for and against Paul's authorship are important on several levels, not least because they help keep those who would engage this extraordinary letter honest. Many of the statements, assertions, descriptions, and arguments within the letter are challenging, and nothing is gained from glossing those over. This commentary proceeds with the presumption, based on a consideration of the modern, scholarly evidence as well as of the text itself, that Paul, along with Silvanus and Timothy, is indeed the author. That hardly resolves the difficulties in understanding the particulars of the letter. It does, however, take seriously the very life situation that Paul was meaning to address in Thessalonica in these back-to-back letters of 1 and 2 Thessalonians and the comfort and challenges that his words presented for the Thessalonians then, and for us now.

In an apparently very short time, the church, or "assembly," that Paul had so praised only months before was showing significant strain both from within and without. By the letter's own testimony, Paul and his team had heard (from an unidentified source) "that some of you are living in idleness, mere busybodies, not doing any work . . ." (3:11). That set of circumstances appears directly related to the matters Paul addresses in 1 Thessalonians 4:10–12 (and perhaps also 1 Thess. 2:9–12; for further context and discussion, see comments on those verses in commentary on 1 Thessalonians, above). Further, "persecutions" and "afflictions" appear to be a serious concern (1:4) here, as in 1 Thessalonians (1:6; 2:14–15; 3:3–4). The difference would appear to be the current circumstance. The overt references to the Thessalonians' experience of persecution in 1 Thessalonians are regarding the recent past, while in 2 Thessalonians these challenges appear all too present: ". . . you are enduring" (1:4; though see Paul's concerns in 1 Thess. 3:3–4). Has a new and more pointed round of persecution begun (for consideration of meaning and scope of "persecution," see esp. comments on 1 Thess. 1:6 and 3:3–4)? A third primary area of concern for Paul and his team is raised thusly: "As to the coming of our Lord Jesus Christ and our being gathered together with him, we beg you . . . not to be quickly shaken in mind or alarmed . . . to the effect that the day of the Lord is already here" (2 Thess. 2:1–2). Here too there is a direct correspondence with 1 Thessalonians 5:1–11 regarding "the day of the Lord" and perhaps also the narrative descriptions of 1 Thessalonians 4:14–17. Why the need for more teaching? Apparently some within the community have become convinced that these "coming" times and events are in some way "already here."

In 1 Thessalonians, as noted in the commentary above, Paul regularly affirms the Thessalonians' understanding of his teachings and consequent actions: "as you learned from us how you ought to live and to please God (as, in fact, you are doing)" (4:1); "For you know what instructions we gave you . . ." (4:2); "Now concerning love of the brothers and sisters, you do not need to have anyone write to you, for . . . indeed you do love all the brothers and sisters" (4:9–10); and, "Now concerning the times and the seasons . . . you do not need to have anything written to you" (5:1). There are some similar statements in 2 Thessalonians: "And you know what is now restraining [the lawless one]" (2:6), and "and we have confidence . . . that you are doing and will go on doing the things that we command" (3:4). However, in contrast to these and to the passages from 1 Thessalonians, above, is Paul's pointed question, "Do you not remember that I told you these things when I was still with you?" (2 Thess. 2:5) and Paul's reminder, "For even when we were with you, we gave you this command ..." (2 Thess. 3:10). Beyond betraying, perhaps, some level of testiness, these also suggest that Paul, after hearing of the deteriorating situation following the Thessalonians' receipt of 1 Thessalonians, does not want to take anything for granted.

It is in such a vein that the whole of 2 Thessalonians 2:2 really resonates: ". . . not to be quickly shaken in mind or alarmed, either by spirit or by word or by letter, as though from us, to the effect that the day of the Lord is already here." For those who argue that Paul did not write 2 Thessalonians, this verse stands as a kind of smoking gun because (the argument goes) surely no forged letter could have arrived in Thessalonica within the few short months between the writing of 1 Thessalonians and the writing of 2 Thessalonians. That does indeed ring true. But, both the posited problem and its resolution are premised on the notion that 2:2 itself refers to a letter other than 1 Thessalonians. A more likely reading (see commentary, below) is that the phrase "as though from us" refers to all three items which precede, and has to do with onsite (at Thessalonica) presentations and interpretations of Paul's prophetic word (so, "spirit"), arguments or reasoning (so "word," which can also be translated as "reasoning" or even "logic"), or letter (that is, 1 Thessalonians, which had indeed arrived recently). In 2 Thessalonians, Paul is correcting whatever misinterpretations are circulating around and influencing the Thessalonian community.

The distinction between correction and refutation is noteworthy for readers of this volume. The situation in Thessalonica appears very different from that in Galatia, for example, in which outside teachers have come in to influence Paul's converts there (see Weidmann, *Galatians*). Here the matter is internal and has to do with local (mis)understandings of Paul's own teachings, whether in person or via 1 Thessalonians, which had recently arrived from him.

What may not be so different from what we find in Galatians is Paul's awareness of, and care for, his distinct proclamation. In Galatians, Paul promotes his "gospel" proclamation in distinction from others, associating his "gospel" with "the gospel of Christ" and indicating concern that any would "pervert" it (Gal. 1:6–8). In 2 Thessalonians Paul's language of choice is "traditions," familiar also from Galatians 1:14 and resonant with Paul's rabbinic background and training. It refers directly to that which he had taught the Thessalonians in person and via 1 Thessalonians (2 Thess. 2:15; see the resonance with 2 Thess. 2:2). In 2 Thessalonians, as in other letters, he exhibits the concern to present and clarify his proclamation and teachings and to do what he can to assure the integrity of that proclamation and those teaching within the "assembly" addressed, in this case that of the Thessalonians.

For discussion of the context of Thessalonica as a city within the Roman Empire and of the activity of Paul's mission there, as well as its movements following the time in Thessalonica, see the introduction to 1 Thessalonians, above. On the matter of those mission activities and movements during and following his time in Thessalonica, it is notable that it is precisely the extended discussion of such in 1 Thessalonians 2:1–3:8 that has no parallel in 2 Thessalonians. Presumably, there was no call for it, since (1) Paul had just recounted it in 1 Thessalonians and (2) the purpose of 2 Thessalonians was a focused one, correcting misinterpretations and misunderstandings arising from, and within, the current circumstance in Thessalonica. Such is the matter that Paul takes up and maintains virtually from beginning to end within the letter.

Commentary

SALUTATION AND ADDRESS
2 Thessalonians 1:1–2

1:1 **Paul, Silvanus, and Timothy,**
To the church of the Thessalonians in God our Father and the Lord Jesus Christ:
[2] **Grace to you and peace from God our Father and the Lord Jesus Christ.**

The authors of this letter are precisely the same as those of 1 Thessalonians. So is the unique (among Paul's letters, with the exception of 1 and 2 Thessalonians) designation of the addressee via indicating the people ("Thessalonians") rather than a location. Concerning authorship, in the discussion of Silvanus in the comments on 1 Thessalonians 1:1, above, it is noted that according to the narrative of Acts and to the evidence of Paul's own letters, it appears that Silvanus, for whatever reason, left Paul's mission after spending some amount of time with Paul and Timothy in Corinth. The collaboration in this letter, then, is certainly Silvanus's last extant written cooperative effort with Paul, but may also be one of their last efforts together of any kind. As to the matter of identifying the addressees, there is extended discussion in the commentary on 1 Thessalonians, above, on the relevance of such a designation, "the church of the Thessalonians," all of which is quite relevant here also. What Paul describes and posits is an alternative "assembly," or "town hall meeting" or "association" of Thessalonians distinct from any recognized, civic authority.

The only change here vis-à-vis 1 Thessalonians 1 is the insertion of the pronoun "our" attendant to "Father." The move, though small, is arguably immediately relevant and potentially impactful for the Thessalonian addressees. Second Thessalonians appears to be picking up where 1 Thessalonians left off. In the first letter, the use of "our" in similar designations appears at 5:23 and again at 5:27, "our Lord Jesus Christ" (see also 1 Thess. 1:2; 2:19; and 3:11; see also "our God" in 3:11). Especially with regard to 5:23, the stress on "our" would appear to drive home the contrast of Jesus, posited as "Lord," with the emperor; the latter being the one who, according to "common sense" and regular understanding, would be recognized as "Lord" by Paul's addressees. That switch of "Lord" from the emperor to Jesus is consistent with Paul's identification of this alternative assembly/church of the Thessalonians. So too, "Father" for God. As discussed in the comments on 1 Thessalonians 1:1, above, "Father" was, according to Caesar Augustus's own testimony, the honorific bestowed on the emperor. As with "our Lord Jesus Christ" in 1 Thessalonians, so "our Father" here in 2 Thessalonians: the "our" underlines and affirms this identity and mission of the assembly/church.

The repetition of "God our Father and the Lord Jesus Christ" would likely appear to be a matter of emphasis. And it surely plays on that level. On closer examination it might also underscore what Paul's language in 1 Thessalonians 1:1 and here suggests: that God's grace and peace are something unique and particular. Especially regarding "peace," the obvious purveyors and maintainers of peace in and for the world of Paul's addressees was the Roman Empire. What was implicit in 1 Thessalonians 1:1 becomes explicit here: genuine, actual "peace" is "from God," who is, again, "our Father." In comments on 1 Thessalonians 1:1 is a consideration of this particularly male language in light of Roman imperial usage.

THANKSGIVING: PERSECUTION AND JUDGMENT
2 Thessalonians 1:3–12

1:3 **We must always give thanks to God for you, brothers and sisters, as is right, because your faith is growing abundantly, and the love of every one of you for one another is increasing. ⁴ Therefore we ourselves boast of you among the churches of God for your steadfastness and faith during all your persecutions and the afflictions that you are enduring.**

⁵ This is evidence of the righteous judgment of God, and is intended to make you worthy of the kingdom of God, for which you are also suffering. ⁶ For it is indeed just of God to repay with affliction those who afflict you, ⁷ and to give relief to the afflicted as well as to us, when the Lord Jesus is revealed from heaven with his mighty angels ⁸ in flaming fire, inflicting vengeance on those who do not know God and on those who do not obey the gospel of our Lord Jesus. ⁹ These will suffer the punishment of eternal destruction, separated from the presence of the Lord and from the glory of

his might, ¹⁰ when he comes to be glorified by his saints and to be marveled at on that day among all who have believed, because our testimony to you was believed. ¹¹ To this end we always pray for you, asking that our God will make you worthy of his call and will fulfill by his power every good resolve and work of faith, ¹² so that the name of our Lord Jesus may be glorified in you, and you in him, according to the grace of our God and the Lord Jesus Christ.

Following the very similar address, 2 Thessalonians proceeds, in a manner similar to that of 1 Thessalonians, with an extended thanksgiving section. As with 1 Thessalonians, one can (and scholars do) debate just how to delineate the thanksgiving section. While in 1 Thessalonians it might be understood maximally to extend through 1 Thessalonians 3:10 or even 3:13, so with 2 Thessalonians it might be seen to extend through 2:13 or even 2:17. As in 1 Thessalonians so here, whether the thanksgiving sections are understood in that extended fashion or more minimally (1 Thess. 1:2–10; 2 Thess. 1:3–12), they establish something of the relationship between the authors and addressees, the mission and identity of the addressees as an assembly/church, and the context for—and content of—the body of the letter to follow. And so here, as in 1 Thessalonians, Paul establishes that he "always give thanks to God for you" and indicates something of the Thessalonian's active "faith" (1:3). He then moves to the community's enduring of persecutions that here, in contrast to 1 Thessalonians 1:5–6, appear to be very much current and, as such, set the stage for much of the content to follow.

In 2 Thessalonians the form and content are each a bit less emphatic than is found in 1 Thessalonians. That is, while prayer and thanksgiving again are very much established, the language of prayer is neither so ardently invoked nor is the community's "work of faith" so extensively detailed as in 1 Thessalonians 1 (though see 2 Thessalonians 1:11). Too, the entrée into the thanksgiving itself is framed differently, captured by the NRSV thusly: "we must always give thanks . . ." (1:3).

Extraordinary for most English speakers is that verses 3–10 form one sentence in Paul's Greek, which means that all of the content through verse 10 provides in some way the occasion for thanks! In light of both the references to the apparently very real "persecutions and afflictions" that the Thessalonians are currently "enduring" (1:4) and the harsh language included in 1:5–9, how can this be? These hardly seem like matters to be thankful for.

The depth of Paul's engagement here, with his own previous teachings to the Thessalonians and with broader tradition, is not to be missed.

On one level, 2 Thessalonians is simply picking up where 1 Thessalonians leaves off. Therein, in the closing exhortations, Paul writes, "Rejoice always, pray without ceasing, give thanks in all circumstances; for this is the will of God in Christ Jesus for you" (5:17–18). Apparently what Paul writes, he means. Recall that this, "you," is clearly referring to the whole community. Just as the community is an assembly/church "called" by "God the Father and the Lord Jesus Christ" (1 Thess. 1:1; see comments on that verse, above), so it is "the will" of that same God "in" the same Christ Jesus who is definitive of the community (2 Thess. 1:1), that "thanks" be given "in all circumstances."

Is this mandated thanksgiving meant to be a burden for the community—something it has got to do, or else? Hardly. God's "will" is for the community's "sanctification" (1 Thess. 4:3; 5:23; see also 2 Thess. 2:13) and such "thanksgiving" as is called for here participates in that, and holds the community—and Paul (2 Thess. 1:3) and, interestingly, God—accountable to that posited divine "will." There is a narrative in place spanning the community's founding and calling "in God our Father and the Lord Jesus Christ" (2 Thess. 1:1; cf. 1 Thess. 1:1 and 1 Thess. 1:1–3:10 broadly) to God's coming salvific activity through Christ (esp. 1 Thess. 4:14–17, 5:9; for further discussion of these two anchoring events, the community's founding/calling and the coming of Jesus Christ, as treated in this section, see discussion below; see also 2 Thess. 2:1). Such thanksgiving as 1 Thessalonians 5:18 calls for and 2 Thessalonians 1:3 models is an ongoing, integral, engaged and engaging, part of that narrative.

In a very different letter to a very different church (though, interestingly, a church located in the very city, Corinth, in which Paul likely composed 2 Thess.), Paul writes words of "thanks" which resonate with these. It is a time of "pain" for Paul and his addressees. Yet, Paul writes, "thanks be to God, who in Christ always leads us in triumphal procession" (2 Cor. 2:1–2, 14). Well, no procession could be more triumphal than that of the coming of Christ as narrated in 1 Thessalonians 4:14–17 (see discussion in the commentary on 1 Thessalonians, above) and referenced again repeatedly in this section (2 Thess. 1:7–8, 10). And notice that in this section that coming is described as occurring in order "to give relief to the afflicted as well as to us." Yes, thanksgiving is a "must" for the community called by God in Christ, especially in a time of suffering.

This "must," as it appears here in the NRSV, is a little misleading. The construction Paul uses suggests not so much necessity as obligation or commitment. It is the same word that the NRSV translates, "owe," in Romans 13:8: "Owe no one anything, except to love one another."

Further, the construction represents an august tradition within Judaism, which is likely the source on which Paul draws (e.g., see Philo, *Special Laws*, 2.173; *The Epistle of Barnabas*, 5.3, 7.1).

As in 1 Thessalonians 1:3, so here Paul recalls the "faith" and "love" that are characteristic of the Thessalonians' response to their founding and calling. The action described at the close of verse 3, "the love of every one of you," is consistent with that described as "taught by God" in 1 Thessalonians 4:9 and reported in 1 Thessalonians 4:10. The "faith" and "love" together result in ("therefore") "boasting."

This "boasting" recalls that of 1 Thessalonians 2:19 regarding this young and active Thessalonian community. There are two significant differences, however. In 1 Thessalonians 2:19 (see also Phil. 2:16 and 2 Cor. 1:14) such boasting is clearly to God and is clearly in the context of the end times. The presumed scene is one in which Paul is meeting God at the coming of Christ and giving an account for himself, during the course of which he cites the Thessalonian community (or, in the case of the other letters cited, those respective communities). Here the context is not the end times but rather the present time, and the recipient of the boast is not God but "the churches of God." On those matters of time frame and recipient, these verses more so recall 1 Thessalonians 1:8–9 than they do Paul's other boasting passages. While in 1 Thessalonians 1:9 Paul's team is the recipient of reports from others, here they are themselves involved in spreading word of the Thessalonians. On that score, it is interesting to note that in 1 Thessalonians 1:8 Paul's team sends the message that "we have no need" to do such reporting or "boasting" (to use the term/concept that Paul uses in 2 Thessalonians) because the word is getting out otherwise. Has such reporting by others stopped? If so, why? Perhaps such "persecutions" and "afflictions" as the Thessalonians are now experiencing have pulled them in, away from any activity beyond the community (whether defined by membership or geography).

Also of interest is the particular word for "boasting" Paul uses here. It is not precisely the one used elsewhere by Paul (such as in the passages cited above) but is a compound word built on the same root. Among the very few uses of this particular word in the Septuagint (the ancient Greek version of Hebrew Scripture), all within the Psalms, is this, in the Septuagint version of Psalm 105:7, whose equivalent in Hebrew Scripture/Old Testament is 106:7: "Save us, O Lord our God, and gather us from among the nations, that we may give thanks to your holy name and glory in your praise." In the Septuagint, the word represented by "glory" is this same word, "boast." Beyond that there are several other words and concepts which resonate with 2 Thessalonians: "gather" (2:1), "thanks" (1:3), and "name" (1:12). Further, and tellingly, verse 41 of this same psalm recalls how enemies "oppressed" God's people, using precisely the root word (in verb form) as Paul does in 1:4 in the noun, translated in the NRSV as "afflictions." Paul employs these allusions to Psalm 106:7 (105:7 in the Septuagint) to help construct the end times context in which he understands the Thessalonians' plight. On that score it is notable that he has here put the Thessalonians in God's place (vis-à-vis the psalm), as the subject of the boasting; that is consistent with his placing of the community in God's place (vis-à-vis Isa. 59–60) as the wearer of the breastplate and helmet in 1 Thessalonians 5:8–9.

The language of "faith" is used dynamically in 1:3–4 (and again at 1:11; see also 1:10, "believed" [twice], a verb built on the same root as the noun, "faith"). Several verses in 1 Thessalonians are called to mind, including 1 Thessalonians 1:3 from the initial thanksgiving section of 1 Thessalonians (the particular phrase therein, "work of faith," is directly paralleled at the close of this initial thanksgiving section, in 2 Thessalonians 1:11 and 1 Thessalonians 3:2–7).

Beginning with the latter, what is immediately noteworthy is the connection there of "faith" with "persecutions." That is a connection that Paul makes again here in 2 Thessalonians 1:4. Further, in verse 4 "faith" is linked with the same word, "steadfastness," that was itself linked to "hope" in 1 Thessalonians 1:3 (for further discussion of "steadfastness," see comments on that verse). And finally, just as Paul left out "hope"—the third member of the important group of three, "faith . . . love . . . hope," which is first introduced in 1 Thessalonians 1:3, so too he does not introduce "hope" here in 2 Thessalonians 1:4 in which both "faith" and "love" are present (for "hope" in 2 Thessalonians, see 2:16). As in 1 Thessalonians 3:6, one strongly suspects that the absence of "hope" here is deliberate, reflective of Paul's assessment of what the Thessalonians might be "lacking" at this time. Though "hope" is wanting, "'steadfastness" is not. And consistent with that, "faith" here resonates strongly in the direction of "faithfulness" (Paul uses an adjectival form of this same word in 1 Thess. 5:24 to indicate that God is "faithful"; see also comments on 1 Thess. 2:4, above). That is, the community is proving itself "faithful," trustworthy, in significant ways even while concerns discussed in the introduction above have prompted this letter.

"Persecutions" and "afflictions" might refer to a range of social, economic, civic, and legal actions discussed in the commentary above regarding 1 Thessalonians 1:6 and 3:3–4 (see also 2:13–14). One can only speculate on what these might have been. That said, given the repeated references to the end times in both 1 and 2 Thessalonians, as well as the repeated indication that Paul's initial teachings to the Thessalonians included significant consideration of the end times (1 Thess. 5:1; 2 Thess. 1:8, 10), it is reasonable to suggest that in part, or perhaps even in full, these "persecutions" and "afflictions" were fueled by the teachings about the end times and attendant, anti-imperial language about God and Jesus (see discussion in introduction to 1 Thessalonians, and esp. comments on 1 Thess. 1:1; 4:14–17, above). Consistent with that, as we have already seen (in the discussion regarding "boast," above), the use of "afflictions" here resonates with descriptions of the end times in Hebrew Scripture.

As noted above, all of verses 3–10 is one sentence in Paul's Greek. That feat may be close to impossible in English, rendering a few sentence breaks understandable. The paragraph break indicated in the NRSV, however, is quite misleading. Simply put, verse 5 follows immediately on verse 4, with no break at all. That said, as verse 4 flows directly into verse 5, precisely what "this . . . evidence" refers to is as unclear in Paul's Greek as it is in the English. Whatever the "evidence" might be, there is no question that it is related to the Thessalonians' "steadfastness and faith" during these trying times.

The language of verse 5 is notably similar to that which Paul writes to the Thessalonians' Macedonian neighbors several years later: ". . . for [your opponents] this is evidence of their destruction, but of your salvation. And this is God's doing, for he has graciously granted you the privilege not only of believing in Christ, but of suffering for him as well" (Phil. 1:28–29). Beyond the use of "evidence" (though not exact, the Greek words rendered by the NRSV in each passage as "evidence" are synonymous and built from the Greek same root), there is the presence of the opponents (see esp. 2 Thess. 1:6, "those who afflict you"); the opponents' "destruction" (see "affliction," 2 Thess. 1:6; "vengeance," 1:8; and "punishment of eternal destruction . . . ," 1:9); the community's salvation (see "relief," 2 Thess. 1:7; the inference that the community will be in "the presence of the Lord," 1:9; and the references to "when the Lord Jesus is revealed from heaven" and "when [the Lord] comes," 1:7, 10, both of which are strongly reminiscent of 1 Thess. 4:14); "believing" (see the note above regarding the faith language in 1:3–4, 11, "faith"; and 1:10, "believing" [twice]), and "suffering" (1:5). Though the broad thrust of 1:5 and more broadly 1:5–10 is relatively clear, verse 5 leaves open the question regarding for whom "this . . . evidence" is intended. In the Philippians passage there is no doubt that it is for the opponents. Given the explanatory clause that closes out verse 5, it seems more likely here that the "evidence" is for the Thessalonian community itself; perhaps not coincidentally, then, putting this whole letter in the same vein as Paul's commitment in 1 Thessalonians 3:10 to "restore whatever is lacking" (3:10; and again, the absence of "hope" in both 1 Thess. 3:6–10 and in 2 Thess. 1:33–4 would appear relevant).

While so much of the first part of verse 5, and the broader text and context of 1:5–10, resonates with the passage from Philippians 1:28–29, many of the particulars of the final clause of verse 5 are found in a passage much closer, and familiar, to Paul's addressees, 1 Thessalonians 2:12: "that you lead a life worthy of God, who calls you into his own kingdom and glory." What is lost in the NRSV is that the Greek construction rendered "that," in 1 Thessalonians 2:12, and "intended to," here, are precisely the same—something that would have been readily apparent to the Thessalonian addressees. Though the words for "worthy" are not the same in each passage, they are indeed built from the same root, which again is readily apparent in Paul's Greek and renders the equivalent translation in the NRSV helpful. The language of "kingdom"—and more importantly, Paul's use of it in the context of such language as "Lord" and "Father" —as indicated especially in comments on 1 Thessalonians 2:12, above, amounts to fightin' words (see also comments on 2 Thess. 1:1). Such language sets Paul's mission enterprise and the Thessalonians' newly formed community "in God our Father and the Lord Jesus Christ" (1:1) in direct contrast to the Roman Empire.

That contrast is too easily lost on readers of Paul's letters and the New Testament more broadly. "Empire" and "kingdom" are precisely the same word in Greek. While those who engage this letter today may well hear and see "kingdom" as a church word, Paul's Thessalonian addressees would have unambiguously heard that same word as indicating "empire," with all its real-world connotations as regards the Roman Empire. So too would those around them have heard the word—which likely goes a long way in explaining the earthly fate of both Jesus and Paul, and of the Thessalonians' own "persecutions."

Paul is (re)establishing the identity and mission of his addressees. What they are "suffering," given who and how they are, is not only understandable, but is part of the very narrative that has been part of their formative teaching from the beginning of Paul's time with them, and of Paul's previous letter (esp. 4:14–17). In 1 Thessalonians 4:6 Paul states, "the Lord is an avenger in all these things, just as we have already told you beforehand and solemnly warned you." As indicated in comments on that passage, such language is familiar from Scripture, particularly in texts regarding the end times. From Paul's own testimony, we know that it is a language and context that has been a part of his teaching to the Thessalonians from early on in his relationship with them, and it will dominate the rest of this section and virtually all of the section to follow (2:1–12). "Vengeance" in 2 Thessalonians 1:8 and "avenger" in 1 Thessalonians 4:6 are, as in English, two variations of the same root word.

Further, and very important to note, as it is hidden from those reliant on English translations, is (1) that the NRSV's "righteous" and "just" as found in verses 5 and 6 represent the same Greek word (in the NRSV and many other translations, the English words "righteous" and "just" serve as alternative translations); and (2) that word is very closely related to the words for "avenger" and "vengeance" (the root word for just/righteous being common to both, recognition of which would have been immediately available to Paul's addressees).

The concept of God's justice is, of course, familiar from Scripture and it may be impossible to isolate any one passage that influences Paul's language and presentation here (and beyond that, his broader teaching to the Thessalonians). Among the candidates would be Psalm 94 (in the Septuagint, this same psalm is numbered 93), whose language of vengeance and justice resonates with Paul's presentation here: "O Lord, you God of vengeance, you God of vengeance . . . O judge of the earth" (vv. 1–2); "for justice will return to the righteous" (v. 15); "evildoers" (v. 16) and "wicked rulers . . . band together against the life of the righteous (vv. 20–21; here, for "evildoers" ["ones doing lawlessness"] and "wicked rulers" [literally, "throne of lawlessness"] the Septuagint employs the word that matches precisely the word that Paul uses in 2 Thessalonians 2:7, "lawlessness"); "[The Lord] will repay them for their iniquity" (v. 23; "repay" translates a word that in the Septuagint is very closely related to that translated "repay" in 2 Thessalonians 1:6; "iniquity" translates the word that in the Septuagint matches precisely "lawlessness" in 2 Thessalonians 2:7). To say the least, Paul, like the psalmist, is assuring all who would listen that God is in charge, and that the addressees are indeed on the side of (real) justice.

Of course, there was an easy and obvious, "commonsense" answer as to who and what dispended justice at the time of Paul's writing and in and for the context in which he wrote: Rome. Indeed, as noted below in the discussion of the legal term "testimony," verse 10, Thessalonica, as the seat of the Roman proconsul, was the site of the regional law courts. As Paul's contemporary, the moral philosopher Seneca, put it, the emperor and imperial justice represent "a security deep and abounding, and justice enthroned above all injustice" (Seneca, *On Clemency* 1.1.7).

Ironically, within several years of making that statement Seneca would be compelled to take his own life by the same emperor he here so effusively praises. Earthly justice—and dependence thereon—can indeed be fleeting! Another contemporary, Epictetus, adopts a stance more resonant with Paul's when he posits the example of a true philosopher, on being oppressed by someone, crying out, "O Caesar, how much do I have to suffer through your peace? Let us go before the Proconsul" (that is, the regional representative of imperial justice, such as was located in Thessalonica). Epictetus, in the voice of the narrator, then quickly adds, "Who is Caesar or a Proconsul other than ... God?" (Epictetus, *Discourses* 3.22.55–56). Such is the question befitting the true philosopher and such is consistent with that which Paul has been teaching the Thessalonians from early on and presents here.

Two of the closest parallels to 1:5–6 within the New Testament are Romans 2:5 and 1 Peter 2:23. The latter is of particular interest because, as noted in the commentary on 1 Thessalonians above (see particularly comments on 1:1), Silvanus, one of the coauthors of 1 and 2 Thessalonians, is also credited with having a hand in the production of 1 Peter (see 1 Pet. 5:12). To what degree does such language as "the righteous judgment of God" (2 Thess. 1:5; cf. 1 Pet. 2:23, "[God] judges justly," using the same root word for "righteous/justice"—see discussion above—and a verb built on the same root word as the noun, "judgment") and the use of "suffering" (which in 1 Pet. 2:19 is coupled with "unjustly") reflect Silvanus's thought and, perhaps, influence on this passage in 2 Thessalonians? That is a fascinating and, likely, unanswerable question, though one that means to take the evidence of 1 Peter seriously and to suggest that 1 Peter may on some level represent a mirror for some of the language and concepts found in 1 and 2 Thessalonians. That said, from this early letter of Paul's to one of his last, Paul shows consistency of language and broader concepts as Romans 2:5–7 presents "God's righteous judgment," and goes on to indicate that God will "repay" "wickedness" (or better, "injustice").

With the close of verse 7, Paul's descriptions begin to narrate in some (sketchy) detail that which will happen "when the Lord Jesus is revealed from heaven." The subject itself recalls the description narrated in 1 Thessalonians 4:14–17 and, to a lesser degree, in 1 Thessalonians 3:13 (see comments on those passages, above). Paul's use of the language of "revelation" invokes a well-established tradition of literature within Judaism regarding the end times as well as a mode of communication between human and divine to which Paul elsewhere indicates he has been privy (see Gal. 1:12, 15–16 and 2 Cor. 12:1–4). Presuming 2 Thessalonians to be written by Paul within a few months of 1 Thessalonians, this phrase represents the earliest recorded Christian use of the technical language of "revelation" to refer directly to "the Lord Jesus." The addition (vis-à-vis 1 Thess. 4:14–17) of "flaming fire" to Paul's description is consistent with scriptural tradition regarding both God's revealing of God's self in the formative stages of Israelite history (e.g., Exod. 19:14; Deut. 5:4) and at the end times (e.g., Isa. 66:15).

The ending of verse 8 is both troublesome and potentially liberating for any individual or church who would mean to follow its implications. On its face, the language will be troublesome for many readers of this volume who tend not to identify their faith around matters of "vengeance" and such. The connection between "justice" and "vengeance" as indicated in discussion above regarding 1:5–6 should not be forgotten. To what degree, granted the harsh language, do passages such as these (within both the New and Old Testaments) reveal something of God's desire for human interaction? That asked, let's not avoid the hard and harsh truth: that some will get theirs. Who are those some?

The language is unclear, not least because of the dual description captured well by the NRSV translation: "Those who do not know God and . . . those who do not obey the gospel of our Lord Jesus" (1:8). Is Paul here describing one group or two? Given the immediately previous discussion, one group is the simple answer, particularly "those who afflict" (1:6). That would appear consistent with Philippians 1:28. Further, the singular, inclusive "these" in 1:9 would seem to resolve the dual description at the close of 1:8 clearly into one. But all of that said, it is perhaps the pointed language regarding "those who do not obey the gospel of our Lord Jesus" that provides the best leverage both on Paul's description here and on the broader relevance of this text.

The language of "obey" returns again toward the close of the letter, 3:14–15: "Take note of those who do not obey what we say in this letter; have nothing to do with them. . . . Do not regard them as enemies, but warn them as believers." Paul's language in this passage at the end of chapter 3 directly mirrors the description of "those who do not obey the gospel" and will clearly suffer "vengeance" and "punishment of eternal destruction" (1:8–9). Further, notice that, in case there might be any doubt, in between these two passages (1:8–9 and 3:14–15), he directly and not surprisingly (given 1 Thess. 1:5) equates "his proclamation" with "the gospel" (2:14, NRSV alternative version). As 3:14–15 opens, Paul posits a group toward which, on first blush, something akin to shunning is appropriate ("have nothing to do with them"). He continues, "Do not regard them as enemies," a directive which is interesting enough given the harsh language of 1:8–9. But he goes further, directing his addressees to continue to concern themselves with these others, even reaching out to them—"warn them" (2 Thess. 3:15) in precisely the same manner indicated in 1 Thessalonians ("admonish," 1 Thess. 5:12, 14, translates the same word as is translated "warn," here). Returning to 1:8–9, the obvious questions are who or what group or groups are being described? Whoever they might be, 3:14–15 indicates at the very least the potential that these are current or former members of the Thessalonian community itself. Perhaps Paul is suggesting that the identification of who is included in 1:8–9 is God's problem, not his or the Thessalonians'. If, as Paul would seem to agree wholeheartedly, "Vengeance is mine"—that is, God's (Deut. 32:35)—then not regarding fellow humans as enemies appears the first and best corollary for any individual or community who would be faithful to God.

All of that said, let readers of this volume not presume to know what it might have been like to be among the addressees of this assembly/church, whose experience would seem to have been all-too-frequently and persistently one of persecution (see 1:4, and discussion thereof, above). Even as Paul's addressees read of these others being "separated from the presence of the Lord and from the glory of his might"—a sort of "might," by the way, that is quite distinct from that readily available through popular notions and imperial propaganda—they will have recalled their formation in the hope that "we will be with the Lord forever" (1 Thess. 4:17), a teaching about which they will shortly be directly reminded (2:1).

In approaching verse 10, it does the reader of the NRSV well to recall, as mentioned above, that one extended sentence in Paul's Greek comprises verses 3–10. And just as this sentence begins with dual references to "your faith" (v. 3) and "your . . . faith during all your persecutions and afflictions" (v. 4), so too does it close with dual usage of that same language ("all who have believed . . . was believed"). The words translated "faith" and "believe" are built on precisely the same root word in Greek, which Paul's addressees would have recognized immediately (see also 1 Thess. 1:7–8; 2:4, 13, and attendant comments). Paul's bookending of the sentence with the language of faith/belief is hardly an accident. This sentence has been crafted to focus on the community's faith and faithfulness (which will be further invoked in the very next sentence, v. 11) and on the foundation of such faith and faithfulness, which is the community's belief in Paul's "testimony." In light of varying and (at least potentially threatening) teachings (see 2 Thess. 2:1–2), Paul is reminding the faithful ones/believers of the "testimony" or "gospel" that serves as the basis of their community's faith.

The word here translated "testimony" would become a technical one in Christianity regarding "martyrdom." For Paul's addressees it would likely ring true as a legal term. Thessalonica was the regional capital and seat of the Roman proconsul. Its law courts regularly heard "testimony." Here the letter's addressees are reminded of the "testimony" of Paul and his mission team, which forms the foundation of and for this alternative "assembly of Thessalonians " (see 2 Thess. 1:1, and attendant comments, above; see also comments on 1 Thess. 1:1).

With verse 11, Paul brings the language and discipline of prayer into 2 Thessalonians (see esp. comments on 1 Thessalonians 1:2–3, 3:10, and 5:17) and marries it, as he does in 1 Thessalonians 1:2–3, with faith/faithfulness. The introductory phrase, "to this end" (a fair representation of Paul's pointed Greek prepositional phrase, which indicates purpose), connects this verse, and Paul's prayer, with that which immediately precedes it. Presumably it is Paul's intent to link the "you" of verse 11 with "[the Lord's] saints and . . . all who have believed" of verse 10. Beyond the word, "prayer" (for discussion of the nuances of this particular term, see comments on 1 Thessalonians 1:2), the use of the adverb, "always," recalls Paul's effusive employment of prayer language at the top of 1 Thessalonians. It also puts a particular emphasis on this prayer.

Important is the degree to which this opening prayer of 2 Thessalonians 1:11 is consistent with the closing prayer of 1 Thessalonians 5:23–24. As already discussed, this prayer of verses 11–12 is linked with verse 10 and its concern for "when [the Lord] comes"; it also immediately precedes the reference to "the coming of our Lord Jesus Christ" in 2:1. First Thessalonians 5:23–24 is also concerned with "the coming of the Lord Jesus Christ." In that prayer, God is the actor who is to "sanctify you entirely." Here, God is the actor who would "make you worthy" (see 2 Thess. 1:5 and attendant comments). In 1 Thessalonians 5:24 it is God who is "faithful." Here it is God who "will fulfill by his power every . . . work of faith." In both prayers there is the reminder to the church/assembly of God's initial and ongoing "call" (at the root of the word for "church" or "assembly" is the word "call"; see discussions at 1 Thess. 1:1; 5:24; and 2 Thess. 1:1). As is clear in the extensive sentence of verses 3–10 (esp. 5–6), it is God who is in charge. All of the community's faithfulness (vv. 3–4; see also v. 10), endurance (v. 4) and suffering (v. 5) are in response to God's call.

In the discussion of 1:5, above, Paul's later statement to the the Philippians is cited (Phil. 1:27). Therein is the direction to "live your life in a manner worthy. . . ." The community, the collective "you," is the actor. Here and in 1:5 it is God who acts to "make you worthy." Does that suggest some shift in Paul's thinking or presentation? Perhaps, but a closer look reveals otherwise. At the end of Philippians 1:28 he writes that "this is God's doing," which, especially in light of the statement that follows in Philippians 1:29, indicates that Paul is crediting God at the very least with the opportunity—or better, "privilege"—granted to the community to act in such a manner in response to the gospel. In 1 Thessalonians 1:4, immediately following Paul's reference to the "work of faith," it is God who chooses the church/assembly, and it is the "word," "power," and "Holy Spirit" that fuels its actions. Paul's focus here on the action of God in making "worthy" and on God's "power" in fulfilling "every good resolve and work of faith" would seem consistent with his previous descriptions and well suited to the prayer form he uses here. Indeed the interaction of the human and divine (i.e., human activity and divine grace, power, and inspiration) that each of these texts suggests in its own way is consistent with the compelling—if dense and slightly awkward—prose of verse 12.

This last sentence of the prayer, and of this whole section, also resonates with Paul's letter to the Philippians. Therein the Christ Hymn of chapter 2 is central. It ends with reference to the "glory" of God (Phil. 2:11). In Philippians 3:21 Paul links the corporate "body" of the community to the "body" of Christ and particularly to "his glory." Also consistent is the focus on "name" in both Philippians (2:9) and here.

WE BEG YOU: THE "COMING OF OUR LORD" AND DECEPTION
2 Thessalonians 2:1–12

> 2:1 **As to the coming of our Lord Jesus Christ and our being gathered together to him, we beg you, brothers and sisters,** [2] **not to be quickly shaken in mind or alarmed, either by spirit or by word or by letter, as though from us, to the effect that the day of the Lord is already here.** [3] **Let no one deceive you in any way; for that day will not come unless the rebellion comes first and the lawless one is revealed, the one destined for destruction.** [4] **He opposes and exalts himself over every so-called god or object of worship, so that he takes his seat in the temple of God, declaring himself to be God.** [5] **Do you not remember that I told you these things when I was still with you?** [6] **And you know what is now restraining him, so that he may be revealed when his time comes.** [7] **For the mystery of lawlessness is already at work, but only**

until the one who now restrains it is removed. [8] And then the lawless one will be revealed, whom the Lord Jesus will destroy with the breath of his mouth, annihilating him by the manifestation of his coming. [9] The coming of the lawless one is apparent in the working of Satan, who uses all power, signs, lying wonders, [10] and every kind of wicked deception for those who are perishing, because they refused to love the truth and so be saved. [11] For this reason God sends them a powerful delusion, leading them to believe what is false, [12] so that all who have not believed the truth but took pleasure in unrighteousness will be condemned.

Somewhat lost in the NRSV translation is the parallelism between the beginning of this chapter and that of chapter 4 in 1 Thessalonians. In Paul's Greek, the "we beg you," which the NRSV buries in the middle of the second line of verse 1, is the first word (it is one word in Greek). It is the same word that the NRSV translates as "ask" in 4:1. Like 1 Thessalonians 4:1, so also 2 Thessalonians 2:1—this verse begins the exhortation within the letter (for further discussion of the relevance of, and shift to, exhortation within the letter, see comments on 1 Thessalonians 4:1 and the introduction to that section of the letter, "Life in Community," p. 135).

As discussed in the commentary on 1 Thessalonians and in the introduction to this letter, above, it is a hallmark of exhortation, and certainly of Paul's practice of exhortation, to remind those being addressed of what they already know. Paul does this regularly throughout 1 Thessalonians 4–5. Here a similar rhetorical move is evident, but with a significant difference. Perhaps reacting to what Paul may now consider to have been a bit of overconfidence, Paul for the most part does *not* affirm the Thessalonians' remembering or knowledge (though see the comment in 2:6, following 2:5). Rather, in a slightly judgmental or testy manner, Paul asks, "Do you not remember that I told you these things when I was still with you?" (2:5; cf. 1 Thess. 2:9, "You remember . . . ," or, in a statement directly pertinent to the subject matter at hand, 1 Thess. 5:2, "you yourselves know very well . . ."). Certainly verses 1–2 and 3 set the tone for this section in which Paul wishes to correct or redirect perceptions within the community.

Paul unambiguously indicates, right from the start, that this section is about exhortation. And he begins with a very familiar topic, "the coming of our Lord Jesus Christ" (see 1 Thess. 2:19; 4:15; 5:2; 2 Thess. 2:10). He then summarizes that topic, via the noun, "gathering," in a manner quite familiar within contemporaneous Jewish and Christian literature and perhaps in his own earlier teaching to the Thessalonians, though he did not use the term in 1 Thessalonians (see Mark 13:27 and 2 Macc. 2:7, 18). *Psalms of Solomon* 17.26–27 is particularly suggestive for this section, and for 2 Thessalonians more broadly, as it uses this term/concept, "gather," to introduce a statement about God's righteousness, judgment, and peoples' unrighteousness: "[God] will gather a holy people whom he will lead in righteousness, and he will judge the tribes of the people that have been made holy by the Lord their God. He will not tolerate unrighteousness . . ." (cf. 2 Thessalonians 1:5–6 regarding "righteous" and "just," and 2:12 regarding "unrighteousness"; regarding "made holy," compare 2 Thess. 2:13, "sanctification").

Second Thessalonians 2:2 is among the more fascinating verses in this letter and perhaps in Paul's letters as a whole. As indicated in the introduction above, it has been used both by those who favor the authenticity (Paul's authorship) of this letter and by those who believe it to have been written by some other(s) to support their arguments. Notable is the dense, suggestive language that Paul uses here to set the tone and context.

The NRSV captures fairly well the purposeful resolve with which the verse opens. The adverb "quickly" speaks deeply to context. There is every indication—as discussed in the introduction above—that the letter was indeed written shortly after 1 Thessalonians. Time is of the essence—Paul is alarmed by the rapidity with which his efforts to fortify the community with 1 Thessalonians have apparently deteriorated. The two verbs "shaken" and "alarmed" are both familiar in contemporaneous Jewish and early Christian literature regarding the end times.

Interesting in light of the reference to *Psalms of Solomon* regarding verse 1, above, is *Psalms of Solomon* 8:33: "May you [God] be pleased with us . . . ; Lord, our savior, we will not be troubled at the end of time" ("troubled" translates the same word the NRSV translates, "shaken"). What the Lord's people assert for themselves in the *Psalms of Solomon*, Paul wishes for the Thessalonians—not to be shaken regarding the end times. The same term, "alarmed," occurs in Matthew 24:6 and Mark 13:7 in an analogous way regarding the end times (see also Luke 24:37, for which most Greek manuscripts use a different word that is a synonym, though the earliest extant manuscript as well as another prominent text tradition use precisely this same word). Given their consistent presence within the tradition of discourse about the end times, one can imagine that Paul would have used these terms in his teaching while present in Thessalonica.

The threefold presentation in the second part of verse 2 is important on three levels, which can be easily missed. First, there is the basic meaning of the three components: each is an important part of Paul's output and of the modes of communication readily available to teachers and preachers at the time. Second, and importantly, is that the comparative marker, "as though," is distributive; that is, it is linked with each of the three components. Third, the final clause, "to the effect that the day of the Lord is already here" is tied immediately to the previous clause. The very same word which is translated "as though" in the phrase just discussed, is repeated here. Were the NRSV's "to the effect" replaced with "as though," it would capture something of Paul's dense rhetoric and close linking of the components of the sentence.

Now, to return to each of the components named. Just as Paul might have regretted his repeated affirmation of the Thessalonians' "remembering" and knowledge in 1 Thessalonians (see introduction to this section, above) so to he might have regretted the simple directives of 1 Thessalonians 5:19–20: "Do not quench the Spirit. Do not despise the words of prophets." Of course, in fairness to Paul he did follow up those directives with "but test everything; hold fast to what is good. . . ." That, in essence, is consistent with what Paul is urging the Thessalonians here. What he is doubtless referring to as "spirit . . . as though from us" is a prophetic word or interpretation (see 1 Cor. 12:10, also 1 Cor. 2:10, 13) based on an earlier utterance of Paul, likely when he was in residence in Thessalonica. Interestingly, Paul ties the word "word" to such prophetic interpretation in 1 Corinthians 2:13 ("we speak of things in words . . . taught by the Spirit") and he may have something along that line in mind here. If so, then the second of the two components would be referring more so to interpretations of, or teachings based on, a prophetic word, while the first component would be referring more directly to a prophetic revelation or utterance, which then would call for interpretation (again, 1 Cor. 12:10). Alternatively, and far more likely is that there is a harder split between "spirit" and "word" with the latter referring to Scripture or teachings of any kind, prophetic or otherwise. That sort of distinction would appear to be precisely what Paul suggests in 1 Thessalonians 1:5: ". . . not in word only, but also in power and in the Holy Spirit . . . ." So, "word . . . as though from us" is likely a teaching or recitation by someone in the Thessalonian community purporting to be precise teaching of Paul or interpretation based on such teaching.

The third component in this list in verse 2 is perhaps the most fascinating. Is Paul—or, for those who argue that 2 Thessalonians is pseudonymous, some other author(s)—suggesting that a pseudonymous letter purporting to be from Paul (but really not) has already been received by the Thessalonians (see also 2 Thess. 3:17). Such a notion stretches credulity especially if 2 Thessalonians is indeed from the hand of Paul within several weeks or a few months following the composition of 1 Thessalonians. Were this in fact a pseudonymous letter from later in the first century, such a notion might work as an interesting fiction or as an attempt to discredit 1 Thessalonians. Of course, that is itself a fascinating notion—for a letter which is itself pseudonymous to forward such a charge against an actual letter; see the discussions of Paul's authorship, pro and con, in the introduction to 2 Thessalonians, above). The simplest and best explanation for this third component and its placement here in 2:2, is that just as Paul is referring to interpretations "as though from us" based on Paul's prophetic utterances ("spirit") and teachings more broadly ("word"), so too with regard to his recent letter (1 Thessalonians). The "letter" referred to is none other than 1 Thessalonians, which very much existed (it had indeed been received only weeks or months earlier) and which, somewhat ironically, has been the source of difficulties around Paul's teachings due to misinterpretations. Paul is righting (interpretations of) Paul's own previous letter as it is being recited and interpreted among the Thessalonians.

With verse 3 one can see the tightrope that Paul must walk in presenting his case. Recall that there is some level of urgency or, at the very least, heightened awareness called for in 1 Thessalonians as regards the end times: "the day of the Lord will come like a thief in the night. . . . So then let us not fall asleep . . . but let us keep awake and be sober" (1 Thess. 5:2, 6). And, of course, as discussed in the commentary on 1 Thessalonians 5:8, the armor imagery draws directly on prophecy regarding the end times. Some of the Thessalonians have apparently been persuaded by those teachings, or some particular spin(s) on them (see comments on v. 2, above) that those end times are indeed somehow "already here" (v. 2). Perhaps outside teachers have played a role in fanning those flames, though there is no indication of such outside influence as there is, for example, in Galatians. Paul is asking his addressees to avoid such extreme understandings of the end times (v. 3), while at the same time asking them to recognize that forces so associated are "already at work" (v. 7). So again: Paul is challenged to accomplish quite a balancing act.

One of the tropes or categories by which Paul forwards his arguably delicate, or difficult-to-define position, is that of deception or deceit. Paul's choice of words here resonates strongly within the letter. Years later, in 2 Corinthians 11:3, he would write to another Christian community, using this same verb, "deceive": ". . . as the serpent deceived Eve by its cunning, your thoughts will be led astray. . . ." Here at the top of verse 3 he does not name the serpent or Satan or anyone or anything directly. The focus is on the negative, "let no . . . ," and on the emphasized "you," that is, the community. But, as the section develops, it becomes clear whom Paul identifies as the one behind the deceiving. The noun, "deception," in 2:10 is built on precisely the same root word as the verb here: ". . . Satan . . . who uses . . . every kind of wicked deception . . ." (2:9–10). Such recognition of the active engagement of Satan in earthly affairs is fully consistent with Paul's previous letter (see 1 Thessalonians 2:18). Further, what is lost in the NRSV's use of "wicked" in 2:10, is that the word by which Paul modifies deception is, in fact, built on the noun "justice" or "righteousness." So the phrase is better rendered, "every kind of deception of injustice," tying it—and Satan—to the theme of righteousness/justice that Paul is developing throughout chapters 1–2 of 2 Thessalonians (see esp. 2 Thess. 1:5–6, "righteous," just," and 1:10, "testimony," also, 2:12, "unrighteousness"; see also the comments on *Psalms of Solomon* cited in the discussion of 2:1, above). And that, in turn, may well inform our understanding of the rest of verse 3 and the section more broadly.

The second part of verse 3 is notably far more forceful and far more nuanced than the NRSV translation suggests, which is not to say that it is easy either to translate or understand. As it stands, there is no resolution to the sentence; that is, there is in the Greek text no equivalent to the phrase, "for the day will not come," which has been supplied by the NRSV translators. That Paul is addressing precisely the matter which closes verse 2, "that the day of the Lord is already here" is clear enough, so on that score the NRSV translation is seemingly consistent with Paul's denser, edgier, more clipped prose. What is lost is Paul's direct statement that "should the rebellion not come first and the lawless one, the one associated with destruction, be revealed *then the day will not come*" (my translation; the phrase in italics is supplied—i.e., Paul's clipped sentence in 2:3 does not include it).

Whatever else is going on here, Paul is at pains to establish in this lawless one a revelation and a coming *prior to* that end time "when the Lord Jesus is revealed from heaven . . ." (2 Thess. 1:7) and "comes" (2 Thess. 1:10). As already discussed, each of these terms, "reveal" and "come," as applied to the Lord regarding the end times, is a technical one. Paul uses each regarding the lawless one: "is revealed" (2:3), "he may be revealed when his time comes" (2:6), "will be revealed" (2:8), and "the coming of the lawless one" (2:9). There is no doubt whose revelation and which coming will be definitive. Paul cuts short any such extended narratives and developed imagery as are found in Jewish and early Christian apocalyptic literature such as the second half of the book of Daniel, the extracanonical book of *4 Ezra*, and the book of Revelation, via the statement that the Lord Jesus "will destroy with the breath of his mouth, annihilating [the lawless one] by the manifestation of his coming" (2:8). In this climactic instance, the identification of Jesus' "coming" is modified with yet another technical term regarding the showing or revelation of God, "manifestation," from whose Greek root we derive our English word, "epiphany."

But first, the lawless one will wreak some havoc. Interesting to note is that the emphatic rhetorical entrée to the second part of verse 3 implies, and the statement of verse 5 affirms, that Paul taught the Thessalonians directly about these matters when he was "still with" that community. The picture of the lawless one's actions in verse 4 draws heavily on Scripture. In Daniel 11:31, an unnamed king sends forces that "occupy and profane the temple. . . ." Further, we learn that that king "shall exalt himself and consider himself greater than any god, and shall speak horrendous things against the God of gods" (Dan. 11:36; these same verses arguably stand behind imagery used in Mark 13 and its parallels in Matthew 24 regarding the end times). In Ezekiel 28:2, these words are put in the mouth of the prince of Tyre: "I am a god; I sit in the seat of the gods." Also of interest in Ezekiel 28 is the prophet's repeated response to the prince's divine presumptions: ". . . yet you are but a mortal, and no god . . ." (Ezek. 28:2) and ". . . though you are but a mortal, and no god . . ." (28:9). Lost in the NRSV—and, for that matter, my (as provided above)—translation of verse 3, is that when the lawless one is first identified in 2 Thessalonians, it is clear in the Greek that he is mortal: "the man of lawlessness" or better, "the human being of lawlessness." In 2 Thessalonians 2:3 Paul uses the very same word for "human being" as is used in the Septuagint version of the Ezekiel text to render "mortal" (this is true for 2 Thess. 2:3 only; in 2:8 a simpler designation is used, which is accurately translated by "lawless one").

The uncharacteristic (for 2 Thessalonians, contra 1 Thessalonians; see introduction to this section) "you know" in verse 6 introduces what might be referred to, quite literally, as an enigma wrapped in a mystery. Paul himself uses the "mystery" language in verse 7, which, in the context of the letter, is of a piece with the other technical language (revelation, coming, and manifestation) used in this section (and discussed above) regarding the end times. In 1 Corinthians 15:51 Paul uses the same term regarding another, happier component of the end-times narrative: "I will tell you a mystery! We will not all die, but we will be changed . . . at the last trumpet." The "last trumpet" is, of course, a reference to Jesus' coming (see esp. 1 Thess. 4:16). Here "mystery" is associated with lawlessness and with the events prior to Jesus' coming. Within that broader mystery, is the matter of something or someone that is "now restraining" the lawless one. What Paul and the Thessalonians "know" has remained, for students of 2 Thessalonians, an enigma.

Before a broader consideration, one needs to recognize a complication on the grammatical level which is captured well by the NRSV translation. Greek, like many languages (of which English is not one), recognizes grammatical gender regularly, including the definite article that precedes nouns and other forms acting like nouns. In verse 6, the grammatical gender of the restrainer is clearly neuter; thus the NRSV's translation, "what is . . . restraining." In verse 7, the restrainer is clearly masculine and not neuter; thus the NSRV's translation, "the one who now restrains."

Now, who or what is this restrainer? We don't know. That has been the honest answer regarding this passage since at least the time of Augustine (*City of God*, 20.19) and probably well before, which is not to say that there are not some interesting and suggestive candidates. Paul himself uses the same root word in his simple directive in 1 Thessalonians 5:21: "but test everything; hold fast to what is good." "Hold fast" translates the verb form of the word for "restrain." Is that which, or the one who, "restrains" or "holds fast" the Thessalonian community itself? Such is an interesting thought, but would appear to stretch credulity on a simple reading of verses 6–7.

A more likely variant on such a notion might be that the Pauline missionary enterprise, or perhaps even the Christian missionary enterprise more broadly serves the role of the restrainer. In Mark 13:10 (see also Matt. 24:14) is the statement that "the good news must first be proclaimed to all nations." Only then will the events of the end times begin, including, as cited above in the discussion of 2 Thessalonians 2:4, the setting of "the desolating sacrilege." In comparing this verse in Mark to 1 and 2 Thessalonians, it is important to recognize that "good news" and "gospel" translate the same Greek word, and it is the very word by which Paul defines and describes his mission (see esp. 1 Thess. 1:5: "our message of the gospel" NRSV). Further, "nations" and "Gentiles" translate precisely the same Greek word, which Paul would come to directly to describe his particular "gospel" (see Gal. 1:16, "among the Gentiles," esp. in light of Gal. 1:6–9) and which he already uses in 1 Thessalonians regarding his particular sense of mission (1 Thess. 2:16). Is it the case that where there's smoke there's fire? These similarities between what we find in Mark 13 and 2 Thessalonians 2 would suggest that the lawless one in 2 Thessalonians or the one associated with the desolating sacrilege in Mark 13 cannot surface until the restrainer has been removed or the gospel has been preached to the Gentiles/nations. Is the mission to the Gentiles the restrainer? That is a much more likely answer than the Thessalonian community itself and gives a broader, more understandable context for Paul's own lack of enthusiasm for seeing/presuming that the end times have already arrived. An interesting and important related conversation—especially if there is merit to this understanding—would be consideration of what relationship there might be, if any, between the "mystery" of 2 Thessalonians 2:7 and that of Romans 11:25, a statement which Paul composed several years after this.

After dispatching the restrainer (v. 7) and doing away with the lawless one at the coming of Lord Jesus (v. 8), Paul then returns to the current context and "the working of Satan" (2 Thess. 2:9). It is a topic with which—at least on some level—the Thessalonians are familiar from Paul's previous letter (see 1 Thess. 2:18). The NRSV translation is helpful here for it allows for the connection between this phrase and the working terms by which Paul defines the community, his time with the community, and his mission team (see esp. 1 Thess. 1:3; 2:9; 3:2, and comments on those passages as well as on 3:10, above; see also 2 Thess. 3:8, 10). Moreover, the language of deception in 2:9–10 picks up directly on that introduced earlier in this section.

In verse 3, as discussed above, that one, or those, who may deceive go(es) unnamed. But here in 2:9–10 Satan is clearly named. As also discussed above, the modifier translated by the NRSV as "wicked" is actually a fairly straightforward term meaning "injustice" or "unrighteousness," which is built from the same root as "righteous" and "just" in 2 Thessalonians 1:5–6. There is no question but that "the working of Satan" is about deception and stands in direct opposition to the justice/righteousness of God. Besides the relationship of "injustice" (NRSV, "wicked") to just/righteous in 1:5–6, what is also lost in the NRSV translation is the presence of a verb and a broader concept familiar from 1 Thessalonians regarding the foundational narrative of the Thessalonian community. Paul repeatedly notes how "in spite of persecution you received the word . . ." (1 Thess. 1:6) and, via a synonym of the verb used in 1:6, "you received the word of God that you heard from us . . ." (1 Thess. 2:13). That same verb as Paul used in 1 Thessalonians 1:6 (and reinforced, via a synonym, in Thess. 2:13) is used here in the second half of verse 10, which is better translated: "because they did not receive the love of truth. . . ." There is no verb "refuse" here—as the NRSV translation would seem to indicate. Rather, the action—or better, nonaction—indicated here is to "not receive."

The move in verse 11, then, is particularly fascinating. Having established that "the working of Satan" is marked by an unjust and un-Godlike "deception" and that "those who are perishing" "did not receive" love of God's truth, Paul now triangulates into the discussion of Satan and non-receivers: "For this reason God sends them a powerful delusion …" (2 Thess. 2:11). Before proceeding further, it is important to note that the word translated here as "powerful" is precisely the same word ("power") as used in verse 9 regarding "the working of Satan." Further, in Paul's Greek God sends, literally, "a working of delusion." So, readily apparent to Paul's addressees was the direct connection of Satan's "working" and God's. Startlingly, each of these workings has to do with delusion or deception.

The word for "delusion" here is familiar in Christian tradition, though not in this particular association as God's own working. Quite to the contrary, in Revelation 12:9 it is "that ancient serpent, who is called the Devil and Satan" who is "the deceiver of the whole world" ("deceiver," here, translating a participle built from the same root as the noun "delusion" in 2 Thess. 2:11). In 1 Corinthians 15:33, Paul uses the term within a simple directive, which itself introduces a quotation from the Greek poet Menander: "Do not be deceived: 'Bad company ruins good morals.'" No word of God's involvement in such deception; though, on another level, the statement that "some people have no knowledge of God, I say this to your shame" (1 Cor. 15:34) is certainly in keeping with the thrust of 2 Thessalonians 2:11–12. The lengthy, complicated first chapter of Paul's later letter to Romans may provide leverage on understanding Paul's presentation of God's role here. Therein, in language that resonates broadly and particularly with both 1 and 2 Thessalonians, Paul writes that ". . . the wrath [see 1 Thess. 1:10] of God is revealed [see 2 Thess. 1–2] . . . against all . . . wickedness [literally, "injustice"; see 2 Thess. 1:5–6 and 2:10]" (Rom. 1:18). As the chapter continues, Paul writes repeatedly how "God gave them up" to their variously un-God-directed activities. Such attribution to God is consistent with scriptural tradition (e.g., Ps. 81:11–12; also Ezek. 14:9. which, in the Septuagint, uses the same word for deceive/delusion that Paul uses here) and speaks to the longstanding theological problem of positing both power and justice/truth to God: (How) can God be in control and there exist evil/injustice as well? Paul provides an answer herein.

Paul closes the section with a reassertion—negatively and profoundly stated—of God's righteousness. The language here is pointed and is captured well by the NRSV, especially if the reader bears in mind the direct equivalence of "righteousness" and "justice" (1:5–6; see also 2:10). From deception of "injustice" (see discussion of 2:10, above) to faith/trust/belief in "what is false," to taking pleasure in/from injustice, those so deluded are beholden to a system which, finally, drags them down. As I write this, an overleveraged economic system, has dragged many down. The economic system has itself used and abused such language as "trust" and "security" to promote policies and activities that were delusional and that ultimately were proven to lack trustworthiness. It is a hard and all-too-real-life lesson of how deeply unjust belief systems can be.

In discussion of 1:5–6 above, it is noted how fleeting worldly—which at the time of Paul's writing, meant Roman imperial—notions of security can be. Whether or not Paul here has the Roman Empire and its agents in his sights, the deep and abiding alternative that he promotes—God's justice/righteousness known in and through Jesus Christ—is one which continues to beguile earthly wisdom, even as its authenticity and "truth" has stood the test of time and experience for those who stand within its traditions.

THANKSGIVING: STAND FIRM AND HOLD FAST
2 Thessalonians 2:13–17

> 2:13 **But we must always give thanks to God for you, brothers and sisters beloved by the Lord, because God chose you as first fruits for salvation through sanctification by the Spirit and through belief in the truth.** [14] **For this purpose he called you through our proclamation of the good news, so that you may obtain the glory of our Lord Jesus Christ.** [15] **So then, brothers and sisters, stand firm and hold fast to the traditions that you were taught by us, either by word of mouth or by our letter.**
>
> [16] **Now may our Lord Jesus Christ himself and God our Father, who loved us and through grace gave us eternal comfort and good hope,** [17] **comfort your hearts and strengthen them in every good work and word.**

In this section Paul returns to that which has marked so much of what he presents in both 1 and 2 Thessalonians: giving "thanks." In 1 Thessalonians 1, the narrative of the community's identity and mission around the "gospel" received from Paul is set in the framework of thanksgiving. Similarly in 2 Thessalonians the community's "steadfastness and faith(fullness)" in a time of "persecution" is set in the framework of thanksgiving. Here via yet another thanksgiving passage, Paul circles back, and responds, to both of those contexts—identity and mission, and current challenges at a time of "persecution"—in order to deliver the basic charge: "stand firm and hold fast." He reminds the community of who and what it is, and moves the letter—and its addressees—toward a call for mutual prayer and support (itself recalling the movement of 1 Thess. 3:9 to 3:10–13) and final exhortation (3:6–15) for the living of identity and mission in these times.

The language of obligation or commitment found in 1:3 regarding prayer is revisited here (see comments on 1:3 for resonances with 1 Thessalonians and with Paul's letters more broadly). What is different here is the emphasis on the "we." Paul and his team model that which they urge (see 1 Thess. 5:18) and what they urge is thanksgiving in all circumstances. So just as "we ourselves" (1:4) give thanks and "boast of you" broadly, even—or especially—at a time of struggle and "suffering" (1:5), so too here following a not-so-pleasant consideration of the workings of Satan and delusions by which the world's systems and understandings of justice are run and to which they are beholden, the "we" again rises to "give thanks" and models appropriate "thanks."

The language of "first fruits" has deep roots in Scripture (e.g., Deut. 26:1–2). Its usage here finds particular resonance among apocalyptic literature and in apocalyptic contexts. In the *Psalms of Solomon* 15.3, the narrative voice refers to "A new psalm . . . the first fruits of the lips from a devout and righteous heart . . ." and contrasts it with the actions of "those who act lawlessly" and "shall not escape the Lord's judgment" (*Pss. Sol.* 15.8; see also 15.10–11 for further uses of "lawless"). In Revelation 14:1–4 the "redeemed" are referred to as "first fruits for God." Meanwhile, in Paul's own letter to Romans, within a passage that evokes the context of the end times ("labor pains," 8:22; cf. 1 Thess. 5:3), it is "we ourselves, who have the first fruits of the Spirit" and "wait for . . . redemption" (Rom. 8:23). As in this Romans passage, so also here, and so from 1 Thessalonians 1:5 on, "the Spirit" is present. Further, the community's "sanctification" is assured via God's (here via the Spirit) activity and presence and the community's "faith(fullness)" (for the latter, see comments on 1:3–4). Such consideration of "sanctification" is consistent with Paul's message throughout both letters (see also 1 Thess. 4:3; 5:23). Especially in light of Paul's reference to "being gathered" in 2:1 (see comments above, including the passage from the *Psalms of Solomon*) reference to sanctification appears apropos as Paul begins to draw this section to a close.

The beginning of verse 14 is a recap, in a sense, of the community's calling and identity. As discussed in comments on both 1 Thessalonians 1:1 and 2 Thessalonians 1:1, the word translated "church," and perhaps better translated "assembly," has at its root the verb, "to call." First Thessalonians 2:12 includes that very verb, along with references to "kingdom" and "glory." This verse is in one sense a commentary on 1 Thessalonians 2:12 and in another sense a commentary on or revisiting of the prayer of 2 Thessalonians 1:11–12. The latter includes just such a direct statement about God's initial call to the Thessalonians, reminding them of their corporate identity with each in mission for the "good news" or "gospel" of "our Lord Jesus Christ." Opting not to use "kingdom" language here, Paul instead revisits "glory" but gives it even great prominence with the stated purpose that "you [here, as always, in the plural, referring unambiguously to the whole community] may obtain the glory of our Lord Jesus Christ." As discussed in comments on 2 Thessalonians 1:12, that language recalls Philippians 3:21, which links the corporate "body" of the community to Christ's glory. Though Paul wrote Philippians several years after 2 Thessalonians, the teachings contained in Philippians are built largely around the Christ Hymn of Philippians 2:5–11, which may well predate all of these letters (see discussion in the commentary on Philippians above). Given the recurrence here of this language regarding "glory" and its particular resonance with what is found in Philippians 2 and 3 (Paul's other extant letter to a Macedonian church, besides 1 and 2 Thessalonians), it is possible that we have here in 2 Thessalonians evidence that Paul's initial teaching to both the Philippian and Thessalonian communities included some reference to the Christ Hymn.

The NRSV captures well Paul's entrée into the directives of verse 15. They are meant to follow directly on what precedes. That is, because of the "purpose" described in verse 14, "now therefore," or, as in the NRSV, "so then" the Thessalonians are to "stand firm and hold fast." These are words and phrases that in both Greek and English suggest *willful* stasis or maintenance in a time of threat (see 1 Thess. 3:8). Paul would use the first, "stand firm," counterintuitively and creatively, in conjunction with the term "strive," in Philippians 1:27. Consistent with this letter's concern for the community enduring heightened threats from outside (2 Thess. 1:4–5) as well as the driving concern of this section *not* to sway from Paul's teachings and grasp onto some other teachings regarding the end times (2 Thess. 2:2), Paul here reinforces "stand firm" with yet another maintenance word. Indeed, the NRSV translates this very term via the term "maintain" in 1 Corinthians 11:2, where it is also used in conjunction with "the traditions": ". . . maintain the traditions just as I handed them on to you."

When Paul refers to "traditions," he knows whereof he speaks. In Philippians 2:5 Paul writes that he is "a Hebrew born of the Hebrews; as to the law a Pharisee." For a discussion of Paul's Pharisaic roots, and

Pharisaic understanding of "tradition" that is "received," see the commentary on Philippians, above. Paul's repeated use of the motif "to receive" (see 1 Thess. 1:6 and 2:13; by way of negative example, see 2 Thess. 2:10) participates in that Pharisaic notion of "tradition." And his use of "tradition" here, especially in light of the motif of "receive" that he has already established with and among the Thessalonians, suggests at least two broad meanings.

First, by way of analogy with the Pharisaic notion of received tradition (see comments on Phil. 2:5 in the commentary on Philippians, above) Paul is establishing another chain of tradition. He, in the place of Moses, received a revelation. He then "handed it down" or, if you will, "traditioned" it to the Thessalonians; in Greek, the word for "tradition" and "hand down" is the same word. In this sense, 2 Thessalonians 2:15 stands in the same vein as 2:14 as something of a recapitulation of the beginning of 1 Thessalonians, in this case particularly 1 Thessalonians 1:5–7. Therein, as discussed in comments on those verses, above, Paul establishes the chain of God/Paul and his mission team/the Thessalonians, and indeed via the good work of the Thessalonians, they themselves become a part of the chain of tradition in becoming an "example" to believers elsewhere. Clearly, the broad outline (1 Thess. 1:5–7) and particular terminology ("receive," 1 Thess. 1:6; 2:13; and 2 Thess. 2:10) are in place to support such an understanding by the Thessalonians. To what degree Paul's own oral teaching to them undergirds it (i.e., did he share his own autobiography in the manner, and with the same words, as Gal. 1:12, 14?) cannot be known.

Second, Paul may be simply using the word as any good and reliable Jewish teacher or layperson might. Repeatedly throughout this commentary and the commentary on 1 Thessalonians are references to Scripture and other Jewish literature regarding teachings, themes, and motifs within the letters. These are "traditions" and would have been referred to as such. It is, of course, characteristic of these letters that there are a very few, if any, direct quotations of Scripture. Indeed we have noted repeatedly, for example regarding the use of righteousness/justice in 2 Thessalonians 1:5–6 or regarding the imagery and language of apocalyptic in 2 Thessalonians 2:1, 9 and other verses, that it is all but impossible to locate any *one* biblical or extrabiblical verse on which Paul may be drawing. That very difficulty indicates that what Paul is sharing is traditional material. By "traditions that you were taught by us," then, this verse is simply indicating the sorts of traditional material, shaped by Paul and Paul's team in light of their (understanding of the) gospel, which is evidenced in the letters themselves and (doubtless) in the earlier teachings to the Thessalonians (so the phrase that follows and closes out the verse). Of course, these two meanings are hardly mutually exclusive.

The close of 2:15 sets up a wonderful balance to 2:2 and, indeed, it is notable that the two verses virtually bookend the section. Clearly Paul has in mind both the oral teachings that he and his team presented in person to the Thessalonians and the letters that follow. In light of 2:2, of course, the strong hope and presumption of 2:15 is that the current letter will have a limiting/defining effect on how Paul's own teachings are interpreted and understood (see discussion of 2:2 as well as the introduction to 2 Thessalonians, above).

Prayer is named, and engaged in, at 1:11–12 and will be named (3:1) and modeled (3:5) again within the next section. In verses 16–17, Paul enters into a prayer which anticipates, on several levels, the next section. First, the movement from "our" and "us" (v. 16) to "your" (v. 17) anticipates the "us" and "you" movement, and mutuality, of 3:1–5. Second, just as the "we" or, more precisely, the "us," of verse 16 have already enjoyed "eternal comfort" as a gift ("through grace gave us") from God, so too does the prayer request "comfort" for "your hearts" and strength "in every good work and word" (v. 17).

This last phrase recalls the foundational narrative of the Thessalonian community in 1 Thessalonians 1:3–7, and in particularly the (multiple) references to "work" and labor in 1 Thessalonians 1:3 as well as to "word" in 1 Thessalonians 1:5–6, and particularly to the *receiving* of the word in 1 Thessalonians 1:6 (see consideration of "receive" in reference to "tradition" in comments on 2 Thess. 2:15, above). Consistent with that, this prayer provides a reminder, and affirmation, of both the identity and mission of this community, founded in the workplace (see esp. 1 Thess. 2:9 and 2:13) for the "work" of faith(fullness) (esp. 1 Thess. 1:3 and 2 Thess. 1:11).

Perhaps anticipating the words of that unnamed saint in the Montgomery Bus Boycott who famously stated "my feets is tired but my soul is at rest," Paul here fuses "comfort" with "work." What is more, and unfortunately lost in the NRSV translation, the word that is here translated, "comfort," is the same that is used at 1 Thessalonians 2:3 ("appeal") and 12 ("urging"; see further comments in discussion of 1 Thess. 2:12, above). Those particular verses frame a section which paints in creative and emotive ways (esp., "nurse caring for her own children," 2:7 and "father with his children," 2:11) the close relationship between Paul and his team and the Thessalonians. That close relationship comes to the fore in 3:1–5.

"FINALLY" . . . STEADFASTNESS
2 Thesssalonians 3:1–5

> 3:1 Finally, brothers and sisters, pray for us, so that the word of the Lord may spread rapidly and be glorified everywhere, just as it is among you, [2] and that we may be rescued from wicked and evil people; for not all have faith. [3] But the Lord is faithful; he will strengthen you and guard you from the evil one. [4] And we have confidence in the Lord concerning you, that you are doing and will go on doing the things that we command. [5] May the Lord direct your hearts to the love of God and to the steadfastness of Christ.

As in Philippians 3:1 (see discussion in commentary on Philippians, above) so also here, Paul marks a significant shift, and an important set of teachings to come, with a particular adverbial construction that is often misconstrued or mistranslated as "finally." Though the letter is starting to move toward its end, there is still a way to go. Indeed, in some sense Paul is just now gaining momentum. Still to come, in this section and the next, are two broad considerations, with general and particular components within them: (1) in this section, following immediately on 2:17, with its nod to the foundational narrative of the community as found in 1 Thessalonians 1:3–10 and under the banner of prayer, there is reaffirmation of the mutual support and care that serves as a foundation for the relationship of Paul and Paul's team with the Thessalonian community; and (2) in the next section, under the banner of a "command," are further remembrances of Paul's relationship with the community, here to reinforce basic rules of engagement for life together in community as the called (1:11) assembly/ church (1:1) of God. This section both begins ("the word of the Lord . . . spread rapidly") and ends ("love" and steadfastness," v. 5) with further recollection of the foundational narrative in 1 Thessalonians 1:3–8.

Prayer holds an important place in both 1 Thessalonians (esp. 1:2–3; 3:10 [and 11–13]; 5:17 [and 5:23]) and 2 Thessalonians (1:11–12 [and 2:16–17]; 3:1 [and 3:5]). Not only named, it is also practiced and modeled, as in the bracketed citations in the previous sentences. It is in the opening thanksgiving section of 1 Thessalonians, in which prayer is placed so prominently (1 Thess. 1:2), that the foundational narrative of the Thessalonian community is told. Therein, after receiving "the word" and becoming "imitators" of Paul's team (1:6), the Thessalonian community, in turn, became "an example" (1:7) to others, so that "the word of the Lord has sounded forth . . ." (1:8). Fascinating, then, that here in 2 Thessalonians is the request that the Thessalonians "pray for" Paul's team, "so that the word of the Lord may spread rapidly and be glorified everywhere, just as it is among you" (2 Thess. 3:1). That sort of inversion—the teacher(s) (i.e., Paul and his team) petitioning that he/they might be as successful as the students (the Thessalonian community)—is unheard of. It is akin to suggesting that, on Paul's departure from Thessalonica, it is not student but the teacher that is in the role of the orphaned child (so 1 Thess. 2:17; see comments, above). Clearly this is a different "Lord" and a different "assembly" or "church" (see esp. comments on 1 Thess. 1:1), and a different community life (see esp. 1 Thess. 4:10–12 and, below, 2 Thess. 3:6–12) than would be expected. Paul is modeling difference from the norms and expectations of the broader society, as well as deference not only to God but to God's people. Though it is a small phrase easily missed by later readers (presumably, the Thessalonians would have picked right up on it) this "just as it is among you" speaks volumes about Paul's deep relationship with the Thessalonians, his nimbleness and creativity in modeling authority and life together (see again 1 Thess. 2, esp. 2:7 and 17, as well as the more traditional 2:12), and his affirmation of the formation and ongoing witness of the Thessalonian community even at this difficult time (see esp. 1:4).

The end to this prayer, in verse 2, is fascinating. From one of Paul's earliest extant letters to perhaps his last, a close parallel to this verse is found in Romans 15:31. There, similar to here, in the context is an appeal to "prayer to God on my behalf" (Rom. 15:30). The prayer is "that I may be rescued from the unbelievers . . ." (the Greek verb translated "rescued" is the same in Rom. 15:31 and 2 Thess. 2; "unbelievers," Rom. 15:31, translates a word built on the synonym of the word, "obey," in 2 Thess. 1:8). The content of verse 1 provides the context for understanding Paul's petition and concern. Just as verse 1 recalls the Thessalonian community's successful missionizing as recounted in 1 Thessalonians 1:3–8, so verse 2 recalls such opposition as the Thessalonians have received from "your own compatriots," in 1 Thessalonians 2:14, and the "persecutions and the afflictions that you are currently enduring," 2 Thessalonians 1:4 (cf. esp. 2 Thess. 1:8–10, and the contrast of "all who have believed," 2 Thess. 1:10, with "not all have faith," 2 Thess. 3:2; lost in the NRSV translation is that "faith" and "believed" share the same root word, which would have been readily apparent to the Thessalonian addressees). Paul is recalling and holding up the Thessalonian community's own experience even as he is asking the members of the community to hold him and his team in prayer.

And then, abruptly, Paul changes focus. In a smoother fashion, the letter takes a similar turn (from "us" to "you) in 2:16–17. An interesting question is raised: in the movement from verse 2 to 3 is Paul looking to comfort the Thessalonians or himself? The simple answer, of course, is the Thessalonians. But they have not been the focus of 3:1–2. Interestingly, in 3:1–2, in the deep, unexpected, and nuanced manner that Paul established in 1 Thessalonians (esp. 2:17), he is measuring himself and his ministry in terms of them (see comments on 3:1–2 immediately above). And so here, as read in light of 1 Thessalonians 3:7–8, this abrupt change appears far less abrupt. Paul's prayer there (1 Thess. 3:9), as here, links the fates of the Thessalonians and Paul and Paul's team. Their "faith" factors greatly in Paul's understanding of his mission (see esp. 1 Thess. 2:19, and comments thereon, above). And, of course, the confident and sure bottom line of any measure of humans' faith(fullness) is that of "the Lord." It is in such light that the confidence expressed in verse 4 is found, as the explanatory "in the Lord" underlines.

The prayer that closes this section likewise draws on the source and example of that which marks the community; "God" and "Christ" (see 1 Thess. 1:1 and 2 Thess. 1:1). Within the Thessalonian correspondences perhaps nowhere is love more directly associated with God than in 1 Thessalonians 4:9, wherein God is portrayed as the teacher of love (see comments on the verse, and the broader section of 1 Thess. 4:9–12, above). In fact, the association of this prayer with that section is deeper than the association of God with love (as if there could be anything deeper than that).

Important to note, given the teachings of both of these letters, is that the word, "command," found on either side of this prayer, is precisely the same word that Paul uses in 1 Thessalonians 4:10 and 11 (something lost, unfortunately, in the inconsistency of the NRSV translation, which uses "urge" and "directed" in 4:10–11 and "command" here; at least the NRSV is consistent in its use of "command" repeatedly in 1 Thess. 3:4, 6, 10, 12). Indeed, the following section, 3:6–15, covers similar territory to that of 1 Thessalonians 4:9–12. There is also the resonance of "love" in passages within each letter having to do with relations within and among the community (1 Thess. 3:12; 2 Thess. 1:3). Worth keeping an eye on is the close relationship of "faith" and "love" from the beginning of the first letter (1 Thess. 1:3) through 1 Thessalonians 3:6 and 2 Thessalonians 1:3–4 to the present section (2 Thess. 3:3, 5).

The "steadfastness" of 2 Thessalonians 3:5 picks up on both the beginning of the first letter (1 Thess. 1:3) and of this one (2 Thess. 1:4). As already noted (in comments on 2 Thess. 1:4, above) it is a particularly apropos characteristic for individuals and communities under persecution to practice. Within Paul's own letters, the point is made perhaps no more forcefully, and akin to the mutuality of 1 and 2 Thessalonians, than in 1 Corinthians 1:6: "you patiently endure the same sufferings that we are also suffering" (here, "patiently endure" translates a short phrase which includes the same noun, "steadfastness," Paul uses in 2 Thess. 3:5; see also 2 Cor. 6:4 and Rom. 5:3–4). The direct association with Christ, here, resonates with other early Christian literature, especially Hebrews 12:1–4 and, noteworthy for its context regarding the end times, Mark 13:13.

NOW WE COMMAND YOU: COMMUNITY BOUNDARIES AND PRACTICE
2 Thessalonians 3:6–15

3:6 **Now we command you, beloved, in the name of our Lord Jesus Christ, to keep away from believers who are living in idleness and not according to the tradition that they received from us. [7] For you yourselves know how you ought to imitate us; we were not idle when we were with you, [8] and we did not eat anyone's bread without paying for it; but with toil and labor we worked night and day, so that we might not burden any of you. [9] This was not because we do not have that right, but in order to give you an example to imitate. [10] For even when we were with you, we gave you this command: Anyone unwilling to work should not eat. [11] For we hear that some of you are living in idleness, mere busybodies, not doing any work. [12] Now such persons we command and exhort in the Lord Jesus Christ to do their work quietly and to earn their own living. [13] Brothers and sisters, do not be weary in doing what is right.**

[14] **Take note of those who do not obey what we say in this letter; have nothing to do with them, so that they may be ashamed. [15] Do not regard them as enemies, but warn them as believers.**

Within the previous section, in the movement from "command" in verse 4 to "the love of God" in verse 5, there is recollection of 1 Thessalonians 4:9–12: "concerning love of the brothers and sisters . . . you yourselves have been taught by God to love one another. . . ." This section continues that movement, beginning with the reintroduction of "command" (v. 6)—here directed in no uncertain terms at "you," as it is in 1 Thessalonians 4:10–11. And, in case it is missed the first time (v. 6), it is repeated in verse 10 and verse 12.

Consistent with the resonances with 1 Thessalonians 4:9–12, with its layered and multitextured language of work, this section puts the readers right back into the workplace, in a way that has been detectable from the beginning of the first letter through such descriptive passages as 1 Thessalonians 2:9–12. As there, so also here, the complementary terms for work and labor underline the workplace setting of Paul's first preaching and teaching to this nascent Christian community. They also show the creative and multiple uses to which any given word can be put by Paul, whether (strictly) the "work" of his and the Thessalonians' trade (so 1 Thess. 2:9, at least in part) or the "work" of his mission and of the Thessalonian church/ assembly called by God (so 1 Thess. 1:3).

First Thessalonians 4:9–12 ends with a statement of purpose for the commands: "so that you may behave properly toward outsiders and be dependent on no one (1 Thess. 4:12; see discussion above). Such would work well here, as well. That said, notable here is Paul's nuancing of community boundaries (see 1 Thess. 5:10, 14, and comments thereon, above) in favor of the broad and permeable, at least regarding those struggling to follow the commands of community life as Paul presents them here.

The exhortation is clearly directed to the community, and its focus is on community life and life with and among community members. Consistent with 1 Thessalonians 4:1 and 4:9, in 2 Thessalonians 3:6 Paul addresses the Thessalonians using family language (as the alternative reading of the NRSV indicates, the Greek behind the [somewhat misleading] "beloved," is, literally, "brother"). As discussed at some length in the commentaries above regarding Philippians 1:12, 14, and 1 Thessalonians 1:4, the word for "brother," in Greek, can be and was used in its plural to refer to a collective of siblings including both male and female. So, either "brothers and sisters" (as often, not always, in the NRSV) or even the underused English word, "siblings," can serve as a fine translation. That said, as discussed in the comments on 1 Thessalonians 4:4, 6, above, there are reasons within the text of 1 Thessalonians, or at least of those specific verses, to consider that Paul may be (apparently uniquely within his letters which elsewhere do address an inclusive collection of siblings) referring more strictly to exclusively male members of the community. Given the resonances of this part of the exhortation with parts of the exhortation of 1 Thessalonians 4:1–12, it is worthwhile to be aware of that possibility.

The NRSV translation is unhelpful in a further sense regarding the identification of the community with this simple familial language, of "brother" or "sibling." Just as the translation, "beloved," is misleading on its face, so too is "believers" (also in v. 6), which also translates that same Greek word for brothers/siblings. More, these individually wanting translations also lose the direct—and awkward—tension between the addressees, who are called brothers/siblings *and* those whom they are commanded "to keep away from," who are also brothers/siblings!

The second set or, better, subset, of brothers/siblings is further defined as those "who are living in idleness and not according to the traditions that they received from us" (3:6). There is a problematic and perhaps telling discrepancy within the textual tradition of verse 6 and of this phrase in particular: is it "they" or "you" who "received from us"? The very fact of this discrepancy here may be indication of the tension in Paul's own Greek—notice that either one makes perfect sense, given the mutivalent use of brothers/siblings in the sentence. The reference to "tradition" brings the addressees back to 2 Thessalonians 2:15 and its evoking of the deep relationship of Paul and Paul's team with the Thessalonians, from their time together and painful separation, through the first letter and up to the present. The particular term that Paul uses for "living" in 3:6 and again in verse 11, calls the Thessalonians back to 1 Thessalonians 2:12, in which this same word is translated "lead a life" (see comments on the term, and its resonances in Greek moral philosophy, particularly regarding action in the face of adversity, there).

As discussed in comments on 1 Thessalonians 5:14 regarding "idlers," above, the Greek root word that the NRSV translates as "idleness" here can indeed mean just that. Here (esp. in light of the first part of v. 8 as well as v. 10), more so than in 1 Thessalonians, some of that sense would appear to come to the fore. But strong still are the resonances discussed in comments on 1 Thessalonians 5:14, wherein both the context and the particular directives indicate for this word something more akin to "disorderliness" or "troublemaking."

Some things never change. Then as now, virtually any given church/assembly or group of any kind will have formal or informal by-laws and customs by which it maintains its structure, functions, and membership. The Thessalonian Christian community was likely founded within, and its membership significantly overlapped with, a professional workplace guild. As discussed in the commentary on 1 Thessalonians, above, the language and substance of the directives in 1 Thessalonians 4:9–12 and 5:14 have particular resonance when read in the context of such by-laws by which professional guilds were organized and run. And, like many teachings of Paul based on the "gospel," the directives do not fit with expectations—see, for example, alternative notions of "peace" (see esp. 1 Thess. 2:12), lordship or rulership (see 1 Thess. 4:16), authority (see 1 Thess. 2:7, 17) and "getting ahead" (to use language very familiar to most readers) or aspiring (1 Thess. 4:11–12). So, here, Paul is calling/reminding/pleading to maintain such practice as they learned from him and his team in person and through the first letter (in other words, "tradition . . . received from us," 3:6).

Accordingly, verses 7–10 bring the addressees back to 1 Thessalonians and, beyond that, to Paul's time among them. The language of "imitate" looms large in the narrative of the founding of the community in 1 Thessalonians 1:3–8. Consistent with the seemingly passing reference to "in the name of our Lord Jesus Christ" in verse 6, that imitation itself links the community, from its inception, through Paul to Christ: "And you became imitators of us and of the Lord . . ." (1 Thess. 1:6). And through its identity as a called church/assembly of God, the community is its own actor and agent of such "work of faith" that would glorify "the name of our Lord Jesus" (2 Thess. 1:11–12).

Beginning with the second part of verse 7, the passage moves from the identity and place of the community in association with Paul's mission and the broader gospel and lordship (see comments on 1 Thess. 1:1) of Jesus Christ, to some particulars of "the tradition . . . received from" Paul and his team. Both language and context point to 1 Thessalonians 2:9–10 and, beyond it, to Paul's foundational preaching and teaching to the community within the workplace setting. Second Thessalonians 3:9 revisits the imitation theme and adds to it the related notion of "example" (see esp. comments on 1 Thess. 1:6–7, above) in light of "that right" that Paul could have exercised. The content of the verse recalls 1 Thessalonians 2:7, which appeals to "demands" that might accompany such "apostolic" status as Paul and his mission assume in order to establish a foil for Paul's counterintuitive (based on expectations) proclamation and teaching of the gospel. The verse is particularly relevant as it leads, through the striking imagery of Paul as wet nurse and mother (see comments on 1 Thess. 2:7) to the very verses being recalled directly in this section (1 Thess. 2:9–10). In a later letter, under pressure and adversity both quantitatively and qualitatively different from that which Paul is addressing here, he will go on at much greater length regarding "that right" (1 Cor. 9:1–15, esp. vv. 4–6; note that the word that the NRSV translates in these verses as "right," standardly is used for "authority").

Beginning with the second part of 2 Thessalonians 3:7, Paul directly recalls 1 Thessalonians 2:9 and his time of initial preaching and practice among the Thessalonians. In 1 Thessalonians 2:9 as here, Paul uses a line of words with overlapping meaning, "toil and labor . . . we worked," to bring his addressees (and by extension, us) back into the real-world context of the workplace in which this God-called church/assembly of

Thessalonians was founded and remains rooted; the phrase "night and day," of course, both conjures that context as well as the same verse, and broader discussion, from the first letter. The reason given is likewise stated here as there, "so that" he and his team might not "burden" others. Here in 2 Thessalonians, as already noted, the imitation language and strategy are stressed and underlined. Paul and his team acted thusly to provide the example for Thessalonian practice going forward.

Indeed, in verse 10 Paul draws on and repeats a "command" (same word here as v. 6, see discussion there; note also, unlike the NRSV, the word is, as in v. 6, a verb) from the time "when we were with you," which does not play (directly) into the first letter. The NRSV translation captures the broad sense, but loses the form of the saying, which is relevant. It is a simple—and very resonant (!), for reasons, importantly, that differ from those which readers of this volume might presume—proposition: "if anyone does not want to work, let that one not eat" (my translation). And, it is followed (in v. 11) by very pointed language, much of which, because of translation and our differing (than those within the world of Paul's Thessalonian addressees) presumptions is lost on our ears.

The matter almost certainly does not have to do with mere idleness of the sort connected with sloth or laziness. As in 1 Thessalonians, Paul is addressing matters of leadership, identity, and mission. And while listening to Paul's teachings in and for that context, some of the Thessalonians have apparently presumed to model their notions of leadership on a mode popular in the moral philosophy of the day—namely, Cynic philosophy. As such, they have begun to detach themselves, at least to some degree, from the normal functioning both of the workplace and of the church/assembly.

Such a phenomenon was hardly unheard of in that society, and drew the malicious humor of a well-known satirist. In a work not coincidentally called *The Runaways*, Lucian writes of the phenomenon:

> You shall see what will happen. . . . All those in the workshops will spring to their feet and leave their trades . . . when they see that by toiling from morning until night, doubled over their tasks, they merely eke out starvation wages . . . , while idle frauds live in unlimited plenty, asking for things in a lordly way, getting them without effort. . . . (Lucian, *The Runaways*, 17; translation slightly amended)

Readers of this volume can draw whatever contemporary analogies they might to individuals who fit such a profile. Whether those whom Paul has in his sights at Thessalonica are, like those Lucian unambiguously and uncharitably characterizes as frauds, are trying to pull one over on others or are acting out of some sense of calling based on their (understanding of their) newfound faith, is an apt question.

Lucian writes from a period approximately one hundred years after Paul. An immediate contemporary of Paul's, cited often above regarding the Thessalonian correspondences, is the moral philosopher Epictetus. Unlike the satirist, Lucian, he does not presume a profiteering motive, but he does look askance at any rash, unconsidered, shallow attempts to follow a call toward leadership that involves detachment from work and society (the latter variously defined as home, family, city, etc.; see the long discussion in *Discourses 3.22*). The one who would take on such a role or understanding of leadership "carelessly" or "without purpose" (3.22.52) had better "Consider the matter more carefully, know yourself, inquire of the divine, and not engage such a decision without God" (3.22.53). It is fascinating, and likely not coincidental, that Paul's consideration herein would fit both Epictetus's baseline orientation toward caution and reserve and his concern for sense of self and God.

The bottom line for Paul is crystal clear as stated in verse 12: "No you don't!" is the message. Yet again using the word "command" as well as "exhort," Paul centers the command/exhortation "in the Lord Jesus Christ." As though recalling the list found in Epictetus, above, Paul provides that which "the divine" and "God" would have "such persons" do. The ruling may seem anticlimactic (at least to readers of this volume): "to do their own work quietly and to earn their own living." In fact, it reflects a deliberate template for the budding Christian community going back to Paul's earliest example and teaching and to the first letter. In setting himself in the workplace Paul was affirming that place as a site of and for the church/assembly. Though calling into question any number of societal and imperially promoted presumptions about power, authority and the like, Paul did not, and does not, call into question the foundation of the workplace or the family (1 Thess. 4:9–12; also 4:4, 6). He does indeed turn on their head some presumptions around how the community might function and how leadership is carried out (again 1 Thess. 4:9–12), but in so doing, he does not intend for any members of the community to strike out on their own to model leadership outside of the community setting (so here, 2 Thess. 3:6–12).

Having recognized the thrust of Paul's teachings and conclusion, we may now see how the allegations of verse 11 fill out the picture. Firstly the word "living," which literally means "walk," resonates in the literature of moral philosophy as well as in the Thessalonian correspondences, around matters of how to conduct yourselves or "behave properly" (the NRSV translation of this word at 1 Thess. 4:12). As the commentary on 1 Thessalonians indicates, Paul's use of the word in the exhortation section of 1 Thessalonians seems particularly rich (4:1 and 12; see esp. discussion of 4:1). Is it mere coincidence that he uses precisely the same term again here, in a discussion that parallels 1 Thessalonians 4:1–12 broadly and 4:9–12 in particular?

The direct reference to "not doing any work" in 2 Thessalonians 3:11 not only sets up well the upcoming command/exhortation in 3:12, but also provides direct and telling context for the charge that those who have opted out of engaging in the community as Paul has taught are "mere busybodies." Lost in translation is that this word in Greek is built on the root word for "work." So, somewhat ironically, all the work language of 3:8 and of this verse provide context and foil for its meaning. It is precisely the word that Epictetus uses in the extended discussion referenced above for those who would in rash and unwarranted discussion opt out of community (*Discourses* 3.22.97). The philosopher's point is that those who are rightly and truly called by God to such leadership are not "busybodies" or "meddlers," but those who merely take it on themselves are. Paul's point in this section is that from his earliest teachings through the first letter and now, his principle for the church/assembly has been life together in and as community (see esp. 1 Thess. 4:9–12). Those who step away from that principle would, presumably, fall under the label "busybodies."

All of that said, life isn't easy, and that is certainly true of life in community and of the demands of work. While verse 12 was directed to "such persons" who would take on for themselves detached forms of leadership, verse 13 is more so directed at the others or, read maximally, for the whole. Lost in the NRSV translation is the stress on the plurality of "you": "But as for you . . ." or even "But as for you all. . . ." Worthy of note is that as written in Greek, "you" is actually the first word in the sentence (a feat virtually impossible to match in English translation), giving it even greater stress. Further, the repetition of the kinship language, "brothers and sisters" (see discussion of 3:6, above), would seem particularly (re)affirmative of the community here.

Finally, the simple—and arguably profound—directive "do not be weary in doing what is right" may well be fitting advice to any community but is particularly apropos for the Thessalonians. This section of the letter has recalled the very real "toil and labor" that set the basis and continues to set the context for community life. Paul uses similar words toward the close of the first letter, "hold fast to what is good" (1 Thess. 5:21). Perhaps it is telling that here the verb is not one of maintenance, "hold fast," but of action, "doing good what is right" or, more simply, "doing good." And, particularly consistent with the acknowledgment of the long haul ("do not be weary"), it is participial in form, indicating continuing action, as is captured well in the NRSV, ". . . in doing [i.e., continuing to do] what is right."

The form(s) and content of verses 14–15 seem to follow directly on the command/exhortation of verse 12. If "such persons" are indeed a "subset" within the broader community (see comments on 3:6, above) then verses 14–15 have in their sights a subset of that subset. More, whereas verse 12 refers to a collective or, at the very least, a plurality—"such persons" (or more literally, "those ones")—here notably, a singular is used: ". . . anyone does not obey." The NRSV is misleading here and in so doing misses the switch from the plural of verses 11–12 ("some . . . such persons") as well as the consistency with verse 10, "anyone." Further, just as verse 11 is structured as a proposition beginning with "if" (which is lost in the NRSV), so too this sentence begins with an "if" (also lost in the NRSV): "if anyone does not obey. . . ."

The commands, then, are in direct response to a hypothetical (perhaps all will obey) and further, as structured in the Greek, both directives do indeed follow the "if." For example, in the Greek of verse 14 it is only after the "if" clause is complete, that the directive is given: "take note of," or better, "mark that one," "in order to have nothing to do with them." There is a give and take within these verses which is very telling if, perhaps, difficult to grasp fully: (1) "take note" and "have nothing to do with . . . so that" shame results—sounds like classic shunning; (2) "do not regard them as enemies, but warn them as believers" (or better, "brothers and sisters," i.e., members of the community; for discussion of the term and its meanings and nuances, see comments on 2 Thess. 3:6, above)—sounds like ongoing, deliberate, relationship. There is something of a parallel in 1 Corinthians 5:9–13 (the repeated directive "not to associate," 1 Cor. 5:9 and 11, employs the same verb translated "have nothing to do with," here), but the upshot for community would seem significantly different in light of 1 Corinthians 5:12–13, which stresses the "outside" status and distance "from" the community of those under consideration. Here it is the inside status, "as believers" (better, "siblings" or community members) that trumps. Importantly, the "all" in the last line of verse 16, below, would seem to further underscore the point.

FINAL PRAYERS AND GREETING
2 Thessalonians 3:16–17

> 3:16 **Now may the Lord of peace himself give you peace at all times in all ways. The Lord be with all of you.**
> [17] **I, Paul, write this greeting with my own hand. This is the mark in every letter of mine; it is the way I write. The grace of our Lord Jesus Christ be with all of you.**

There were no section breaks in the letters as the Thessalonians received them. The prayer in verse 16 follows immediately on the complicated and nuanced directives of verses 14–15 and would seem to comment directly on them (see esp. "all of you" in verses 16 and 18). At the same time, the prayer appears a suitable closing to both letters as a whole, picking up, as it does, on such important themes as prayer itself, as well as "peace," and the ongoing struggles of the community. "Peace" similarly appears toward the close of the first letter (1 Thess. 5:23) as does virtually the same final benediction (1 Thess. 5:28; though see the added "all" here). Even the pointed reference to the letter itself has something of a parallel in the first letter (1 Thess. 5:26).

The reference to "the Lord of peace himself" is a close parallel to 1 Thessalonians 5:23, including the self-reflexive pronoun. What the sub-stituting of "Lord" for "God" (vis-à-vis 1 Thess. 5:23) may indicate is not completely clear. The "Lord" is, of course, used regularly for "God" in the Hebrew Scripture, and the language here may be reflecting that. But, from the first verse of the first letter, "Lord" has been used for Jesus Christ (as is the case generally in Paul's letters; see esp. discussion of Phil. 2:11 in the commentary on Philippians, above). Here at the close of the second letter, Paul would appear to be recalling and affirming the initial reference to "peace" associated with "God our Father and the Lord Jesus Christ" and placing the emphasis on the alternative (to Caesar) "Lord" of this alternative "assembly" or "church" of the Thessalonians (see comments on 1 Thess. 1:1).

The phrase "at all times and in all ways" is captured well in the NRSV. Paul is being a bit overabundant in his prose here. And why not? He and his team and the Thessalonians have been through a lot together and also separate from each other. There are the highs of the community's initial conversion, growth, and spreading influence (1 Thess. 1:3–8), the initial and intimate teach-ins with Paul (2:9), the pain of separating (2:17), the contact afforded by Timothy's visit (3:2–6), the first letter, the ongoing prayers (1 Thess. 1:2–3; 3:10; 5:25; 2 Thess. 2:16–17; 3:1, 5). All of that, along with the added press of increased adversity (2 Thess. 1:4) and complications with the community (2 Thess. 3:6–12), suggest that "all" of these "times" and "ways" covers a lot of ground and circumstances.

Striking is the reassertion of lordship and of the "all" in the last phrase of verse 16. The first, in the earlier part of the verse, would appear a simple, if profound (in context), assertion about Jesus Christ. The second, the "all," in light of the immediately preceding verses (vv. 14–15) appears to be sure affirmation of the expansiveness of the reach of the community's "Lord," Jesus Christ, and of the community itself to include, at the very least, concern for those currently outside its immediate boundaries of regular practice.

What precise relationship, if any, that 2 Thessalonians 3:17 has with 2 Thessalonians 2:2 is an open question. Surely, consistency and confidence are of concern. With repeated references to "traditions that you were taught by us" (2:15) and "the tradition . . . received from us" (3:6), direct reference to his initial teaching to the Thessalonians (3:10), as well as the many allusions to that early period and to 1 Thessalonians, this letter is intent on (re)establishing and (re)building the understanding of, and actions undertaken by, the community. This letter carries Paul's voice and his teachings (on both those scores, 2 Thess. 2:5 rings strongly).

A fascinating verse within Paul's letters is Romans 16:22 in which Tertius, "the writer," or stenographer, of the letter names himself and sends his greetings. Who the stenographer may have been for 2 Thessalonians or for most of Paul's letter is unknown (though see 1 Pet. 5:12 and comments on 1 Thess. 1:1 for association of Silvanus with that, or a similar, role). In 1 Corinthians 16:21 Paul, similar to here, makes it clear that "I, Paul, write this greeting. . . ." What of the other letters? If Paul did in fact pen the greetings directly, they do not contain overt statements to that effect. Of course, included in that camp is 1 Thessalonians (e.g., perhaps in the autograph of 1 Thessalonians Paul physically wrote 1 Thessalonians 5:26 or 27 through 28). Also of interest is the reference to "every letter of mine"; were 1 Thessalonians indeed the very first letter Paul wrote, the statement would make little, if any, sense. That Paul wrote letters prior to 1 Thessalonians, which is Paul's first *extant* letter, would be quite likely given the many years of mission work and travel that precede the writing of 1 Thessalonians (see further discussion in introduction to 1 Thessalonians).

Perhaps a very fitting close to 2 Thessalonians is the final benediction familiar from 1 Thessalonians 5:28 and from Paul's letters generally (Rom. 16:20; 1 Cor. 16:23; 2 Cor. 13:13; Gal. 6:18; Phil. 4:23, Phlm. 15). What stands out is the "all." Consistent with 3:14–15, 16, Paul's sights are on, and his vision for community includes, "all."

Philemon

Introduction

In a volume on the shorter epistles of Paul, the Letter to Philemon takes a kind of pride of place in at least this sense: it is unquestionably the shortest letter of Paul's that we have. No chapter distinctions are needed; it is a letter, simply, of twenty-five verses. Often ignored or overlooked, the letter has much to offer those who would understand Paul and his mission, not to mention broader matters of Christian faith and life itself. What is it about and how is it to be understood?

Often, Philemon is understood as Paul's—or, more broadly, an early Christian—response to slavery. It may be a brilliant example of such. That said, it is important to recognize that it makes no pretense of being a treatise or sustained treatment on slavery or any other matter. Further, as will be discussed below, it is important to recognize that there are broad and specific aspects of slavery as practiced, and legislated, then, which differ significantly from the experience of slavery in the United States.

Readers of Philemon will miss much if they ignore aspects of the letter that tie it immediately to the others letters of Paul. These include—importantly—the descriptions, and affirmations, of identity and mission together in Christ. The three main sets of characters in this letter are (1) Paul and the mission team that writes the letter, (2) Philemon and the other named addressees and the whole (local) "church," and (3) Onesimus. These, and their circumstances, will be considered in order, with much attention paid to Onesimus, because it is his circumstances and plight that are the reason for the letter.

As in the Letter to the Philippians, so here, Paul is in prison. Regarding Paul's identity and the mission enterprise, all that pertains regarding Philippians pertains here, too (see the introduction to Philippians). Though he is in prison, Paul neither presumes nor settles for a halting of the work of his mission. Such "sharing of . . . faith" as marks life in and around (Christian) community continues to connect the addressees with the imprisoned Paul and set a standard for mission and community action (v. 6). Regarding the imprisonment itself, the discussion in the introduction to Philippians is immediately relevant here. By far the most likely possibilities for the place of imprisonment are Rome and Ephesus. If the former, the letter is written in the early 60s CE, and if the latter, it is written in the mid 50s CE. For the reasons outlined in the discussion of Philippians as well as the close proximity of Ephesus to Colossae (the likely location of Philemon's household), this commentary proceeds under the assumption of an Ephesian imprisonment. That said, little or nothing in the commentary rises or falls on that decision.

Concerning the letter's addressees, something that surfaces immediately is that the traditional title is something of a misnomer. Though Philemon is indeed the first named and primary addressee, there are two other named recipients, Apphia and Archippus, as well as "the church in your house" (Phlm. 2). While Apphia is not known elsewhere in the New Testament, Archippus is named in the Letter to the Colossians (4:17), as is Onesimus (4:9). That connection to Colossae makes it likely that "the church in your house" is a reference to a church community at Colossae. Colossae is a regional city in western Asia Minor (western Turkey on today's map) within the sphere of Ephesus.

Philemon 19 suggests strongly that Paul is responsible for Philemon's association with the Christian faith. If that is so, what about the church that is meeting in Philemon's house? It would stand as likely, or at least as possible, that Paul founded the church there. But Colossians 1:4–7 seems to indicate a certain Epaphras as founder of the church at Colossae. And that said, Philemon 23 indicates a close association of Paul with Epaphras, which may suggest a role for Paul and the Pauline mission in the founding of the church. Even granted the Colossian report of Epaphras's role as founder, how does one weigh the evidence? Unfortunately Philemon simply does not provide sufficient background information for us (presumably because its addressees did not need such; they already knew Paul's relationship to Philemon and to the church in his house). And Colossians, whatever the strength and accuracy of the supplementary (vis-à-vis Phlm.) information it provides, may postdate Paul and be written by other(s) in his name (see the *Colossians, Ephesians, 1 and 2 Timothy, and Titus* volume within this series). Given these factors, we cannot know for sure the circumstances of Paul's relationship to Philemon or to the broader church referenced herein, presumably at Colossae.

Similarly, we cannot know for sure the circumstances of Paul's relationship with Onesimus either. The broader circumstances surrounding

Onesimus's association with Paul, his presence with Paul (in Paul's place of imprisonment), and his relationship to Philemon, the other named addressees, and to the church in Philemon's house, are unclear. Most who read this letter (at least since the fourth century, from which we have written comments) have presumed that Onesimus is a runaway slave. Notice that in that presumption there are actually two separable presumptions: "runaway" and "slave." Neither is stated clearly in the text.

An approach that is gaining some recognition within New Testament scholarship is forwarded by Allen Callahan: that Onesimus is not a slave at all but in fact Philemon's (actual) brother (see *Embassy of Onesimus* for sustained treatment and for further bibliography). How could this be? Such an understanding rests on the premises that nowhere in the letter is Onesimus directly identified as a slave and that the phraseology regarding the acceptance of Philemon as "a beloved brother . . . both in the flesh and in the Lord" (v. 16) is a reference to the literal fraternal relationship of Onesimus and Philemon. The flipside of that same coin, regarding verse 16, is to take the "slave" language therein as figurative. Such a reading, while fascinating and worthy of consideration, stretches credulity given the flow of verses 10–16.

Another fairly recent proposal, which veers less from the runaway slave approach, is that of Sara Winter, who proposes that Onesimus, a slave, had been sent by the Colossian church to be of service to Paul while the latter was in prison (Winter 1987). The strength of this position is that it breaks the presumption that Onesimus's "slave" status necessarily implies or requires that he is a "runaway." The weakness is that this suggestion does not well explain the broad thrust and particular language of the letter. For example, regarding verse 11, who among us would send a "useless" individual to carry out some service for someone we care for? And regarding verses 13–14, is not this precisely the circumstance that Winter's proposal forwards as being the case? If so, why would Paul name it as a *wish*, but not a reality?

So, are we back, then, to the runaway slave theory? No. There is a weakness in this theory. Though slavery in the Roman Empire and slavery in the United States were significantly different both in terms of legislation and practice (as will be discussed briefly, below), there was certainly this in common: runaway slaves risked and regularly received severe treatment. On that fact alone, that a runaway Onesimus would willingly go to a place of imprisonment to seek succor stretches credulity. On a different but related note, that Paul and Onesimus might have been brought together via a coincidence of capture and imprisonment also stretches credulity. However harsh his imprisonment and experience of chains (see commentary on Philippians, above), simply on the surface of it Paul seems to be enjoying at least some of the benefits that a citizen could presume—accepting visitors and writing and accepting letters. A runaway slave could not have anticipated such treatment and would not likely have been placed in the presence of one such as Paul.

Another interesting matter arises if, indeed, Onesimus is a runaway. Though Roman law would commit Paul to returning the fugitive, Jewish Scripture indicates quite the opposite. Deuteronomy 23:15–16 forbids handing over fugitive slaves who seek asylum: "Slaves who have escaped to you from their owners shall not be given back to them. . . ." At the very least, the arrival of a fugitive slave to Paul would have pitted his Jewish training and commitments against his Roman citizenship and networks. Paul considers none of that in this letter. What Paul does do, herein, is act consistently with—and forcefully and creatively within—a legally established and recognized set of relationships within Roman law that has no counter in Scripture or Jewish—including earliest Christian—tradition.

Gaining ascendancy among students of Philemon is the understanding that Onesimus was indeed a slave, and that he did, by choice, leave his legally established master and place of assignment. However, he did not do so as a fugitive. As discussed by both B. M. Rapske and S. Scott Bartchy, Onesimus acted consistently with Roman legal precedent that recognized exceptions under which slaves might flee *without* being or becoming a fugitive. It was an important consideration and set of legal rulings since the imperial economy was based so heavily on slavery, and slaves held such a variety of positions and responsibilities within society (Rapske 1991; Bartchy 1992).

Here is one of the areas in which slavery in the Americas and that of the Roman Empire differ significantly. The horrible conditions of the plantation South are paralleled most closely in Rome in the contexts of mining and agriculture. But slavery in the Roman Empire was more broadly prevalent throughout society and far more varied than in the American context. Many slaves held positions such as teachers, writers, doctors, accountants, managers, and agents of various kinds. Further, both entry into slavery and manumission were very different from the American context. First, though people were indeed born into the status of slave in Rome, important sources of slaves were prisoners of war and individuals who sold themselves, or were sold by family members, into servitude. Second, manumission was more far more regular and even, to some degree, expected, especially for those in more urban contexts and less menial tasks. Writing a few generations prior to Paul, the historian Dionysius of Halicarnassus provides some insight on how these matters played out: ". . . how many people, both Barbarians and Greeks, from being slaves had become free; and how many, from being free, had become slaves. . . ." (*Roman Antiquities* 4.23).

In the Roman context, manumission did not mean full freedom of obligation, according to both unwritten and, increasingly, written law. Rome was a society of patronage. Freedmen, or persons who had purchased freedom, remained under the patriarchal influence of the individual or household with whom or with which they had been associated when slaves. Indeed, the Roman historian Suetonius tells us that just a few years prior to the writing of Philemon, the emperor Claudius "reduced to slavery any [freedman] who failed to show due gratitude or about whom their former owners had cause for complaint . . ." (*Claudius* 25; see introduction to 1 Thessalonians for other actions of Claudius). That act alone indicates something of the complicated depth and breadth, and flexibility and rigidity, of the institution of slavery within the empire.

Several first-century Roman jurists attempted to define and deliminate precisely what were the acceptable circumstances and practices of physically taking leave of one's legal master or assignment. Their deliberations are recorded in that famous archive of Roman law, *The Digest of Justinian* 21.1.17. The jurist Vivian would appear to move from some manner of common sense and some level of humanity: ". . . a slave who flees from an enemy or brigand, a fire, or the collapse of a building, certainly runs away, but . . . is not a fugitive. In the same way, a slave who runs away from the instructor to whom he was entrusted for training is not a fugitive, if the reason for . . . running is intolerable treatment." He goes on to state that the same holds true if the intolerable treatment comes not from an agent of the master (such as "the instructor") but from "someone who borrowed" the slave. Another jurist, Proculus, pushes the matter further, broaching the matter of the (possible) actions of the masters themselves, and also providing a broader context: "he would not be a fugitive . . . who, having in mind that his master wished physically to chastise him, betook himself to a friend whom he induced to plead on his behalf."

This latter statement offers a context and a legal precedent that neatly fits the Letter of Philemon as we have it. A fascinating parallel involves a much younger contemporary of Paul, Pliny the Younger. He writes to a certain Sabinus, "You have done the right thing in taking back into your home and favour the freedman who was once dear to you, with my letter to mediate between you both" (*Letter* 24; the "letter" to which Pliny refers is recorded as *Letter* 21; see further discussion of Pliny's correspondence, and other parallels, in the commentary, below). Paul's Letter to Philemon and the broader community at Colossae is just such a letter of mediation. That, and much more, as we shall see.

Commentary

SALUTATION AND ADDRESS
Philemon 1–3

> 1 **Paul, a prisoner of Christ Jesus, and Timothy our brother,**
> **To Philemon our dear friend and co-worker,** ² **to Apphia our sister, to**
> **Archippus our fellow soldier, and to the church in your house:**
> ³ **Grace to you and peace from God our Father and the Lord Jesus Christ.**

From the first sentence it is clear that this is a letter that presumes and promotes a broader mission and network. The designation "prisoner of Christ Jesus" is unique among the openings of Paul's letters. Though Paul does not use the term, "prisoner," or the broader phrase, "prisoner of Christ Jesus," in Philippians, the designation is consistent with several descriptions found near the beginning of that letter (see Phil. 1:7, 13, 17). As do "imprisonment" and "prison" in English, the Greek words that Paul uses in Philippians and here share the same root (and indeed differ by only one letter). The same designation, "prisoner," is used with similar phraseology in Ephesians 3:1; 4:1; and 2 Timothy 1:8.

The designation here resonates immediately with the broader description in verse 13, "my imprisonment for the gospel." As a "prisoner of Christ Jesus" and "brother" to Timothy, Paul is part of a mission whose head and goal and purpose are summed up in "Christ Jesus." Presumably Paul's addressees are well aware of that, and they (or at the very least, Philemon; see v. 19) may well have received teaching directly from Paul regarding "Christ Jesus," perhaps including (consideration of) the Christ Hymn (see Phil. 2:5–11 and the commentary on Philippians, above). Paul does not embellish or further describe or define his role along the lines found in other letters, such as, for example, "apostle" (see Rom. 1:1; 1 Cor. 1:1; 2 Cor. 1:1; Gal. 1:1) or "servant" (or better, "slave," see Rom.

1:1; Phil. 1:1). The latter, "slave," might have been a particularly effective choice here, or perhaps it would have been too charged. In any event, Paul chooses the quite literal designation "prisoner."

Timothy, though present, is not imprisoned with Paul and so does not share his designated title (see below regarding Epaphras, v. 23) as he does in Philippians 1:1, where both are named "servants," or better, "slaves." In that sense, this salutation shares the pattern of 2 Corinthians 1:1 where Paul, there designated as "apostle," is followed by "and Timothy our brother." There as here no "our" is, in fact, stated, though according to Greek usage a "my" or "our" could be supplied and one or the other may well have been presumed by Philemon and the other addressees. In any event, as with the identity of "Christ Jesus," they were doubtless familiar with Paul's usage and broader understanding of familial language for the members of the community (which will figure greater in this letter; see also Phil 3:1, 13 [NRSV alternative reading], and 17). The designation here seems particularly apt and suggestive, as Paul moves throughout the salutation and address, prayer section, and body of the letter toward the purpose statement ("so that") in verses 15–16, and the use of "brother" in verse 16. (For further consideration of "Timothy" see esp. comments on Phil. 1:1 and 1 Thess. 1:1, above.)

The "to" section of the address is a complicated one, involving four distinct addressees. The first is Philemon, identified as "our dear friend and co-worker." The first designation is a vitally important one in the letter and its relevance is completely lost, unfortunately, in the NRSV translation. The one Greek word here translated "dear friend" and that translated "beloved" in verse 16 are precisely the same. This correlation would not have been lost on Philemon or the other addressees. Philemon is simply, and unequivocally, "beloved" to Paul.

What Paul accomplishes, then, in two short, back-to-back turns of phrase—"Timothy brother" and "Philemon beloved" (remember, as indicated above regarding Timothy, there is no "our" in Paul's Greek)—is to present and use precisely the same designations that he will urge on Philemon vis-à-vis Onesimus in verse 16: "beloved brother." That is Paul's wish; indeed it is the reason for the letter.

And, following these back-to-back phrases Paul extends his description of Philemon to included "co-worker." To be sure, via this letter he is calling Philemon directly to carry out the "work" of expanding Christian community and expanding his own capacity for recognizing Onesimus, to include full acceptance and status as "beloved brother" and, perhaps, "even more" (v. 21). "Co-worker" is itself a term Paul uses elsewhere and uses in direct conjunction with "brother": 1 Thessalonians 3:2 regarding Timothy and Philippians 2:25 regarding Ephaphroditus (wherein the designation "fellow soldier" is also used; for further uses of "co-worker," see Phil. 4:3; Rom. 16:3, 9, 21; 2 Cor. 8:23; also Col. 4:11; see also comments on vv. 23–24, below).

That the "work" of welcoming and expanding the circle of the "beloved" is essential to Christian community is at least hinted at, if not bolstered and reinforced, through consideration of "love" within in the thanksgiving section (vv. 4–7, see vv. 5, 7) and at the top of the body of the letter (vv. 8–22; see v. 9).

What relationship, if any outside of Christian community, the next two addressees have to Philemon or each other is a matter of speculation. An obvious possibility regarding Apphia is that she is Philemon's wife. Primary for Paul is that she is "sister" (again, no "our" in the Greek), a direct indication and affirmation of her place in Christian community and more particularly in the church named shortly. If one presumes (literal) familial relations as Paul runs through this line of individuals en route to the naming of the fourth addressee, the church, then it is certainly possible that Archippus, clearly a male name, is the son of Philemon and Apphia; other relations are possible. What is certain is that he, like Philemon and Apphia is one of the Christian community. For him, Paul uses the same designation, "fellow soldier," that rounds out the description of Epaphroditus in Philippians 2:25 (see discussion of "co-worker," above). Whether his particular responsibilities vis-à-vis Paul or within the local community would match those of Ephaphroditus in any way (see comments on Phil. 2:25 in commentary of Philippians, above) is a matter of speculation.

The designation "your" regarding the "church in your house" (v. 2) is singular and most naturally refers back to Philemon. Close parallels are found in Romans 16:3–5 and 1 Corinthians 16:19 wherein both the male and female heads of the house church are named. In Colossians 4:15, of particular interest given the connections of Philemon with that letter, it is a woman, Nympha, whose house is identified (see also 1 Cor. 1:11 where Chloe, clearly a woman's name, may be the host of a house church). For consideration of the meaning of "church" as both a community "called out" and as an "[alternative] assembly" see the discussion of 1 Thessalonians 1:1 in the commentary on 1 Thessalonians above.

The greeting itself (v. 3) is identical to that in Philippians (see comments on Phil. 1:2, above; for further discussion, see also comments on 1 Thess. 1:1). Here the "our" *is* found in the Greek text before "Father." Among other things, then, the greeting affirms what is clear from the start.

Paul and his mission, and the individual addressees and the local church, are part of something much bigger, something that offers the possibility of God-directed, God-blessed community or assembly, in which individual and corporate identity are built on alternative standards to those of the empire (see comments on 1 Thess. 1:1). Paul's purpose in writing this letter is certainly consistent with that alternative community, and it is inconsistent, to say the least, with accepted and expected legalities and norms.

THANKSGIVING
Philemon 4–7

4 When I remember you in my prayers, I always thank my God [5] because I hear of your love for all the saints and your faith toward the Lord Jesus. [6] I pray that the sharing of your faith may become effective when you perceive all the good that we may do for Christ. [7] I have indeed received much joy and encouragement from your love, because the hearts of the saints have been refreshed through you, my brother.

Paul has already introduced several elements into this letter. As discussed above, "brother" (Timothy) and "beloved" (Philemon) loom large already, given Paul's description/wish/purpose regarding Onesimus as described in verse 16. But, Paul hardly waits until that resolution to revisit and reinforce these notions. Within the thanksgiving Paul draws on and builds on each in particular ways.

The thanksgiving section begins in a way familiar particularly in Philippians and 1 Thessalonians: that is, the fusing of thanksgiving and remembrance. Not unlike those letters, Paul then begins to introduce or—as the case here—reintroduce items that he will build on throughout the letter. As in English, the Greek word used for "beloved" regarding Philemon in verse 1 and for "love" here share the same root and sound alike (see above for discussion of "dear friend" which misleadingly translates the same word that is correctly translated "beloved" in v. 16). That would not have been missed on Paul's addressees. Paul is here beginning to flesh out what the "beloved" community is and does and how "beloved" individuals treat each other within community.

Before proceeding, a word about the letter's addressees and the focus of Paul's pointed rhetoric. The NRSV footnote regarding "you" in verse 4 is important: "From verse 4 through verse 21, *you* is singular." This is a unique situation within Paul's letters wherein Paul is wont to address the whole of the community via a consistently plural usage of "you" and "your" (see, e.g., comments on Phil. 1:4–5 and Phil. 2:2). On that score, the matter of the NRSV footnote regarding "we" in verse 6 warrants comment: "Other ancient authorities read *you* (plural)." As a matter of fact, the plural forms of "you" and "we" vary little in both written and oral expression in Greek—*if* Paul did indeed use "you" (plural) in verse 6, it would stand as an exception to the NRSV footnote just cited. While the matter is up for scholarly debate given some notable variance in the textual tradition, the preponderance of the evidence favors the "we," as is found here. Either way, the essential point would remain the same: "you"—Philemon—are a valued, key, unique instance and agent of the expression of Christian community found and experienced among "you all" at the local church at Colossae and among "we" all who are Christ's.

Indeed, that creative tension between individual "you" and plural "you all" or "we" all is set up in a particular way via the greeting and four-part address (which establishes the broader church and network of which Philemon is a part) and the use of, and orientation toward, the individual "you" (i.e., Philemon) through the greater portion of the letter (and see discussion of the transitional v. 22, below). Further, the indication broadly of "the good that we [or, "you" all (plural)] may do for Christ" in a corporate sense is focused in verse 14 in a particular way around that which Philemon might do.

Within this pointed thanksgiving section, the "beloved" of verse 1 becomes an instantiation of Christian "love" in verse 5. What the NRSV tears asunder, Paul has put together. There is no separation, in the Greek, of either "love" from "faith" or of the direction of that "love" and "faith": both are "toward the Lord Jesus and for the purpose of all the saints" (my translation). The phrases appear in that order, and in that simple manner, in the Greek. The beauty and (theo)logic of that phraseology speaks volumes—the individual and community formed in Christ and believing in Christ acts on behalf the greater community of "saints" or "holy ones." Faith and love in and toward Christ result necessarily in love and faith (or faithfulness) for the purpose of community (see commentary on Philippians regarding Phil. 3:9).

With "sharing" in verse 6, Paul introduces a term and broader concept familiar in Philippians (1:5, 7; see also 4:15). That, plus the "co-" word, "co-worker," used in verse 1, establish a strong link between this letter, and particularly its presentation of Christian community, with Philippians. (For discussion of the use, and abundance, of "co-" words in Philippians, see discussion of Phil. 1:7 in the commentary on Philippians). As the comments on Philippians 1:5 indicate, the "sharing" therein is "for the purpose of the gospel," a phrase that uses the same construction indicating purpose that Paul uses in verse 5 here: "toward the Lord Jesus and for the purpose of all the saints" (my translation). In 1 Corinthians 1:9, Paul uses both "faithful" (for God) and "sharing" (there translated "fellowship") in the same sentence: "God is faithful; by him you were called into the fellowship of his Son, Jesus Christ our Lord." The resonance of both the Philippians and 1 Corinthians usages with that here is clear: "sharing," which is God-blessed, Christ-directed and "for the purpose of the gospel" of Christ is necessarily outward-directed and on behalf of Christian community. Tellingly, the word that Paul uses for "partner" (v. 17) shares the same root as the word for "sharing" (see comments on v. 17, below).

In verse 7 Paul now speaks of, and from the place of, receiving such Christ-directed "love"—love that is purposed *and* outward-directed, towards others. And notice, Paul, himself an individual, deigns to speak on behalf of "the saints" generally.

The two particular terms/concepts identified here, "joy" and "encouragement," are also key within Philippians. For "joy," see comments on Philippians 1:4 (and also Phil. 1:25, where it is linked directly with "faith"). For "encouragement," see comments on Philippians 2:1 and 4:2 (regarding "urge," a verb formed from the same root as the word translated "encouragement"; "appeal," in Phlm. 9–10 translates this same verb). Worthy of note, is that "joy" and this verb form of "encouragement" (translated as "urge" in Phil. 4:2; "appeal" in Phlm. 9–10) are closely linked at Philippians 4:1–2. These differing translations of the noun and verb form—"encouragement" (noun) and "urge" and "appeal" (verb)—as well as the urgency evident in Philippians 4:1–3 provide some sense of the depth and meaning of the concept of encouragement/urge/appeal for Paul. Repeated and varied use of the encouragement/urge/appeal root throughout 1 Thessalonians provide even further insight (see comments on 1 Thess. 4:1). Along with, and part and parcel of, the joy found in community is the varied, sometimes complicated, always meaningful action of encouraging, comforting, urging and appealing.

Also resonant with Philippians is the use of a particular term, here translated "hearts." The actual term is at once more earthy (or "bodily") and more idiomatically Greek than "heart" suggests. Though "hearts" fairly captures something of an equivalent English idiom, as discussed in comments on Philippians 1:8 above, the term means, literally, "guts." It is used to express the seat of, and sense of, real and deep feeling. Its repeated usage in Philemon offers a depth of feeling and intensity to Paul's purpose and reasoning within the letter. Notice that its use in verse 20, particularly in conjunction with "refresh" (see "hearts . . . refreshed," v. 7, and "Refresh my heart," v. 20) stands as a call for a particular expression or instantiation of that sort of activity "from your love," which is remembered and offered up for thanks in verse 7 herein.

And, also consistent with that same verse 20, is the naming/identifying of Philemon as "brother" (as in v. 1, no "my" is stated here). The NRSV captures well the manner in which Paul draws this verse, and section, to a close: "through you . . . brother." As is Timothy (v. 1), so is Philemon (v. 7 and 20) and, as we (and he, Philemon) will see, so, according to the norms and implications of Christian "love" and community, is Onesimus (v. 16).

APPEALING ON THE BASIS OF LOVE
Philemon 8–16

> 8 **For this reason, though I am bold enough in Christ to command you to do your duty,** [9] **yet I would rather appeal to you on the basis of love—and I, Paul, do this as an old man, and now also as a prisoner of Christ Jesus.** [10] **I am appealing to you for my child, Onesimus, whose father I have become during my imprisonment.** [11] **Formerly he was useless to you, but now he is indeed useful both to you and to me.** [12] **I am sending him, that is, my own heart, back to you.** [13] **I wanted to keep him with me, so that he might be of service to me in your place during my imprisonment for the gospel,** [14] **but I preferred to do nothing without your consent, in order that your good deed might be voluntary and not something forced.** [15] **Perhaps this is the reason he was separated from you for a while, so that you might have him back forever,** [16] **no longer as a slave but more than a slave, a beloved brother—especially to me but how much more to you, both in the flesh and in the Lord.**

The body of the letter follows immediately and seamlessly on the thanksgiving as Paul has crafted it. Even as he continues to develop notions of "love" and familial relationship begun at the top of the letter (see "beloved," v. 1 and "brother," v. 1 and 7), so too he provides a direct appeal on behalf of, and narrative about, Onesimus. Everything—the development of notions of "love" and familial relationship, the appeal (which itself develops the "encouragement from . . . love"), the development of a narrative regarding Onesimus—is intertwined with each other and with the salutation and greeting and thanksgiving, already provided.

The NRSV captures well Paul's clear and smooth transition from "love." The thanksgiving has been all about "love," and it is the "beloved" Philemon, a "brother" in Christian community, whose "love" has been so active and has so impressed Paul. And, it is "for this reason" that Paul will "appeal" to Philemon and will do so on the "basis of love" already established (vv. 9–10; see v. 7 for discussion of the root of "appeal" and its association with "love" there as well as here). The framework, the foundation, and content ("love") are consistent. They are consistently expressive of the relationship that Paul and Philemon share in "Lord Jesus" (v. 5; see similarly vv. 1, 3; a relationship for which, Philemon will be reminded, Paul is responsible, v. 19). And they are evidenced by the "beloved" Philemon's own activity of "love" to date (esp. v. 7).

As central as the ethos developed by Paul within this letter is to the Christian expression of life in community, the rhetorical posture of the letter also borrows from the broader culture, as becomes particularly evident in this section. At the close of the introduction to this letter, above, is a discussion about the correspondence of Pliny the Younger and a certain Sabianus. Pliny has taken it upon himself to mediate between Sabianus and one of his freedmen (for the status of a "freedman" vis-à-vis the former owner in the Roman Empire, see the introduction to this letter). Pliny, writing in Latin, constructs his presentation and uses terms and figures of speech in a manner that resonates instructively with Paul's usage here. Writing after the fact regarding Sabianus's reception of the freedman back into his household with favor, Pliny states: ". . . . You will be glad of this, and I am certainly glad, first because I see you are willing . . . , and then because you paid me the tribute of bowing to my authority, or, if you prefer, to granting my request" (*Letter* 24).

Just as Paul could "command" but would rather seek an alternative "appeal" (vv. 8–9; in Paul's case, "love" rooted in Christian community), so Pliny, after citing his authority, offers that his mediation be recognized as a "request." One might pause to note how clearly Pliny's rhetoric marks the poles of a patriarchal society, which trades in honor and shame: from "bowing to authority," on the one hand, to "request" or even "begging" (the word can mean either or both) on the other hand. Contrast that with the rhetoric of Philemon: rooted in the "love" reflective of the community's expression of dear and familial relationship, Paul's request goes for neither pole but is founded on another basis (see discussion of "church" as an alternative community, in comments on v. 2, above).

Further, Pliny is careful to underscore that Sabianus himself is "willing" to work things out. Paul indicates his preference for the same regarding

Philemon (v. 14). Moreover, Pliny provides indication of the shared, and even equal, consequence to both himself and Sabianus—Pliny is already "certainly glad," and assures Sabianus of the same. So too Paul assures Philemon that the new familial status of, and relationship with, Onesimus, which Paul has already experienced and which he presents for Philemon's consideration, is already, "now . . . useful . . . both to you and me" (v. 11). Indeed, by way of revisiting and putting a twist on the family motif and engaging in rhetorical abundance, Paul goes on to state that Onesimus is "a beloved brother—especially to me but how much more to you" (v. 16). Now, going beyond balance or equality, Paul indicates that Philemon has even more to gain.

Though Paul's singular voice has been evident from the beginning (so v. 4, "I,") it comes out with particular strength in verse 9: "I, Paul, . . ." What follows builds not a sense of immediate or necessary authority, but pathos, and perhaps some sense of playfulness. Resonant with Philippians (see esp. Phil. 1:7, 12–14, and associated comments in the commentary on Philippians) and with Philemon 1, above, Paul does not shy from his status as a "prisoner of Christ Jesus." At the very least, that immediate and deep connection with and to "Christ Jesus" renders him a member of the community or, following the lead of his language thus far ("brother," v. 1, 7; "beloved," v. 1), a member of the family. Paul's use of "old man" is considered problematic or unsure by some scholars (as is evidenced in the NRSV alternative reading, "ambassador"). There is little or no ambiguity regarding the Greek word or its literal meaning. That said, it is a matter of fact that the word for "old man" varies by one letter from a standard Greek word for "ambassador," and itself appears to take on such a meaning in some circumstances. However, it is more likely that Paul intends the simple and literal meaning here since he has avoided any titles or honorifics of any kind. Further, the use of "old man" may provide some winsomeness given the content of verse 10.

Before even naming the subject for whom this letter is written, and for whom this "appeal" is being made, Paul presents that one as "my child." The "old man" has a "child"? Where has anyone ever heard of that before? Well, the Septuagint (ancient Greek) version of the Hebrew Scriptures uses precisely this same designation, "old man," for Abraham (Gen. 25:8) who fathered a child in old age (Gen. 17:1, 18:9–14, 21:1–2). Whether that (perhaps playful) allusion to Scripture was alive for Paul in this usage or would have resonated with his addressees, the colorful descriptions keep coming. Where does the "old man" Paul's unlikely entrée into fatherhood occur? In prison! As in Philippians (see esp. 1:12), so here, Paul's time in prison proves fruitful for the continuation of his mission and of the continuing establishment and expansion of Christian community.

There is clear playfulness in Paul's introduction of "Onesimus" into the body of the letter. Lost in the NRSV translation is the way Paul structures that introduction—"Onesimus" is the last word in verse 10; the name itself sets up and leads directly into the statement of verse 11. As the NRSV footnote rightly indicates, "The name Onesimus means *useful* or (compare verse 20) *beneficial*." Having introduced the name, Paul then plays on its meaning and on some perceived lack vis-à-vis Onesimus' on-the-job production. Whether this lack is perceived by Philemon, Paul, Onesimus himself, or others in the broader church community we cannot tell. That's how we might put it—"on-the-job production." But, of course, this is a slave society and Onesimus is owned; he is a commodity as far as the system of the slave society is concerned.

The wordplay is on the meaning of the root word of Onesimus' name. That word is itself used in verse 20, there translated "benefit." Here, Paul uses a particular synonym for that word, on which he can easily add one prefix meaning "not"—so, rendering "not beneficial" or, as per the NRSV, "useless"—and another that enhances the root meaning in a positive sense—so, rendering "quite beneficial" or, as the NRSV translates, "useful."

Paul uses this synonym of choice in its bare form—that is, without any prefix—in two other places within the extant letters. In one of these, he is quoting from the esteemed Greek poet Menander: "Bad company ruins good morals" (1 Cor. 15:33; what the NRSV translates "good" is the same word here translated "useful"). In the other, Romans 2:4, Paul uses the same word twice (translated in the NRSV as "kindness" in each case), the second instance being, "Do you not realize that God's kindness is meant to lead you to repentance?" Isn't the Menander quote interesting if overlaid on the situation in Philemon? Might the notion in verse 11 that Onesimus was formerly "useless" say less about him than about the "company" or context within which he found himself at Philemon's house? And what about the passage from Romans? Is Onesimus's new-found or newly recognized kindness/usefulness "meant to lead [Philemon] to repentance"? Paul spells none of this out and the suggestions here are little more than speculation. They are forwarded, in part, to highlight that the traditional notion that there must have been something inherently "useless" about Onesimus himself is likewise speculation. At least the suggestions here draw on Paul's own use of the same word in other letters. To be clear, verse 11 does not say that Onesimus was "useless"; rather, it indicates that something in the former relationship of Philemon and Onesimus was blocking the potential for usefulness or benefit to Philemon.

Paul goes on in verse 12 to provide a further term of endearment, and like so much in this section it resonates with what comes before and after (see comments on v. 7, above, for its literal meaning, its sense herein and in other of Paul's letters, and its appearance in v. 20). In verse 7 Paul writes of, and to, Philemon: "the hearts of the saints have been refreshed through you. . . ." Here he designates Onesimus as his, Paul's, "own heart." Already he has set the stage: Will Philemon live up to his previous track record by acting on behalf of this particular "heart,"—Onesimus?

Initially, in verses 13–14, Paul takes the argument in the direction of one person of status writing or speaking to another about a third party who may or may not share that same status. That is, for the moment, Onesimus might yet be considered a commodity. So, verse 13: "I wanted to keep him with me, so that he might be of service to me in your place." Notice how neatly that sentence can fit with the statement of verse 7. The (one Greek) verb translated "might be of service" can and does indicate functions carried out by slaves, particularly waiting on tables. Such usage is captured neatly in Luke 12:37, which draws on that broad and standard usage in presenting a striking image of the slave-master relationship. That said, the same verb was also used by Paul in a much more focused and particular sense for Christian ministry or service (so Rom. 15:25 regarding himself; the noun form of the word, from which the English, "deacon," is derived, is used regarding Jesus in Rom. 15:8 and regarding Phoebe in Rom. 16:1). Following verse 14, on which we have already commented, Paul turns the tide completely away from descriptions that may accrue to slaves—never to look back.

As presented in the introduction to this letter, Onesimus has come to Paul not as runaway or fugitive; rather he sought out Paul, a "friend" of his master, "to plead on his behalf." In verse 15 Paul deftly handles the matter of Onesimus's vacating of his place of assignment via use of the passive, "he was separated," and gently (via "perhaps") introduces a proposed reason for that separation: "so that you might have him back. . . ." Paul's statement trades on a range of meaning that his chosen verb, "have . . . back," enjoys within the sphere of business and other transactions. It can and does carry the simple meaning "have . . . back," which makes some sense here (after all, the letter is regarding Onesimus's return *back* to Philemon). It can and does also carry the meaning to "receive" or "have fully." That latter sense may draw on the lack indicated in verse 11 as well as prefigure the discussion in the next section, particularly verses 18–19. And regarding the little "while" that Onesimus was away—well, the new order of things has implications that are "forever."

It is in verse 16 that Paul clearly spells out his "appeal" (vv. 9–10; see also comments regarding "encouragement" in v. 7). Picking up on the verb of verse 15, "have . . . back" or perhaps better, "have fully," he continues: "no longer as a slave but more than a slave, a beloved brother." That there is nothing cheap or easy or flippant in this phraseology is evident in the way Paul has presented and developed the language of "love"/"beloved" and "brother" throughout (see discussion of "dear friend," or better, "beloved," v. 2, also vv. 5, 7, 9; for "brother," see vv. 1, 7). Paul is faced with a particular situation with legal implications and attendant socially expected and accepted norms. He responds fully and forcefully from within the ethos of Christian community. There is no stronger bond evident than the familial (besides "brother," see "child . . . father" in v. 10) and no more deeply or broadly applicable than "brother" (vv. 1, 7; and, to that, one ought quickly to add "sister," v. 2). "Brother," or more broadly, "sibling," is simply and profoundly the applicable bond and posture for Philemon to adopt vis-à-vis Onesimus.

The almost passing phrase by which Paul draws verse 16 to a close is not to be missed. As discussed in comments on verse 3, "the Lord Jesus Christ" or, simply, "the Lord" (so here), indicates the alternative (to the broader society and all its attendant expectations) to and for which this community is formed (see also comments on "church" in v. 2, above). In case there could be any doubt, Paul is clear: "the reason" for the current circumstance and its resolution herein is that Onesimus be "a beloved brother . . . in the Lord." Fair enough. So too, Paul establishes that Onesimus be "a beloved brother . . . in the flesh." That is, in the sphere of outward relationship, action, and accomplishment (see Gal. 6:12; Phil. 3:3).

The NRSV provides a particularly marvelous example of Paul's usage here in the translation of 2 Corinthians 11:18. As indicated in the *alternate* reading there, the text reads, "according to the flesh"; the NRSV translation is "according to human standards." That begins to get at the strength of Paul's phraseology here: the purpose is that Onesimus be to Philemon, now, as "a beloved brother" according to, or in the manner of, human standards as well as vis-à-vis Christian community. It is an all-encompassing charge. Indeed, the focused charge is coming in the next verse.

DO EVEN MORE: PARTNERSHIP IN ACTION
Philemon 17–22

17 So if you consider me your partner, welcome him as you would welcome me. [18] If he has wronged you in any way, or owes you anything, charge that to my account. [19] I, Paul, am writing this with my own hand: I will repay it. I say nothing about your owing me even your own self. [20] Yes, brother, let me have this benefit from you in the Lord! Refresh my heart in Christ. [21] Confident of your obedience, I am writing you, knowing that you will do even more than I say. [22] One thing more—prepare a guest room for me, for I am hoping through your prayers to be restored to you.

It is in this section that Paul directs Philemon to act on the case that Paul has built. The opening of the previous section notwithstanding—"though I am bold . . . to command . . . , yet I would rather appeal" (vv. 8–9), Paul does indeed present a command here at the beginning of this section, though couched in an "if" statement. On what basis is the command (and for that matter, the others to follow in vv. 18, 20, 22)? And on what basis is the partnership referred to in verse 17? And what are the limits, if any, of that partnership? These are among the questions addressed in the following verses.

The NRSV captures well the connecting word that begins Paul's statement in verse 17. "So," "therefore," "based on what has been said"—any or all of these would indicate the simple but vital particle found in the text at this point. Attendant to it is another small but vitally important word, "if." Paul is about to present a command—at least, a word put in the grammatical form of a command—but he takes care to do so within a simple conditional sentence: if . . . then. The choice is Philemon's. He is the subject or agent. And the word translated "consider" in the NRSV is even simpler, meaning "have"; this conditional phrase, then, might be more directly translated: "if you will have me as partner," or, "should you have me as partner."

Having eloquently affirmed the close Christian tie between himself and Philemon and the local community meeting at Philemon's house, and having introduced and affirmed the same bond between himself and Onesimus, Paul now puts it all on the line. And he puts Philemon in the key role of agency to tip that "if" one way or the other. "If" Philemon opts to have Paul as "partner," then . . . (we will get to that momentarily). Importantly, the word for "partner" here and the word for "sharing" in verse 6 share the same root and are virtually identical (see comments on v. 6, above). That connection would not have been lost on Philemon and the other addressees. Indeed, this verse and the section more broadly, and further the letter as a whole and the actions to stem from it, are an expansion of, and acting out of, the prayer in verse 6.

Regarding grammatical structure and meaning, the fact that the command word, "welcome," follows an "if" softens or tempers the sense of the command. Philemon is in the position of pushing that "if" one way—making it real—or the other—leaving it lie as a mere possibility, therefore rendering the (potential) command moot. The word itself involves the sense of "welcome" but is a bit simpler and more graphic: "take in," "receive" even, "hold close" or "bring toward" oneself or community. It is used rarely by Paul (besides Rom. 15:7, quoted in the next sentence, see also Rom. 14:1). Its sense here is captured very well in Romans 15:7, which itself might serve as a commentary on this verse: "Welcome one another, therefore, just as Christ has welcomed you."

"Welcome," is followed shortly by another imperative, following another "if," in verse 18: "charge." In Greek as in English, the word trades on financial usage and the matter of keeping accounts. The drama of Paul's seizing of the scribal pen (see discussion of 2 Thess. 3:17) introduces yet another financial term, "repay," which leads to yet another, "owe" (verse 19). That term is a compound form built on the same root word used for "owe" in verse 18. But here the similarities between the two uses of "owe" ends.

The second use of "owe" is meant to put the question of a "charge" to rest. The particular matter(s), if any, that Paul might be referring to in verse 18 are left unstated. Theoretically left unstated—though, via the old rhetorician's trick, by stating that one will not state something, one has in fact stated it—is that Philemon owes Paul nothing short of his ". . . own self"; that is, simply and profoundly, his identity in "the Lord Jesus Christ" and within Christian community (see comments on vv. 2–3, above).

Just as profoundly, Paul's whole appeal throughout the letter has been about Onesimus's identity within the same community defined by "the Lord Jesus Christ." The simple and important use of "brother" at the top of verse 20 directly connects Philemon (v. 7) and Onesimus (v. 16) and their common identity.

The first verb in this verse, as indicated in comments on verse 11 is built on the root word from which Onesimus's name is derived and expresses the "benefit" that Paul can derive "in the Lord" based on Philemon's actions. In the NRSV translation it is not evident that in the Greek, "benefit" is a verb form. It is what grammarians call an optative. Its use here expresses something along these lines: "would that I might have benefit." The optative form allows for a range of likelihood that the wish will be realized. So

Paul's winsome, whimsical, hopeful, and immediately available wish for "benefit" is dramatically followed by yet another simple command word.

However, unlike what we see in verses 17 and 18, this command is not immediately preceded by an "if. Simply, directly, and tellingly (see v. 7: "refreshed," "hearts") Paul writes, "Refresh my heart." With that, verse 20 stands as a bookend to verse 17 and further teases out verse 6 (prayer, see comments on v. 17) and verse 7 (report of action). Paul's direct message, which cannot have been missed on its recipient, is this: what the saints and I have come to count on you for, do here and now with regard to Onesimus.

Consistent with verses 15–16, the stated purpose of this letter is not one, demarcated request. Like Christian community, it is about "love" and relationship (see esp. comments on vv. 1 and 16, and on vv. 5, 7, 9 ["love"]; for consideration of Christian community or "church," see discussion of v. 2). There is certainly no (human) limit that one would want to put on that. All of that said, verse 21 leads with assurance that Paul is "confident" regarding, *not* community or "love," but "your obedience." In Philippians 2:12 (see the commentary on Phil. 2:12, above), Paul closely links Christian community and relationship (via the word "beloved," so Phil. 2:12) with "obedience." Clear in Philippians is that such "obedience" is no floating principle, and certainly no simplistic call to bow to some recognized earthly authority. Nor is it some external principle. The model for obedience is none other than "Christ Jesus" (Phil. 2:5) as described in the Christ Hymn of Philippians 2:6–11 (see esp. "obedient," v. 8). Philemon 21 plays off of this same linking of community membership with "obedience" (see also 2 Cor. 7:1, 15 for the linking of "beloved" with "obedience"). Of particular relevance regarding Philemon is that it was very possibly written at about the same time, and during the same imprisonment, as was Philippians.

The final sentence of this section provides a marvelous transition, which is both deeply personal and deeply and broadly connected to Christian community and mission. Further, like the sentence before it, it includes lively echoes of Philippians. Following the richly open-ended "knowing that you will do even more" of verse 21, the final command of the letter is delightfully concrete: "prepare a guest room for me." The poignancy and optimism of the command derive from, and build on, the first words of the letter, "Paul, a (literal) prisoner. . . ." That poignancy and optimism are then folded directly into Christian hope and community with the explanatory "for I am hoping through your prayers to be restored to you." Virtually each of these words is loaded and carries rich connotations here.

Paul does not use a verb meaning "restored" here at all. Rather, he uses a verb based on the noun with which he will begin the final sentence of the letter: "grace." He is "hoping" to be "granted" or even (in light of the NRSV translation of the noun in v. 25) "graced" to Philemon and his community. He is hoping for a God-given resolution to his imprisonment and to a future meeting with Philemon and his community. For Paul, God's "grace" (vv. 3, 25) is no abstract or detached thing; it effects activity and affects the relationship, networking, and mission of Christian community.

Consistent with that, "your" and "you" here are clearly plural: Paul anticipates being with the whole community, and he cites the prayers of the whole community. That is consistent with the more fleshed-out narrative of his imprisonment and hoped-for release and return to community as found in Philippians (see esp. Phil. 1:25, 27), wherein Paul also cites the community's prayers (Phil. 1:19).

FINAL GREETINGS
Philemon 23–25

23 **Epaphras, my follow prisoner in Christ Jesus, sends greetings to you,** [24] **and so do Mark, Aristarchus, Demas, and Luke, my fellow workers.** [25] **The grace of the Lord Jesus Christ be with your spirit.**

As noted in discussion of verse 22 above, there are significant consistencies between Philippians and the window on his imprisonment that Paul allows in Philemon. That said, whereas by way of final greetings in Philippians Paul references "all the saints . . . especially those of the emperor's household" (Phil. 4:22; cf. Phil. 1:13), Paul here includes a list of particular names. The close association of the names in Philemon with The Letter to the Colossians is discussed in the introduction to Philemon. Epaphras in verse 23 (see discussion in introduction) and all the names in Philemon 24 are also found in Colossians 4:10 and 14.

Regarding the designations, "fellow prisoner" and "fellow workers" used herein, they both employ a prefix, translated here as "fellow," which is analogous to the English "co-." Such usage is familiar throughout Paul's letters, especially Philippians (see esp. comments on Phil. 1:7).

Interestingly, "fellow prisoner," or co-prisoner, is itself used of Aristarchus in Colossians 4:10. Why not here? Epaphras is imprisoned with Paul. Presumably the others who are named as "fellow workers" or "coworkers" (precisely the same term, though in the plural, as is used of

Philemon in verse 1, where it is translated, "co-worker") are not imprisoned but are involved in carrying out Paul's mission even as they visit him in his imprisonment.

The all-encompassing and energizing sense of "grace" is discussed regarding the use of the verb "granted" or "graced," translated by the NRSV as "restored" in verse 22. Not to be missed here—at the very close of a letter that has so deeply and profoundly (re)established and (re)affirmed the depth and breadth and implications of Christian community—is the plural "your." All of you, the "community" of verse 2, are presented as having one, corporate, spirit. That is consistent with Philippians 1:27 (for further resonances with Philippians 1:27, see comments on verse 22, above) and with endings of both Galatians and Philippians.

What different letters! And yet, how directly do both Galatians and Philippians speak to aspects of Philemon. We have already discussed the matters of "co-sharing" and "obedience" that, among other consistencies, link Philemon with Philippians. With Galatians there is the profound matter of at least one part of Galatians 3:28, "no longer slave or free." The positing of one spirit of the community is consistent too with that profound chapter of Romans 8 in which Paul writes, "When we cry, 'Abba! Father!' it is that very Spirit bearing witness with our spirit that we are children of God, and if children, then heirs, heirs of God and joint heirs with Christ" (Rom. 8:15–16). In that one corporate spirit, who could or would deny the status of "beloved brother" or "sister" to another? May it be so.

Works Cited

All quotations from the Bible, including the Apocryphal/Deuterocanonical Books, are from the NRSV unless otherwise noted.

All quotations from Pseudepigraphical texts are available in James H. Charlesworth, ed., *The Old Testament Pseudepigrapha*, vols. 1 and 2 (Garden City, NY: Doubleday, 1983, 1985).

All quotations from ancient Greek and Latin literature, including Philo, Josephus, and the Apostolic Fathers, unless otherwise indicated, are from the editions of the Leob Classical Library (Cambridge, MA: Harvard University Press) except those from:

The Digest of Justinian, vol. 2. Mommsen Theodor, with Paul Krueger, ed. Trans. Alan Watson. Philadelphia: University of Pennsylvania Press, 1985.

Priene Inscription. As cited in James R. Harrison. "Paul's Dishonoured Benefactor: Responses from Augustan Rome (posted at www .vanderbilt.edu/AnS/religious_studies/SBL2003/Harrison.htm).

Soranus. *Gynaecology*. As cited in Jennifer A. Glancy. *Slavery in Early Christianity*. Oxford: Oxford University Press, 2002.

All citations from the Dead Sea Scrolls are available in G. Vermes, trans., *The Complete Dead Sea Scrolls in English*, rev. ed. London: Penguin, 2004.

A version of the *Pirke Avot* or *Fathers of Rabbi Nathan* may be found at http://ultimasurf.net/bible/pirkeavot/pirke-avot-1.htm.

Bartchy, S. Scott. "Philemon, Epistle to." *Anchor Bible Dictionary*, 5:3054–310a. New York: Doubleday, 1992.

———. "Slavery [Greco-Roman]." *Anchor Bible Dictionary*, 6:65b–73b. New York: Doubleday, 1992.

Bauer, Walter, Frederick W. Danker, W.F. Arndt, and F.W. Gingrich (BDAG), *Greek-English Lexicon of the New Testament and Other Early Christian Literature*, 3rd. ed. Chicago: The University of Chicago Press, 2000.

Danker, Frederick W. *Benefactor: Epigraphic Study of a Graeco-Roman and New Testament Semantic Field*. St. Louis: Clayton Publishing House, Inc., 1982.

Heen, Erik M. "Phil. 2:6–11 and Resistance to Local Timocratic Rule: Isa Theo and the Cult of the Emperor in the East," pp. 125–53 in Richard A. Horsley, ed., *Paul and the Roman Imperial Order*. Harrisburg: Trinity Press International, 2004.

Krentz, Edgar M. "Thessalonians, First and Second Epistles to the." *Anchor Bible Dictionary*, 6:515a–523a. New York: Doubleday, 1992.

Lutz, Cora. *Musonius Rufus: The Roman Socrates*, vol. 10. Yale Classical Studies. New Haven: Yale University Press, 1947.

Malherbe, Abraham J. *Paul and the Thessalonians: The Philosophic Tradition of Pastoral Care*. Philadelphia: Fortress Press, 1987.

Rapske, B. M. "The Prisoner Paul in the Eyes of Onesimus." *New Testament Studies* 37 (1991): 187–203.

Segal, Alan F. "Response: Some Aspects of Conversion and Identity Formation in the Christian Community of Paul's Time," in *Paul and Politics: Ekklesia, Israel, Imperium, Interpretation*, ed. Richard A. Horsley. Harrisburg, PA: Trinity Press International, 2000.

Winter, Sara. "Paul's Letter to Philemon." *New Testament Studies* 33 (1987) 1–15.

Introduction

Ascough, Richard S. *What Are They Saying about the Formation of Pauline Churches?* Mahwah, NJ: Paulist Press, 1998.

Bassler, Jouette M. *Navigating Paul: An Introduction to Key Theological Concepts*. Louisville, KY: Westminster John Knox Press, 2007.

Horsley, Richard A., ed. *Paul and the Roman Imperial Order*. Harrisburg, PA: Trinity Press International, 2004.

Park, Eung Chun. *Either Jew or Gentile: Paul's Unfolding Theology of Inclusivity*. Louisville, KY: Westminster John Knox Press, 2003.

Segal, Alan F. *Paul the Convert: The Apostolate and the Apostasy of Saul the Pharisee*. New Haven, CT: Yale University Press, 1990.

Philippians

Droge, Arthur J., and James D. Tabor. *A Noble Death: Suicide and Martyrdom among Christians and Jews in Antiquity.* San Francisco: HarperSanFrancisco, 1992.

Fee, Gordon D. *Paul's Letter to the Philippians.* New International Commentary on the New Testament. Grand Rapids: Wm. B. Eerdmans, 1995.

Wansink, Craig S. *Chained in Christ: The Experience and Rhetoric of Paul's Imprisonments.* Journal for the Study of the New Testament, Supplement Series 130. Sheffield: Sheffield Academic Press, 1996.

Weidmann, Frederick W. "An (Un)Accomplished Model: Paul and the Rhetoric of Philippians 3:3–17," pp. 245–257 in Virginia Wiles, Alexandra Brown, and Graydon F. Snyder, ed. *Putting Body and Soul Together: Essays in Honor of Robin Scroggs.* Valley Forge, PA: Trinity Press International, 1997.

Witherington, Ben, III. *Friendship and Finances in Philippi: The Letter of Paul to the Philippians.* The New Testament in Context. Valley Forge, PA: Trinity Press International, 1994.

1 and 2 Thessalonians

Donfried, Karl P., "The Imperial Cults of Thessalonica and Political Conflict in 1 Thessalonians," pp. 215–223 in Richard A. Horsley, ed., *Paul and Empire: Religion and Power in Roman Imperial Society.* Harrisburg, PA: Trinity Press International, 1997.

Fatum, Lone. "Brotherhood in Christ: A Gender Hermeneutical Reading of 1 Thessalonians" pp. 183–197 in Halvor Moxnes, ed., *Constructing Early Christian Families: Family as Social Reality and Metaphor.* London: Routledge, 1997.

Furnish, Victor Paul. *1 Thessalonians, 2 Thessalonians.* Abingdon New Testament Commentaries. Nashville: Abingdon Press, 2007.

Gaventa, Beverly Roberts. *Our Mother Saint Paul.* Louisville, KY: Westminster John Knox Press, 2007.

Krentz, Edgar M. "Thessalonians, First and Second Epistles to the." *Anchor Bible Dictionary,* 6:515a–523a. New York: Doubleday, 1992.

Malherbe, Abraham J. *Paul and the Thessalonians: The Philosophic Tradition of Pastoral Care.* Philadelphia: Fortress Press, 1987.

———. *The Letters to the Thessalonians: A New Translation with Introduction and Commentary.* The Anchor Bible 32B. New York: Doubleday, 2000.

Philemon

Bartchy, S. Scott. "Philemon, Epistle to." *Anchor Bible Dictionary*,
   5:305b–210a. New York: Doubleday, 1992.
———. "Slavery [Greco-Roman]." *Anchor Bible Dictionary*, 6:65b–73b.
   New York: Doubleday, 1992.
Callahan, Allen Dwight. *Embassy of Onesimus: The Letter of Paul to Phi-
   lemon*. The New Testament in Context. Valley Forge, PA: Trinity
   Press International, 1997.
Glancy, Jennifer A. *Slavery in Early Christianity*. Oxford: Oxford Univer-
   sity Press, 2002.
Winter, Sara. "Paul's Letter to Philemon." *New Testament Studies* 33
   (1987) 1–15.

CPSIA information can be obtained
at www.ICGtesting.com
Printed in the USA
JSHW020542270523
42351JS00002B/58

9 780664 238520